Islamists of the Maghreb

In 2011, the Maghreb occupied a prominent place in world headlines when Sidi Bouzid, Tunisia, became the birthplace of the so-called Arab Spring. Events in Tunisia sparked huge and sometimes violent uprisings. Longstanding dictatorships fell in their wake. The ensuing democratic reforms resulted in elections and the victory of several Islamist political parties in the Arab world.

This book explores the origins, development and rise of these Islamist parties by focusing on the people behind them. In doing so, it provides readers with a concise history of Sunni Islam in North Africa, the violent struggles against European colonial occupation, and the subsequent quest for an affirmation of Muslim identities in its wake. Exploring Islamism as an identity movement rooted in the colonial experience, this book argues that votes for Islamist parties after the Arab Spring reflected a universal human need for an authentic sense of self. This view contrasts with the popular belief that support for Islamists in North Africa reflects a dangerous "fundamentalist" view of the world that seeks to simply impose archaic religious laws on modern societies. Rather, the electoral success of Islamists in the Maghreb, like Tunisia's *Ennahdha* party, is rooted in a reaffirmation of the Arab-Islamic identities of the Maghreb states, long delayed by dictatorships that mimicked Western models and ideologies (e.g., Socialism). Ultimately, however, it is argued that this affirmation is a temporary phenomenon that will give way in time to the fundamental need for good governance, accountability, and a stable growing economy in these countries.

Written in an accessible format, and providing fresh analytical perspectives on Islamism in the Maghreb, this book will be a valuable tool for students and scholars of Political Islam and North African Politics.

Jeffry R. Halverson, PhD, is an associate professor of Religious Studies (Islamic Studies) in the Department of Philosophy and Religious Studies at Coastal Carolina University (USA). He previously served as an assistant research professor at Arizona State University (USA).

Nathaniel Greenberg, PhD, is an assistant professor of Arabic at George Mason University and an affiliate member of the Ali Varul Ak Center for Global Islamic Studies. His research centers on modern Arab intellectual history and aesthetics. His work includes *The Aesthetic of Revolution in the Film and Literature of Naguib Mahfouz (1952–1967)*.

Routledge Studies in Political Islam

This series provides a forum for the latest research on all aspects of political Islam. It includes a range of approaches and studies on individuals, movements, theory and practice.

For a full list of titles in the series: www.routledge.com/middleeaststudies/series/SE0520.

1 **The Flourishing of Islamic Reformism in Iran**
Political Islamic Groups in Iran (1941–61)
Seyed Mohammad Ali Taghavi

2 **The Political Thought of Sayyid Qutb**
The Theory of Jahiliyyah
Sayed Khatab

3 **The Power of Sovereignty**
The Political and Ideological Philosophy of Sayyid Qutb
Sayed Khatab

4 **Islam and Political Reform in Saudi Arabia**
The Quest for Political Change and Reform
Mansoor Jassem Alshamsi

5 **Democracy in Islam**
Sayed Khatab and Gary D. Bouma

6 **The Muslim Brotherhood**
Hasan al-Hudaybi and Ideology
Barbara Zollner

7 **Islamic Revivalism in Syria**
The Rise and Fall of Ba'thist Secularism
Line Khatib

8 **The Essence of Islamist Extremism**
Recognition through Violence, Freedom through Death
Irm Haleem

9 **Religious Authority and Political Thought in Twelver Shi'ism**
From Ali to Post-Khomeini
Hamid Mavani

10 **Islamism and the West**
From "Cultural Attack" to "Missionary Migrant"
Uriya Shavit

11 **Islamists of the Maghreb**
Jeffry R. Halverson and Nathaniel Greenberg

Islamists of the Maghreb

Jeffry R. Halverson and
Nathaniel Greenberg

LONDON AND NEW YORK

First published 2018
by Routledge

2 Park Square, Milton Park, Abingdon, Oxfordshire OX14 4RN
52 Vanderbilt Avenue, New York, NY 10017

Routledge is an imprint of the Taylor & Francis Group, an informa business

First issued in paperback 2019

Copyright © 2018 Jeffry R. Halverson and Nathaniel Greenberg

The right of Jeffry R. Halverson and Nathaniel Greenberg to be identified
as authors of this work has been asserted by them in accordance with
sections 77 and 78 of the Copyright, Designs and Patents Act 1988.

All rights reserved. No part of this book may be reprinted or reproduced or
utilised in any form or by any electronic, mechanical, or other means, now
known or hereafter invented, including photocopying and recording, or in
any information storage or retrieval system, without permission in writing
from the publishers.

Notice:
Product or corporate names may be trademarks or registered trademarks,
and are used only for identification and explanation without intent to
infringe.

British Library Cataloguing in Publication Data
A catalogue record for this book is available from the British Library

Library of Congress Cataloging in Publication Data
Names: Halverson, Jeffry R., author. | Greenberg, Nathaniel, 1979- author.
Title: Islamists of the Maghreb / Jeffry R. Halverson and Nathaniel Greenberg.
Other titles: Routledge studies in political Islam ; 11.
Description: Milton Park, Abingdon, Oxon : Routledge, 2018. |
Series: Routledge studies in political Islam ; 11 | Includes bibliographical
references and index.
Identifiers: LCCN 2017026423 | ISBN 9781138093522 (hbk) |
ISBN 9781315106762 (ebk)
Subjects: LCSH: Islam and politics–Africa, North–History–21st century. |
Arab Spring, 2010- | Political parties–Africa, North–History–21st century. |
Sunnites–Africa, North–History. | Africa, North–Politics and government–
21st century.
Classification: LCC JQ3198.A979 H35 2018 | DDC 324.2/1820961–dc23
LC record available at https://lccn.loc.gov/2017026423

ISBN: 978-1-138-09352-2 (hbk)
ISBN: 978-0-367-89078-0 (pbk)

Typeset in Times New Roman
by Wearset Ltd, Boldon, Tyne and Wear

Contents

Note on transliteration		vi
Introduction		1
1	The victory of Sunni Islam	12
2	Occupation	30
3	Algeria	46
4	Tunisia	64
5	Libya	84
6	Morocco	100
7	The Maghreb beyond Islamism	117
	Index	128

Note on transliteration

In this book we employ a modified version of the system for the transliteration of Arabic words into English as provided by *The International Journal of Middle East Studies* (IJMES). We render the Arabic *ta marbuta* as "a" unless contained as part of an *idafa* sentence. In the case of names, which are often pronounced differently in the Maghreb than other parts of the Arabic speaking world, we have pursued a method that favors the "most conventional spelling" of an individual's name. This spelling is typically derived from its usage in a public forum (i.e., a recognized news organization, or international summit), or other documentation that indicates direct participation of the individual in question. This method goes beyond the parameters of IJMES which allows for alternate transliterations of a name only in the case of an individual's 'preferred' spelling. In those instances where there exists no conventional model for spelling an individual's name in English, or a preferred spelling in English, we defer to the IJMES system. In all cases, however, in accord with IJMES, we have retained the letters *'ayn* (rendered ') and non-initial *hamzas* (rendered ').

Introduction

This book examines the Islamist political parties that rose to power and prominence in the wake of the Arab Spring in the Maghreb. To clarify at the outset, the Maghreb is the region of northwest Africa comprised of Libya, Tunisia, Algeria, and Morocco, as well as Western Sahara and Mauritania. We emphasize those first four nation-states when using the term, *Maghreb*. For anyone unfamiliar with it, *Maghreb* is an Arabic word that simply means the "Western place," and generally refers to the lands of North Africa west of Egypt. Today approximately 90 million people live spread out over some 1.8 million squares miles of land, but over 69 percent now live in cities.[1] Most of the land is harsh and uninhabitable desert—Libya has no natural rivers. By 1912, all of the Maghreb was under the rule of European Christians, principally the French, Spanish, and Italians. Some Europeans imagined their imperialist ambitions in the Maghreb as a rightful reclamation of lands once part of Christendom. It was in Algeria, after all, that Augustine of Hippo had laid the theological foundations for the Latin Church in the fifth century (CE).

For centuries before their conquest of the Maghreb, Europeans called this vast Muslim region "Barbary." That name derives from the time of the Romans, who described the "uncivilized" (i.e., un-Romanized) peoples inhabiting the frontiers in all directions as barbarians (*barbarus* in Greek and Latin). The indigenous non-Arab inhabitants of the Maghreb hence came to be known as Berbers; a name still commonly used today. Meanwhile, the Berbers, or *Imazighen*, called their homeland *Tamazgha*.

The identity of this region, both in its components and as a composite, represents one of the most complex regions in the world today. Among the *Imazighen*, the region is home to several distinctive indigenous subgroups, including the Tuareg and Kabilye. Over the centuries, the *Imazighen* have lived under the rule of Romans, Arabs, Turks, and Europeans, who all occupied land in the Maghreb. This long history of imperialism has generated, in turn, a virtually unceasing cycle of conflict, ranging from wars of sedition to revolutions and civil wars, as well as struggles over identity.

While the region is home to Judaism, Christianity, and a number of indigenous religions, perhaps the single defining cultural dimension of the contemporary Maghreb is the preeminence of Islam, particularly the Sunni-Malikite

2 Introduction

sect. Since the initial Arab conquests under the banner of the Umayyad Caliphate by the early eighth century (CE), successive Muslim imperial dynasties, including the Abbasids and Fatimids, emphasized Islam as a basis for social cohesion and political legitimacy. From the colonial era onward, however, no such coalescence has existed. The contemporary nation-state system embedded itself and engendered additional layers to already contested and complex multivalent identities.

In 2011, new upheaval brought historic change. The Maghreb occupied a prominent place in world headlines when Sidi Bouzid, Tunisia, became the birthplace of the Arab Spring. Events in Tunisia sparked huge and sometimes violent uprisings. Longstanding dictatorships fell in their wake. The ensuing democratic reforms resulted in elections and the victory of several Islamist political parties in the Arab world, such as Ennahdha in Tunisia, the Freedom and Justice Party (FJP) in Egypt, and the Justice and Development Party (PJD) in Morocco. The origins, development, and rise of these Islamist parties in the Maghreb are the core subject of this book.

Since the Arab Spring revolution in Egypt, the Muslim Brotherhood (*Ikhwan al-Muslimin*)—grandfather of all Islamist groups—rose to power through democracy, albeit with great subsequent turmoil under the reign of President Mohamed Morsi. After only one year in power, Morsi was overthrown in a military coup on July 3, 2013. Morsi and large numbers of Muslim Brotherhood members now sit in prison and face execution amid international outcries. As noted at the onset, Egypt is not part of the Maghreb. Rather, Egypt is typically designated as a key part of the obscure transcontinental and historically fluctuating entity known as "the Middle East." Depending on who uses the term, it may even include countries like Pakistan. The fact that Egypt is discussed periodically in this book should not confuse readers into thinking that the Maghreb and the Middle East are the same. They are not, and, geography aside, the two regions have significant historical and cultural differences. In fact, Egypt is the only "Middle East" country located in Africa, unless one chooses to include countries such as the Sudan, Eritrea, or Djibouti. However, this study does not envision "the Middle East" in this manner.

At present, there is a controversial view in the United States of America that Islam, the dominant religion of the Maghreb, is not a religion but a political ideology. A similar view has been espoused in parts of Europe, such as the Netherlands. This is a problematic and provocative thesis tied to Islamophobic and anti-immigrant political agendas. But the fact that such a claim exists at all illustrates how pervasive secular assumptions about religion have become in the United States and elsewhere. The thesis rests on the assumption that the existence of laws and political institutions in Islamic thought and texts (e.g., Qur'an, Hadith) somehow removes Islam from the contested category of "religion." And by "religion," proponents of this view appear to mean a set of beliefs ("faith") about transcendent matters that inform ethics, morality, rituals and a set of communal activities, but little or nothing else. Obviously, if we were to apply this litmus test to all the religions of the world, including Judaism and Catholicism,

Introduction 3

very few (if any) religions would meet such a narrow and deliberately restrictive definition.

On one hand, this problematic conception of "religion" reflects the prevailing Protestant culture of its proponents (which includes non-Protestants). As we know, beginning in the sixteenth century, Protestants in Europe stressed salvation through faith alone (*sola fide*) and not through works, nor through the intermediary role of the Pope (an absolute monarch) and the Roman Catholic Church. But this is only part of the story. Protestantism was not a revolt against the role of religion in politics in general (but against the papacy), and it was never about keeping religions restricted to the private sphere; reducing religion to a set of beliefs, moral platitudes, and weekly worship services. Far from it. John Calvin and the Protestant Grand Council of Geneva saw no such separation between religion and politics. Indeed, they saw fit to execute the Spanish polymath Michael Servetus at the stake for his heretical rejection of the Trinity and infant baptism. Likewise, the Protestant Pilgrims and Puritans who settled in New England saw no separation, and looked to the Bible as the basis of their laws and political institutions. The examples are numerous. Hence, the idea that religion is only a set of beliefs, separate from the realm of law and politics, is not a product of the sixteenth century Reformation but the eighteenth century, the Age of Enlightenment. And it came about through fierce and violent struggles, such as the Thirty Years' War.

Religion has always been intertwined with law, politics, and all other areas of individual and communal life. It is only in cases where religions have failed to attain a level of dominance and power (e.g., Jainism) that we find little attention given to such matters. But for Islam, Christianity, Judaism, Hinduism, Buddhism, and many others, the idea of separating religion from public life is a break from historical precedent and tradition. It is a modern European innovation. Separating religion from public life is the outlier. Not Islam. That said, we must ask an important question. What exactly do scholars mean when they refer to "political Islam" as something distinct from traditional Islam or Islam in general? This is the question we now seek to address.

In the seventh century (CE), the "Arabs of Muhammad," as they are called in the earliest Syriac sources, were led by a caliph (*khalifa*) who served as a political, administrative, and legal authority over the community (*umma*). According to the Sunni version of events, the earliest caliphs were pious statesmen with close ties to the Prophet Muhammad during his lifetime (all *sahaba* with bonds to him by marriage), but lacked infallibility and ongoing divine guidance. The Shia tradition, rejecting the first three (conventionally recognized) caliphs as illegitimate (or simply inferior in the case of the Zaydis), insisted that God's guidance continued through 'Ali and Fatima in the form of divinely-appointed, infallible, sinless imams from the *Ahl al-Bayt* (i.e., Muhammad's family). As the office of the caliphate developed in the coming decades and centuries under the auspices of proto-Sunnis and Sunnis (to the exclusion of the Shia until the rise of the Ismaili Fatimids—as discussed in Chapter 1), the caliph became a monarch comparable to his rival in Christian Byzantium. And, indeed, the Umayyad

4 *Introduction*

dynasty of Damascus (661–750 CE) borrowed heavily from Byzantine and Sassanian customs and institutions to run the Arab empire, filling numerous gaps or matters left unattended by the Qur'an and *sunna*. As a world empire stretching from Spain to North Africa to Central Asia, the diverse multiethnic populace of the empire was organized according to religious affiliation with differing tax brackets, obligations and legal jurisdictions. For the Muslims living in the empire, a system of jurisprudence (*fiqh*) and courts took shape that referred to the Qur'an and sunna (later codified in the books of Hadith) for judgements. The resulting legal formulations produced by Muslim scholars or *'ulama* are known collectively as *shari'a*. The Jews and Christians in the empire were governed by their own legal traditions, such as *halakha*. Nowhere do we find religion divorced from the public sphere and the realm of politics and law, whether among the Muslims, the Christians, or the Jews.

When contemporary scholars speak of "political Islam," they juxtapose a particular expression of Islam with modernity. They view Islam through the lens of the European Enlightenment and delineate religion as a discernable entity with its own contours and features, apart from other areas of human life and society. Such conceptions have been the target of scholars like J. Z. Smith, who famously argued that "religion is solely the creation of the scholar's study … [It] has no independent existence apart from the academy."[2] Let us take this observation as a starting point for establishing the manner in which we discuss "political Islam" or Islamism in this study. As scholars, we discern the start of Islamism in the colonial era during the early twentieth century, specifically in British-occupied Egypt and India.

In these contexts, Muslim activists like Hassan al-Banna in Egypt and Abul A'la Mawdudi in India (neither a member of the *'ulama*) reacted to the growing privatization and disregard for religion in their societies. More specifically, the removal of Islam as the bedrock of public life. The British Empire was in fact not secular; the monarch remained the head of the Anglican Church. Religious missions and institutions were established wherever the empire spread. But in practice, British Protestantism had been reduced to a supremacist cultural identity, a set of symbols and casual moral maxims. Indeed, as sociologists of religion have long argued, the growth of nationalism, such as "Britishness," assumed a role previously held by religion. And as historian Hilary M. Cary argued in her study, *God's Empire: Religion and Colonialism in the British World,* c. *1801–1908*, "Britons in the [nineteenth] century tended to define themselves less by their belligerent Protestantism than by their religious toleration and love of liberty."[3] This was the Enlightenment at work, bolstered by a series of British legislative reforms.

The British Empire, more so than anything else, valued their vast colonial holdings for their commercial and strategic value. Indeed, Britain's entire occupation of Egypt was motivated largely (if not entirely) by investments and the Suez Canal, without which access to British India ("the Jewel of the British Empire") was very difficult. The indigenous peoples of territories like Egypt were an afterthought and perceived as a burden and an inconvenience. Colonial

Introduction 5

administrators like Evelyn Baring acted as though they were reluctant foster parents, tasked with managing vast irrational masses in desperate need of manners, education, and discipline, including the strike of the rod when necessary. If the colonial subjects of the British Crown might be put to some good use in the mines, the farm fields or the battlefields then all the better. But colonial agents like Baring believed that Islam was an obstacle that hindered Muslim ("Mohammedan") subjects of the empire. As Baring wrote in his two-volume tome, *Modern Egypt*, he believed that Islam "as a social system has been a complete failure."[4]

Hassan al-Banna was a child when Baring left Egypt in 1907, but the British would remain until after al-Banna's assassination in 1949. According to the dominant narrative, the Muslim Brothers were established by al-Banna in Ismailia, a town in the British-fortified Suez Canal Zone, in 1928. The original goals of the group were to support Egyptian independence from British colonial rule and to counteract the European cultural impact on society. Christian missionaries were active in Egypt. Saloons had set-up shop. Al-Banna and his peers lamented a perceived shift toward secularism that separated Islam from public life. Women were encouraged to discard the *hijab*. Men defiantly neglected their prayers. Meanwhile, most of the traditional religious establishment—except for a few like the students of the late reformist *shaykh* Muhammad 'Abduh (d. 1905)—did little to confront these profound challenges. Al-Banna, a school teacher by trade (not a *shaykh* per se), mobilized. He preached in coffee shops, travelled from village to village, met with Azhar *shaykhs* and Arab nationalists alike, all in the cause of building an Egyptian state that was true to its own heritage and people (as he envisioned it). As a Muslim majority country with a long and rich history in the Islamic era, the land of Egypt—for al-Banna and the Muslim Brotherhood—must be an "Islamic state" (an ambiguous concept from the start). And it must be free from colonial occupation and economic exploitation at the hands of foreign powers (e.g., Britain).

Contemporary academic scholars have offered many definitions of political Islam or Islamism; the ideology behind the modern concept of the "Islamic state." For instance, Asef Bayat defined political Islam or Islamism broadly as "ideologies and movements that strive to establish some kind of an 'Islamic order'—a religious state, *shari'a* law, and moral codes in Muslim societies and communities [in association with the state]."[5] In particular, Bayat emphasizes the state and state power as the framework for Islamist politics; the key distinction between it and other Islamic movements or earlier political formulations. Similarly, Jeffry R. Halverson defined Islamism in another study by stating:

> If the modern nation-state represents (among other things), as Crawford Young has written, the marriage of the state with the idea of nationalism, then (in my view) the emergence of Islamism in the first half of the twentieth century, whether in Egypt or India, represents the marriage of [Athari-imposed creedalism] with the modern nation-state.[6]

6   *Introduction*

The modern state, therefore, lies at the heart of political Islam. It is the framework for the construction of what Bayat described as an "Islamic order."

The Islamist parties of the Maghreb are rooted in this same historical experience of colonial occupation as those in Egypt and India, albeit under different European powers. While certain dogmatic factors do have a role (discussed below) in political Islam, the primary concern of the Islamists was not simply the notion that God (*Allah*) demands a certain ancient law imposed. Rather, the Islamists saw Islamic law (*shari'a*) and governance (i.e., a nation-state with *shari'a*) as an indigenous system that does not emulate a European colonialist's system (at least explicitly). This observation brings us to the core analytical lens of the book—identity. All of the Maghreb countries were ruled (by force) for decades by European colonial powers who compelled the peoples of these lands to conform to their foreign dictates. That dark history is explored in detail in Chapter 2. For now, it suffices to say that colonial rule fundamentally deracinated and humiliated the Muslim peoples and societies of the Maghreb. Those experiences still reverberate on the geopolitical scene today. Islamism in the Middle East and North Africa, starting in Egypt, has always been a reassertion of Muslim identity in pro-independence revolutionary terms. Its significance was enhanced when rival twentieth century modernist ideologies, such as Pan-Arabism, socialism, and communism, failed to deliver on many bold promises and restore a sense of dignity to these nations, especially when it came to the conflict over Palestine (e.g., 1967 Six-Day War). Slaheddine Jourchi, a co-founder of the Islamic Tendency Movement in Tunisia (French acronym MTI) and first appointed head of the Constituent National Assembly (ANC) in 2011, described the situation by stating:

> While other parties were busy dealing with the effects of the crisis from the Sixties—the result of the failure of the country's experiment in socialism— a small group of individuals, in the early seventies, began meeting in one of the mosques of the capital forming the first nucleus of the Islamic Movement. Its direction was formed by clear and simple orations of ideology. Even when some of elements of the movement began migrating to the public realm, the political elite, though suspicious, never saw it as anything more than a "passing trend." They paid little attention to the seriousness of the issues or the "significance" of the movement to the development and balance of power. It was only with the Iranian revolution and the overthrow of the Shah that the warning became real.[7]

In 2012, Rachid al-Ghannouchi, the chief ideologue and spiritual guide of MTI, now known as Ennahdha, crystalized the group's longstanding political mission. Speaking at the annual conference for the commemoration of the 1948 Palestinian *Nakba*, he stated: "Every development witnessed by the nation in the direction of freedom, justice and democracy, is a step in the direction of the liberation of Palestine." Lost to the British Empire in 1917, Palestine (in al-Ghannouchi's view) is the last Arab-Muslim state under European colonial rule (i.e., Israel).

Introduction 7

Toward this point, al-Ghannouchi addressed criticism of an article added to Tunisia's draft constitution that banned all normalization with Israel by explaining that "we are not against Jews, but rather, all forms of colonialism," reiterating his position (and connecting the postcolonial regime to French colonialism) that "the Arab Spring was inspired by the Palestinian resistance."[8] As Tunisia's elections revealed, Ennahdha's anti-colonial message was broadly supported.

In the first election since independence from France, Tunisia elected a temporary constituent assembly tasked with drafting a new constitution. Winning over 37 percent of the vote, Ennahdha won 89 out of 217 seats; the highest of any party participating in the election. Ennahdha's secretary-general, Hamadi Jebali (an engineer by trade), was selected as prime minister. In neighboring Algeria, three of the country's Islamist parties formed an alliance to participate in parliamentary elections. The alliance finished third and an additional Islamist party, the Justice and Development Party, finished seventh. The party of the ostensibly leftist ruling regime, the National Liberation Front, was the biggest victor and added 72 seats. In Morocco, parliamentary elections resulted in the victory of the Islamist Justice and Development Party led by 'Abdelilah Benkirane, winning 107 out of 305 elected seats. Benkirane was subsequently chosen as prime minister. Meanwhile, Libya saw the greatest outbreak of violence among the Maghreb states. After the capture and extra-judicial execution of Mu'ammar al-Gaddafi in 2011, a general national congress was elected. The largest number of seats (120 out of 200 seats) was won by independent candidates without a party affiliation, some of whom would be described as Islamist. Among officially organized parties, the Muslim Brotherhood-affiliated Justice and Construction Party finished second in the election, winning 17 seats.

The results of the post-Arab Spring elections present us with a question: Why has Islam reasserted itself in the political sphere of the contemporary Maghreb? The responses to this question are myriad. On one hand, one may argue that Islam already permeated government in the Maghreb on a variety of levels (some less visible than others), particularly in the case of Morocco. On the other hand, one might suggest that the prevailing strength of the secular tradition, a carryover from European colonialism and bolstered by the military force of the postcolonial state, consciously kept Islam out of the public sphere, save for opportune moments when the state found it advantageous. We contend that the most compelling explanation is a deep modern disconnect between political elites and the citizenry, which is part of a broader contest over the nature of Muslim identity. For instance, does Muslim identity rest on the profession of a certain orthodox dogma, or by performative association with a particular narrativized cultural heritage? Or some combination thereof?

In his study *The Failure of Political Islam*, Olivier Roy argued (perhaps prematurely) that Islamism was on the decline and destined to evolve into mainstream political parties or a type of evangelical personal piety disinterested in politics.[9] In a subsequent study, *Globalized Islam*, Roy continued his thesis and argued that globalization and the migration of Muslims to countries with non-Muslim majorities, like the United States or Great Britain, were steadily

8 *Introduction*

diminishing the relevance of the nation-state as a framework for the affirmation of Muslim identities.[10] In contrast to his intellectual foe Gilles Kepel, Roy has argued throughout that Islamism has little to do with Islamic doctrine. And, indeed, we too contend that doctrine is often over-exaggerated in Western analyses of political Islam and most certainly in popular media discourses (which often seem preoccupied with a smattering of Qur'anic verses). Yet, as Halverson argued in his study *Theology and Creed in Sunni Islam*, doctrine has played a role in this complex phenomenon; albeit in a far more complicated, historically embedded and nuanced manner than popular media discourses would ever have it.

On this note, it is appropriate to provide a few remarks about the relationship between Muslim belief and politics, particularly as the Islamists perceive it. Like Islam as a whole, the core of Islamism as a distinctive modern ideological movement is the doctrine of monotheism or *tawhid*. This is the foundational principle that there is one and *only* one god, *Allah*. The supreme deity is the primordial point from which everything derives. *Allah* is not divisible or comparable to anything created (which is everything in existence but God). In Sunni Islam (the dominant sect in the Maghreb), accepting the Oneness of God is the key to eternal salvation. Nothing can exist without God and there is no power but God's power in existence. Thus, nothing can exist in God's absence and annihilation (i.e., Hellfire) is a given, despite a person's individual merits. Since this idea is so pivotal, the biggest sin that a person can commit is rejecting *tawhid*, whether by being polytheistic (believing in many gods) or rejecting the idea that God exists at all.

Muslims further believe that *Allah*, the One God, has reminded and guided humanity to the true monotheistic reality of things through revealed knowledge conveyed to special individuals known as prophets. As most readers will already know, these prophets include Abraham, Moses, Jesus, and Muhammad, among many others. When we look at the content of those revelations given to the prophets, we find that God dictated many specific rules and duties for human beings. In the Qur'an, for example, God dictates to the Prophet Muhammad that human beings should abstain from consuming wine (or alcohol) due to its intoxicating effects. This is a dictate traditionally subsumed under the label of *shari'a*. That means that the One God—the sole power and source of existence—has resolved a question that needs no further debate (as the majority of Sunni *'ulama* would have it). This point brings us to a political question. Does a human being or a democratic society have the right to disagree with God? If human beings decide through legislation that alcohol is legal for consumption, does that mean they are placing themselves on par with *Allah* and committing the grave sin of idolatry (*shirk*)? According to the Islamists (but not most Muslims), the answer is "yes." And as they see it, this imperils individuals and societies as a whole— perhaps something the colonial powers wish to do.

Such deep notions of monotheism have many repercussions. *Tawhid* means that everything comes from God. That means that God is the source of the good and the bad. There is no Manichean dualism where an evil deity struggles against

Introduction 9

a good deity (as Zoroastrianism has it) and causes all the problems for individuals and societies. The issue of free will is thus problematic when approached in terms of strict monotheism. For instance, if all power comes from God, how do human beings—mere finite creations—act independently (against God's Will)? Historically, some Muslims have stressed God's omnipotence and advocated predestination (*jabr*). This claim is problematic if one believes in divinely dictated laws that punish people for sins and crimes. For example, how does the state punish a person for adultery if it was God's Will that the person commit adultery? The answer proposed by Sunni theologians like Abu Hamid al-Ghazali (d. 1111) is called the doctrine of acquisition (*kasb*). The doctrine of acquisition states that God creates every conceivable action (since He alone can brings things into existence), and human beings possess only the ability to choose or acquire an act (whether righteous or sinful). This makes people responsible (and punishable) for their choices in this world and the afterlife (thus preserving God's power over all things). Accountability for individual actions and conduct is important to the ethos of Islamist thought, even if Islamists are not particularly well-steeped in theology (*kalam*). Indeed, Halverson has argued that *kalam* as an active discipline largely collapsed in the Sunni Muslim world by the fifteenth century (CE), displaced by a creedalism that discouraged dynamic theological inquiry as new needs arose, such as the challenges of postcolonial statecraft.[11]

The ideological premise we find behind Islamism is that the modern state (a European innovation) should function as a tool to enforce *shari'a* and cultivate a virtuous or "true" (whatever that may mean) Islamic society. Not only does it presuppose strict monotheism (*tawhid*), but also the existence of divine law and human accountability for following it. In addition, Muhammad was the final prophet (marking the end of revelation), which means that the world is left with millions of Islamists trying to figure out how to live correctly with no direct channel to God. That means that there are now parties in power in the Maghreb trying to determine how to apply a 1400 year old classical Arabic book (the Qur'an) and 1200 year old books of prophetic traditions (Hadith) to their twenty-first century nation-states. This is a daunting and perplexing task. And as the son-in-law of the Prophet and Fourth Caliph/First Imam, 'Ali ibn Abu Talib, once said (as recorded in the *Nahj Balagha*): "The Qur'an is a book between two covers; it does not speak and must therefore have an interpreter." In other words, if there are 1.6 billion Muslims in the world, there are probably 1.6 billion different interpretations of the Qur'an, and thus Islam.

In the run-up to the vote on a new constitution in 2012, Rachid al-Ghannouchi laid out how Ennahdha might mitigate this dynamic by instituting a network of local *shura* councils, each capable of exercising discretion in the application of *shari'a*. These local councils would remain subordinate to the authority of al-Zaytouna in Tunis, the country's oldest center of Islamic jurisprudence.[12] The Muslim Brotherhood of Egypt advanced a similar idea in their own constitutional draft, which was revealed just months later. Article 4 of Part 1 of the document stated that "senior scholars from al-Azhar," the country's oldest center of Islamic learning, would "be consulted in matters pertaining to Islamic law."

10 *Introduction*

Since Islamic law was to be the "principal source of legislation," the clause attempted to ensure that all local legislation was subordinate to the authority of al-Azhar. Despite these nods to local autonomy in the application of *shari'a*, attempts to centralize Islamic jurisprudence under the banner of the modern nation-state have proven challenging and often hazardous.

When it comes to the Islamists of the Maghreb, matters of doctrine and jurisprudence are ultimately only part of the story and a relative afterthought. This is particularly true insofar as the millions of everyday people who cast votes for the Islamists are concerned. In this study, we go beyond ideology to explore the people behind the Islamist parties of the Maghreb and how local history shaped their political visions and aspirations. Behind millions of votes, it is these Islamists who have risen to power through democratic channels in the wake of the Arab Spring. Despite the trials that inevitably occur in every nation-state (including the United States), the challenges faced by these parties are necessary steps forward. In particular, this is the time for the peoples of the Maghreb to explore their own cultural identities; an essential component of any viable nationhood. It is a step that was repressed, often with bloody force, for decades by postcolonial, anti-democratic, autocratic regimes in the interests of power and privilege. As the present study proceeds, we concisely review the historical contexts to put these important developments into place. Local history and culture are important, although this book is still fundamentally about identity. In Chapters 3, 4, 5, and 6, the study takes readers from country to country across the Maghreb and discusses the Islamist parties and key Islamist personalities in each of these states. After that journey, we conclude with a broader analysis of the rise of these parties and offer some speculation about the future of Islamism in the Maghreb.

Notes

1 According to 2015 data by the World Bank, accessed August 27, 2016, http://data.worldbank.org/indicator/SP.URB.TOTL.IN.ZS.
2 See Smith (1982, xi).
3 See Cary (2011, 10).
4 See The Earl of Cromer (1916, 34:134).
5 See Bayat (2013, 4).
6 See Halverson (2010, 62).
7 From the collection *Min qabḍat Bin 'Ali ila Thawrat al-Yasamin: Al-Islam al-siyasi fi Tunis* [From the Grip of Ben 'Ali to the Jasmine Revolution: Political Islam in Tunisia] (Dubayy: Markaz al-Misbar lil-Dirasat wa-al-Buḥuth. Markaz al-Misbar lil-Dirasat wa-al-Buḥuth, 2011).
8 The speech, titled, *"Tahrir al-sh'aub al-'Arabiyya min al-istibdaad khatuwwa 'ala tariq tahrir Filistin"* [The Liberation of the Arab Peoples: Stepping Stones to the Liberation of Palestine] was posted on the group's Facebook page and party website on May 17, 2012, but later removed. A copy of the remarks can be found at *Turess*.com: www.turess.com/infosplus/11450, accessed September 1, 2016.
9 See Roy (1998).
10 See Roy (2004).
11 See Halverson (2010, 33–81).

12 Al-Ghannouchi clarified this position in his interview with a*l-Jazeera* host Teymoor Nabili on September 22, 2012.

References

Bayat, Asef, ed. 2013. *Post-Islamism: The Changing Faces of Political Islam*. New York: Oxford University Press.

Cary, Hilary M. 2011. *God's Empire: Religion and Colonialism in the British World, c. 1801–1908*. New York: Cambridge University Press.

The Earl of Cromer. 1916. *Modern Egypt, Two Volumes in One*. New York: Macmillan.

Halverson, Jeffry R. 2010. *Theology and Creed in Sunni Islam: The Muslim Brotherhood, Ash'arism, and Political Sunnism*. New York: Palgrave Macmillan.

Roy, Olivier. 1998. *The Failure of Political Islam*. Translated by Carol Volk. Cambridge, MA: Harvard University Press.

Roy, Olivier. 2004. *Globalized Islam: The Search for a New Ummah*. New York: Columbia University Press.

Smith, Jonathan Z. 1982. *Imagining Religion: From Babylon to Jonestown*. Chicago: The University of Chicago Press.

1   The victory of Sunni Islam

The surviving historical sources for the Arab-Islamic expansion across the Maghreb are few and generally date from centuries after the events they describe. This is not uncommon for the time or the region. Furthermore, the Arabic language was not developed into a literary language until after Muhammad's death, as attested by the earliest surviving fragments of the Qur'an. The records that historians of the Maghreb rely on generally date from the ninth century and after. There is therefore a high probability of embellishment, politicization, and folk legend present in the narratives. Nevertheless, scholars have sought to assemble the most reliable history of the period, based on all known information and data. We have relied on the consensus of those findings for the narrative recounted in this chapter. The history of Islam's arrival in the Maghreb and the rise of Sunni Islam as the dominant sect in the region is the subject we now explore.

In the first decades of the seventh century, North Africa's coastal regions were the domain of the Byzantine Empire. A Christian empire with its capital in Constantinople (now Istanbul, Turkey), the Byzantines had endured a bloody and protracted war against the Zoroastrians of the Sassanian Empire of Persia for years. This left Byzantium in a weakened state by the time the Arabs emerged from the desert so unexpectedly. Only a decade after Muhammad's death, the Arabs were snatching away major Byzantine holdings in Egypt and Syria and creating garrisons for further imperial expansion in every direction.

Away from the North African coast and Byzantine urban centers, such as Carthage, the Maghreb was inhabited by Berber (*Amazigh*) tribes and confederations, led by chieftains (sometimes monarchs), who were largely nomadic, mostly pagan, and engaged in periodic military raids. These tribes proved to be the greatest challenge to Islam's advance into the Maghreb. The Byzantines, after all, were separated from their centers of power, like Constantinople, by the Mediterranean Sea. But the Berbers, even after converting to Islam, proved to be a source of political instability over the ensuing centuries that shaped the history of Islam in the region.

After the Muslim conquest of Egypt, a garrison city was established on the Nile called al-Fustat, encapsulated by Cairo today. In the seventh century, the city served as the staging ground for the coming military campaigns. The westward expansion out of al-Fustat fell under the leadership of 'Abdullah ibn Sa'd,

The victory of Sunni Islam 13

an unpopular governor of Egypt, appointed by the caliph in Arabia, 'Uthman of the Umayyad clan.

Politics was a turbulent business in the Muslim community from the start. Three of the first four caliphs, the political rulers of the Muslim empire, were assassinated, and they were all close companions (*sahaba*) or disciples of the Prophet Muhammad. Sunni Muslims call these first four leaders the "Rightly Guided Caliphs." Obviously, some of their contemporaries in the seventh century disagreed. Unlike those four men, 'Abdullah ibn Sa'd was not a close disciple of the Prophet, but rather a kinsman of the caliph, 'Uthman. This is how he received his post in Egypt. He reportedly converted to Islam, apostatized, and returned to the pagans of Mecca during the 620s. In fact, one tradition says that the Prophet wanted 'Abdullah ibn Sa'd killed after the conquest of Mecca in 630.

In 642, Arab armies started capturing sparsely populated regions of modern Libya. A year later, the important Byzantine port city of Tripoli was taken. At the time, the central coastal region of North Africa was under Gregory, the Byzantine Exarch of Africa. The fall of Tripoli led Gregory to build his forces in anticipation of future Muslim advances into his domain. But in 647, the year that 'Abdullah ibn Sa'd and his army invaded modern Tunisia, then known as *Ifriqiyya*, Gregory declared that his Exarchate, protected by the Mediterranean, was a separate empire apart from Byzantium. He would face the Arab armies alone, without Byzantine reinforcements and hemmed in by the great sea.

At Sbeitla, his independent capital in central Tunisia, Gregory made his last stand. The city's inland location offered some strategic advantages, but it lacked substantial walls or fortifications. The region around Sbeitla also held valuable farm lands. The strategy, therefore, was to engage the Muslims before they reached the city. Gregory's army consisted of North African feudal lords (probably of Roman-Byzantine extraction) and their clients, as well as auxiliary Berber units from allied tribes and possibly Numidian light cavalry.[1]

Among 'Abdullah ibn Sa'd's Arab and Berber forces were many notable early Muslims, including the son of 'Umar (the second "Rightly Guided Caliph"), a future Umayyad caliph, and 'Abdallah ibn al-Zubayr, a rebel leader who later proclaimed himself caliph in Mecca.[2] Sources also suggest that the Muslims were accompanied by Coptic Christian allies from Egypt.[3] Under the advice of 'Abdallah ibn al-Zubayr, the Muslims carried out ambushes, skirmishes, and feigned flights throughout the day, until hours before sunset when a direct assault was launched against Gregory's fatigued defenses. Poorly trained auxiliaries fled and core units were decimated in combat. Tradition relates that Gregory himself was killed by 'Abdallah ibn al-Zubayr, although no one knows for certain. The Muslim victory at Sbeitla sent shockwaves throughout North Africa and opened the gates for the caliphs to take hold. Raids and skirmishes continued throughout the region for the next year or so, until the local population was so desperate that they agreed to pay a huge tribute to the Arabs in exchange for a peace treaty. Permanent settlement though was still some years away.

Nothing remains of Sbeitla today but ruins. Signs of 'Abdullah ibn Sa'd's presence have vanished too. After his short stint in *Ifriqiyya*, he returned to

14   *The victory of Sunni Islam*

Egypt, where he lived in luxury and ruled harshly over the people. He was so unpopular, in fact, that a delegation of Muslims in Egypt traveled to Medina in Arabia to share their grievances and seek his removal from office. After much discussion, 'Uthman reluctantly agreed and selected the son of Abu Bakr, the first "Rightly Guided Caliph," as the new governor. But traditions relates that a letter attributed to 'Uthman ordering 'Abdullah ibn Sa'd to retain his post and kill the new governor was discovered. This created intense scandal among the Muslims. It also delayed and complicated any plans to further expand into the Maghreb.

The caliph 'Uthman, now over 80 years old, was suddenly in danger of being overthrown by fellow Muslims, who felt he was corrupt and being exploited by his own clan. Muslim rebels concluded that the letter in question was written by the caliph's close kinsman, Marwan ibn al-Hakam, and they demanded his surrender. 'Uthman, however, refused. A siege of 'Uthman's house ensued and he was murdered, spending his final moments seated inside, reading piously from the Qur'an.

'Abdullah ibn Sa'd, meanwhile, was traveling east in support of his kinsman and master, 'Uthman. However, upon hearing news of the turmoil in Medina, he traveled north into Syria, where the Umayyad clan remained in firm control. Living in Damascus, he enjoyed the protection of the governor there, Mu'awiyya (son of the Prophet's arch-foe Abu Sufyan), who was also appointed (or retained) by 'Uthman. After the caliph's murder in 656, Mu'awiyya became the head of the Umayyad clan and refused allegiance to the new caliph, 'Ali. Now, less than 30 years after the death of the Prophet Muhammad, politics was driving the Muslims into an all-out civil war.

'Uthman's clan, the Umayyads, led by Mu'awiyya in Syria, were not the only faction that refused to accept the caliphate of 'Ali. One of the Prophet Muhammad's widows, Aisha (daughter of Abu Bakr, the first "Rightly Guided Caliph"), also opposed 'Ali's reign and led an army against him at the so-called Battle of the Camel in Basra, Iraq, in 656. She and her supporters, including the father of 'Abdullah ibn al-Zubayr (who killed the Exarch Gregory at Sbeitla), were easily defeated by 'Ali's army. But the Umayyads were a far more formidable enemy for 'Ali. The climatic confrontation between the two sides occurred in the summer of 657 at the Battle of Siffin in northern Syria along the waters of the Euphrates River.

The Battle of Siffin is a major turning point in Islamic history with wide-ranging ramifications. However, the separation between Islam and politics was not one of them. The battle lasted for months, beginning with reluctant skirmishes and tense negotiations, and then steadily increased into greater combat and bloodshed (Muslims killing Muslims). Finally, when the indecisive battle seemed to lean in 'Ali's favor, soldiers from Mu'awiyya's army marched out with manuscripts of the Qur'an tied to their lances. They called for God's Word to decide. This meant that they wanted arbitration based on Islamic law to end the conflict. 'Ali reluctantly agreed, believing that it was likely a trick concocted by Mu'awiyya. Negotiations, however, commenced. The terms were unfavorable to 'Ali and his willingness to negotiate with the treacherous rebel Mu'awiyya angered some in his ranks. After all, the Qur'an states that: "If two parties from the believers are fighting each other, make peace between them; but if one of them rebels against the other, then fight against the rebels until they follow the command of God" (49:9). Still, 'Ali's defenders would retort, the Qur'an also states immediately afterwards that: "The believers are one brotherhood so make peace between your brothers and fear God" (49:10). The most zealous opponents of the arbitration insisted that those following Mu'awiyya must be fought as sinful rebels. The majority in the ranks wanted an end to the bloodshed though. It was a conflict that could have threatened the very existence of Islam. Rival empires, like the Byzantines, would have liked nothing better than to see the Muslims implode on themselves.

From Siffin, 'Ali and his forces withdrew to Kufa in Iraq, while Mu'awiyya remained in Damascus. Delegates for the two sides met to discuss settlement terms in the ensuing months. It was not a fruitful process. At the heart of the negotiations was Mu'awiyya's demand for vengeance against those who killed 'Uthman. Ultimately, it resulted in a stalemate, neither side yielding, and Syria, as well as other territories, remained under Mu'awiyya's rule, outside of 'Ali's caliphate. Meanwhile, a portion of 'Ali's supporters who opposed the arbitration withdrew from 'Ali altogether and renounced both sides as unbelievers. These pious but zealous (even extremist) Muslims are known as the Kharijites (*al-khawarij*).

The Kharijites, who produced several sects including Ibadi Islam (one of the three main branches of Islam), gathered at Nahrawan in Iraq. They believed that true believers should live separately or dissociate from apostates, heretics, and sinners elsewhere in the Muslim empire. They also recognized only the first and second caliphs, Abu Bakr and 'Umar, as "Rightly Guided," condemning 'Uthman, 'Ali, and the rebel Mu'awiyya as sinners. Faith, they believed, was evident in a person's actions, so sin could nullify a person's status as a believer. Among the most extreme Kharijites, this meant that sinners should be killed as apostates. This strict emphasis on righteous behavior applied to everyone in the community too, including (or especially) the caliphs. Egalitarianism was a core element of the Kharijite movement, and it made their teachings very appealing to Berbers in the Maghreb who felt discrimination under the Arab aristocracy.

In the winter of 661, 'Ali was praying in a mosque in Kufa when he was struck in the head with a poisoned sword by a Kharijite assassin. He died days later and was buried in the adjacent city of Najaf, Iraq. A Kharijite assassin tried to kill Mu'awiyya as well, but failed. The death of 'Ali ended the era of the four "Rightly Guided Caliphs," a period of time revered by Sunni Muslims, especially Islamists, as a golden age under a true "Islamic state." Admittedly, for the outside observer, it would seem that the Islamists could hardly have chosen a worse political environment to extol as a model for a modern nation-state.

After 'Ali's death, Mu'awiyya claimed the throne of the caliphate. His coronation was held at Jerusalem in 661, beginning the Umayyad dynasty of caliphs that would last until the middle of the eighth century. To his credit, he succeeded in unifying the Muslim empire again and proved to be an astute administrator.

16 *The victory of Sunni Islam*

But his changes to the office of the caliphate (making it a hereditary monarchy), his innovations and his disregard for Islamic teachings proved unpopular. As the Umayyads asserted their newly attained power, the Muslims once again were able to turn outward and engage the Byzantines. And the Maghreb was once again a battleground, as earlier gains there had been lost amidst the civil war.

The caliph designated a veteran Arab commander, 'Uqba ibn Nafi, as the general in charge of the campaign in the Maghreb. 'Uqba is a major character in the story of Islam's expansion into the Maghreb. In fact, he is often known as "Sidi 'Uqba" or Saint 'Uqba for his important efforts and achievements. In 670, 'Uqba led his army into Tunisia with little resistance and founded a new garrison city to serve as a base of his operations.[4] The city was called Qayrawan (Kairouan) and it remains one of the holy cities of Islam today.

Kairouan sits inland around the center of Tunisia. It is hot and arid there, unlike the fertile lands around Tunis to the north. In the middle of the old medina, only a few paces from a café, one can find a most obscure attraction. Going up a narrow set of stone stairs, visitors reach a floor with a café and an adjacent chamber under a white dome. In this chamber one will find a fully grown camel wearing blinders over its eyes and bunches of colorful scarves affixed to a body harness. Over its back, the harness connects to a large wooden lever, about 12 feet long. It attaches to a system of pulleys and large wheels and a water-well decorated with ornate tiles, known as Bir Barouta, which sits in the center of the chamber. When the camel walks around the well, the wooden lever turns the system of pulleys and wheels. Water is pulled up out of the well. In order to get the camel to walk, a man with a stick taps on the wooden lever and calls out "Zamzam! Zamzam!" The water is then gathered and placed in clay cups for people to drink. According to local belief, it is holy water from the same source as the well of Zamzam in the holy city of Mecca in Arabia.

Legend says that 'Uqba ibn Nafi and his army discovered a lost golden chalice from the holy city of Mecca (another version says Medina) there in the desert sand. When the chalice was pulled from the ground, water began to bubble up on the spot. Amazed at the fresh drinking water coming up from the sand, they soon made the even more miraculous discovery that it was from the same source as the Zamzam water in Mecca. Due to this miraculous spring, an encampment was created and it grew into the city of Qayrawan (Kairouan). In his new city, 'Uqba built an administration house and a mosque, portions of which still remain.

The grand mosque in Kairouan today, known as the Mosque of 'Uqba, remains on the site of the original structure and still contains original parts in the mosque's fascinating and eclectic architecture. However, it was remodeled and expanded several times over the early centuries, most notably under the Aghlabid *amirs* (kings) in the ninth century. Accessible seemingly only by foot, the lanes around the imposing brown buttressed exterior walls of the mosque are spacious, to accommodate large crowds on Fridays. The doorways to the mosque are elegant arches with heavy wooden doors. Inside of the mosque, there are hundreds of ornate stone pillars (legend says 600). They support a roofed brick

The victory of Sunni Islam   17

porch that surrounds a large open air courtyard paved with white stones, probably marble. The carpeted *musalla* (prayer space) on the south end is cordoned off with ornate wooden dividers. The venerable al-Azhar mosque in Cairo also has a large open air courtyard paved in white marble, similar to 'Uqba's. On the north end of the 'Uqba mosque stands an enormous minaret, where men once climbed up five times a day to proclaim the *adhan* or call to prayer. The distinct architectural style of the minaret is uniquely Maghrebi. Even the minarets in Egypt differ from them. The traditional minarets of the Maghreb are square and recall large clock or bell towers. At the top, there is a flat level with a smaller structure (or two) on top, capped by a dome or pointed roof.

Another classic example of the Maghrebi style of minaret is found at the Zaytouna mosque in the old medina of Tunis. It too is reached by foot. The Zaytouna mosque is the second most important mosque in the country, after 'Uqba's mosque. Just outside of Zaytouna, the Ottoman Turks (who conquered Tunisia in the sixteenth century) built a mosque with its own distinctive Ottoman minarets, baring no resemblance to the Maghrebi ones. Ottoman minarets are pointed, more decorative than functional, and usually come in pairs. The skyline of Istanbul, once the Ottoman capital (formerly the Byzantine capital), still demonstrates this distinctive style.

After almost five years in Kairouan, the caliph in Damascus, Mu'awiyya, forcefully recalled 'Uqba ibn Nafi to the east. He was replaced in the Maghreb by Abu al-Muhajir Dinar, who preferred to settle in a place called Takirwan instead of Kairouan. Under their new general, the Umayyad armies pushed westward into Algeria. There the army encountered a Christianized Berber tribal confederacy led by a king named Kusayla, who ruled from the city of Tilimsan (Tlemcen).[5] Abu al-Muhajir managed to negotiate an alliance with Kusayla, who accepted Islam in the process. This arrangement remained intact until 681, when the new caliph, the infamous Yazid (son of Mu'awiyya), reinstated 'Uqba ibn Nafi and dispatched him again to the Maghreb.

When 'Uqba reached Tunisia, he settled in Kairouan and had Abu al-Muhajir shackled as his prisoner. He also showed no deference to Kusayla at all. 'Uqba's behavior was likely equal parts revenge, arrogance, and disdain for Berbers, who were often treated as second-class citizens under the Umayyad Arab aristocracy. Whatever the case, he mobilized against the tribes and charged westward with his army and Abu al-Muhajir in tow. Traveling all the way to the coast of Morocco on the Atlantic Ocean, legend says that 'Uqba cried out: "Oh God! If this ocean had not stopped me, I would have continued to the farthest corners of the earth to extol Thy Name and fight the unbelievers!" Or something to that effect. Afterwards, he turned east to return to Kairouan, dividing his forces into two traveling parties.

During 'Uqba's surge toward the Atlantic, the Berber king Kusayla renewed ties to the Byzantines and apostatized from Islam. He hated 'Uqba and awaited his return from the coast. When 'Uqba and 300 of his warriors crossed Algeria, near the Roman fortress of Tahuda, Kusayla and a combined army of Berber and Byzantine troops ambushed them.[6] 'Uqba, Abu al-Muhajir, and virtually all the

18 *The victory of Sunni Islam*

Muslim warriors traveling with them, were slaughtered near Biskra. The year was 683. 'Uqba's tomb is now a revered shrine in a town named after him, Sidi 'Uqba (Sidi Okba), southeast of Biskra in northeastern Algeria.

The death of 'Uqba left his appointed deputy back in Kairouan, Zuhayr ibn Qays, as the leader of the Muslims in the Maghreb. Horrified by the news of 'Uqba's death, Zuhayr had his forces evacuate Kairouan until reinforcements could arrive from the caliph in the east. In the meantime, Kusayla continued his campaign against the Umayyads and took Kairouan. The Muslim capital now became the capital of Kusayla's Berber kingdom and he reportedly treated the Muslims who remained there, including the Arabs, in a just and fair manner.[7] His reign was relatively short-lived however.

Sometime in the next five years, probably around 686 or 687, Zuhayr returned to Tunisia at the head of a large Umayyad army from the east. One historian relates that the army consisted of 6000 men (4000 Arabs and 2000 Berbers), which was substantial for the time.[8] Confronted by this new army, Kusayla apparently decided to abandon Kairouan and pull back west into the mountains to create a better defense. The Berber king's strategy failed though. He and his warriors were destroyed by Zuhayr's army in 688 or 689 at a place called Mams or Mammas. After Kusayla's death, Zuhayr's victorious army pursued the remnants of the Berber resistance all the way to Morocco and picked off a number of Byzantine forts in the process. Zuhayr did not stay though. He pulled back into eastern Libya where the Byzantines had made a naval incursion and seized some Muslim territory. He died there fighting the Byzantines with hardly a chance to bask in his victory over Kusayla.

The Berber resistance to the caliph's control over the Maghreb did not end with the death of King Kusayla. Far from it, in fact. A new leader emerged shortly thereafter in the Aurès mountains of northeastern Algeria and Tunisia. Her name was Dahya, but she is known in Muslim tradition as *al-Kahina*, or "the prophetess." There is much mystery and folklore around her. Tradition says that she was a member of the Jawhara tribe of Berbers, which may have been a Jewish tribe that converted to Christianity, or some eccentric form of it. She was probably of mixed Berber-Byzantine descent too, and apparently married a Greek man who fathered one of her sons.[9] And, most importantly, she could see the future through ecstatic divination, which is why the Muslims called her *al-Kahina*.

After the death of Zuhayr ibn Qays, the banner of Islam was carried for the Umayyads into the Maghreb by the Arab general, Hassan ibn al-Numan. It was Hassan who was destined to face the infamous al-Kahina in battle. After marching his army across Libya into Tunisia, facing little Byzantine resistance, Hassan laid siege to the important fortified Byzantine city of Carthage, capturing it, and followed his victory with success in Bizerte on the northern coast.[10] From there, Hassan took his army south and westward to engage the infidel Berber prophetess. He found al-Kahina and her Berber tribal warriors at her primary encampment near Baghai, which is a small town today in northeastern Algeria. She outmaneuvered Hassan though, and engaged the army further east at Meskiana.

The victory of Sunni Islam   19

And there she won, sending Hassan and his surviving army into a retreat. When Hassan regrouped his forces, there was a second battle against al-Kahina at Gabès and again the prophetess was victorious, now taking many Arab prisoners. Hassan fled to eastern Libya to wait for reinforcements from the caliph, 'Abdul-Malik.

As Hassan waited, al-Kahina sought to deter the Umayyad armies from returning and to encourage submission to her reign among the settled inhabitants of the region. She initiated what historians have described as a "scorched-earth policy," wreaking havoc and destruction throughout the countryside. This backfired. The people encouraged Hassan to return and bring order to the area. And in the year 697, Hassan marched into Tunisia at the head of a new army. Outmatched, al-Kahina fled west to her homeland around Baghai in Algeria. Perhaps sensing the grim future awaiting her, al-Kahina sent her two sons to surrender to Hassan, where they converted to Islam and joined the Umayyad army.[11]

Taking defensive positions in the Aurès Mountains, al-Kahina went out for a final battle, even participating in the fighting herself. Legend says that she was more than 120 years old at the time. Her final moments, probably around the year 703, came at Tarfa or Tubna, northeast of Baghai, where she was slain by Hassan's army and likely decapitated. A water-well in the area was known as Bir al-Kahina for centuries afterwards, presumably because of its proximity to the spot where she died.

After the death of al-Kahina, the Berber tribes of the Maghreb were increasingly pacified and incorporated into the Muslim empire. In 705, the Maghreb was designated as its own province by the Umayyad caliphate, separate from Egypt. The new governor there, dispatched by the caliph's brother (governor of Egypt) to replace Hassan ibn al-Numan, was Musa ibn Nusayr. He was a shrewd and competent general, who established himself at Kairouan. Thereafter, Musa launched military campaigns westward and brought Muslim rule to the ancient city of Tangier on the northern coast of Morocco, overlooking the narrow strait (8.9 miles at its closest) that separates the Maghreb from Europe. In Tangier, Musa appointed a Berber Muslim general, Tariq ibn Ziyad, as his deputy. It was this Berber general who would become perhaps the most famous Muslim warrior in the entire Maghreb.

At the time of Tariq's appointment, the Iberian Peninsula, consisting of modern-day Spain and Portugal, was a divided kingdom ruled by the Catholic Visigoths. They were only a generation or two removed from the Arian Church, which rejected the Trinitarian Nicene Creed. But records indicate that pagan practices were still widespread among the populace too, especially among the rural peasantry.[12] Iberia or *Hispania* was home to a Jewish minority as well, later known as the Sephardim, who suffered persecution under the Catholic Visigoths. For instance, Visigoth Catholic bishops issued a decree in 694 that the Jews were traitors and should have their wealth confiscated and face perpetual slavery.[13] The Fourth Council of Toledo even described the Jews, who were allegedly proselytizing their beliefs, as "the Antichrist's ministers."[14]

The city of Toledo, which emerged during the Roman era, served as the Visigoth royal capital. It was the city of Saint Ildefonso, a Visigoth Catholic

20   *The victory of Sunni Islam*

monk who later became Toledo's patron saint, and, as a central city in the peninsula, a major religious, cultural, and administrative center among the five Visigothic provinces. A fortified city located along the Tagus River, Toledo was the foremost ecclesiastical seat in Iberia and an important target for the Muslim expansion into Western Europe.

In the spring of 711, Tariq ibn Ziyad crossed the strait at Tangier into southern Spain. The mountainous peak at the traditional crossing point of Tariq's troops is known as Gibraltar, deriving from the term *Jabal Tariq* ("Mountain of Tariq").[15] Arabic sources differ on the size of his initial army, ranging from 7000 to 12,000 men.[16] Whatever the size, among the army were the two sons of the slain prophetess, al-Kahina. News of Tariq's arrival led the controversial King Roderick (Rodrigo in Spanish or *Luthariq* in Arabic) to come south with his own army, where it was swiftly defeated by Tariq and the Muslims at the Battle of Guadalete. A Latin chronicle dating from 754 states that King Roderick and several other Visigoth nobles were killed in the battle. Further Muslim victories quickly followed the battle. In October, Córdoba surrendered to a detachment of 700 horsemen under Tariq's deputy Mugayth (Mugit) al-Rumi and the city later became the capital of Islamic Spain.[17] The Muslims called their new imperial province in Iberia, *al-Andalus*, which likely derives from the name "Vandalacia" referring to the time of Vandal rule.[18]

Following the death of King Roderick at Guadalete, his widow Egilona married the son of Musa ibn Nusayr, 'Abd al-'Aziz. Tradition relates that Egilona encouraged her new husband to break with the Umayyad caliph in Damascus and declare his own sovereignty in Iberia, leading to his assassination. Both Latin and Arabic chronicles emphasize the destructive role of Egilona in these events.[19]

The most notable Arabic chronicle of Tariq ibn Ziyad's conquest is the tenth-century treatise, *Tarikh Ibn al-Qutiyya*, which is kept in the Bibliothéque Nationale de France in Paris. The *Tarikh* ("History") relates that Tariq entered Iberia in Ramadan of 711 and claims that he was encouraged to do so by a Christian Visigoth noble or merchant named Julian (*Yuliyan*) seeking revenge against Roderick.[20] The king had raped or seduced (accounts vary) Julian's young and beautiful daughter. So, traveling to the Maghreb, where he conducted business in the past:

> *Yuliyan* met with Tariq and incited him to come over to *al-Andalus*, telling him of its splendor and the weakness of its people and their lack of courage; so Tariq wrote to Musa ibn Nusayr and informed him of that, whereupon Musa told him to invade.[21]

The narrative further relates that Tariq had a dream during his journey on a boat to the Iberian coast in which he encountered the Prophet Muhammad. Thereafter, Tariq reached land and took *Qartajanna*, thought to be Carteya, in the province of *al-Jazira* [Algeciras] and sent out the survivors to spread the news of his fearsome army and all they had done.[22] Shortly thereafter, Tariq faced

The victory of Sunni Islam   21

Roderick in battle. The *Tarikh* relates: "The confrontation between Tariq and *Ludhariq* [Roderick] occurred at the *Wadi Lakuh* [Rio Guadalete] in the province of *Shaduna* [Sidona] and God defeated *Ludhariq*."[23] It further adds: "Weighed down with weapons, [Roderick] threw himself in the river and was never found."[24]

A legend recorded in the *Tarikh* relates how Roderick violated sacred protocol in the Catholic temple (perhaps a shrine or cathedral) of Toledo prior to the Muslim conquest. The story relates that a sacred ark (*tabut*) containing the four Gospels sat inside the temple, and custom held that when a Visigoth king died, his name was inscribed on it. This holy precinct was always kept closed. Some Muslim traditions even state that the altar in the temple once belonged to King Solomon.[25] But when Roderick claimed the throne, he placed the royal crown on his head and entered the sacred temple and opened the ark, thus breaking the sacred rules. The *Tarikh* states:

> He opened the temple and the ark, although this was forbidden by Christianity. Inside the ark he found pictures of Arabs with bows on their shoulders and turbans on their heads. On the wooden base was written: "If this temple be opened and these pictures taken out, then *al-Andalus* [i.e., Iberia] will be invaded by the people shown in the pictures and conquered by them!"[26]

And thus Roderick lost his kingdom to Tariq ibn Ziyad and the conquering Muslims of the Maghreb. This odd legend clearly reads as an explanation invented by Christians to explain how the Catholic kingdom could fall to the "infidel" Muslims, but it was nevertheless recorded in the Muslim sources for posterity.

The advance of Tariq's army northward from Guadalete to Ecija (Estadja), east of Seville, resulted in a fierce battle. But again Tariq was victorious. From there Tariq advanced further north to the Visigoth capital of Toledo and sent his aforementioned deputy Mugayth to Córdoba. Various traditions, in both the Latin and Arabic chronicles, report that the Jews of the city "opened the gates of Toledo" to Tariq, but some note that the city was abandoned and still others that a siege ensued. All agree though that Toledo was conquered by Tariq. The thirteenth century Kurdish historian Ibn al-Athir al-Jazari reports that Tariq found Toledo abandoned and "installed there Jews, together with a certain number of his soldiers."[27] Meanwhile, the seventeenth century historian, Abu'l-Abbas al-Maqqari, relates that Mugayth assembled all the Jews of Córdoba and left them in charge of the city, "trusting them in preference to the Christians, on account of their hatred and animosity towards the latter."[28] When Tariq's master, Musa ibn Nusayr, arrived later with a large Arab force and took Seville, he too entrusted the city to its Jewish inhabitants until his return.[29] Musa reportedly met Tariq at Almaraz on the Tagus River near Toledo, where they passed the winter before advancing on Saragossa.[30] After their armies had reached the northern regions of Iberia, the Umayyad caliph al-Walid summoned Tariq and Musa to Damascus in 714, and Iberia was left under the control of Musa's son in

22 *The victory of Sunni Islam*

Seville.[31] Neither Tariq ibn Ziyad nor Musa ibn Nusayr ever returned to *al-Andalus*.

The narrative of Tariq's heroic conquest of *al-Andalus* is famous throughout the Maghreb. In fact, it is common to come across contemporary Islamist writings where the Muslims of the Maghreb are addressed as "sons of Tariq." For example, the Libyan al-Qaeda ideologue, Atiyatallah al-Libi, recited a poem in a video from September of 2011, wherein he related the verse: "The sons of Tariq went to the middle of the desert and wore the garments of war!" Such language is an attempt to encourage Muslims in the Maghreb to recall their great history and identify with a military figure who inflicted great defeats against the West. Of course, it also glosses over the tensions that existed between the Arab aristocracy and the Berber majority at the time. Islamists also generally prefer not to mention the role that Jews (synonymous with Zionism today) played in helping the Muslim conquest either. History is often an inconvenience for ideologues.

Although Tariq was a Berber, frustration and discontent with the Arab aristocracy and the Umayyad caliphs' policies was still widespread among Muslim Berbers in the Maghreb. This made the Berbers ripe for the message of the Kharijites, the egalitarian rebels who rejected 'Ali and Mu'awiyya during the first Muslim civil war (*fitna*). Tradition says that two Kharijite missionaries, one from the Ibadi sect and one from the Sufri, arrived at Kairouan in 719.[32] The representative of the Ibadi sect was Salma ibn Sa'd, who was trained in Ibadi doctrine at Basra, Iraq. The Ibadis are still found in pockets of the Maghreb today, including the island of Djerba in Tunisia. Little is known about the events after Salma's arrival though. What is clear is that by 740 there were Kharijite Berber tribes across the Maghreb from Tangier to Tripoli.

Djerba is located off of the southeastern coast of Tunisia near the Libyan border. Coming to the island from the north, visitors take one of several ferries across the water with names like "Hannibal." In addition to members of the Sunni majority in Tunisia, Djerba is home to Ibadis and Jews (although many left for Israel after 1948). The two groups have long coexisted on the island. Both groups are also wary of outsiders. In fact, it was an outsider in April of 2002 who carried out a suicide-truck bombing at Djerba's oldest and most famous synagogue, El-Ghriba. The attack killed 21 people, and the synagogue, one of the oldest in Africa (although most of the current structure is only a century old), was seriously damaged. Thus, even a decade later, visitors now pass through metal detectors manned by armed Muslim guards to enter the synagogue complex. Legend says that a Jewish virgin who came from Palestine carrying sacred scrolls was buried on the site. Visitors to the synagogue are obligated to remove their shoes (recalling the Muslim custom) and cover their heads (men and women).

The Berber rebellions of the mid-eighth century coincided with anti-Umayyad revolts elsewhere in the empire, carried out under the black banner of the Abbasids, a rival claimant to the caliphate. The Abbasids claimed to represent the family of the prophet, thus playing on the sympathies of many. The rival Umayyads, after all, were among the most vicious adversaries of the prophet's

The victory of Sunni Islam 23

family. The most infamous incident took place in 680, when the caliph Yazid in Damascus sent an army to attack the prophet's grandson Husayn, his family, and supporters in Iraq. The Umayyads saw Husayn and the prophet's family as a threat to their hold on power. Hence, at Karbala, an Umayyad army slaughtered Husayn, his family, and their supporters in the desert and sent his severed head back to Yazid. The martyrdom of Husayn at Karbala has since held profound cosmic significance for Shia Muslims. And it is annually commemorated with passion plays, self-flagellation, and even bloodletting on the day of Ashura.

For Sunni Muslims, Husayn's death was a bitter tragedy, but devoid of deeper theological meaning. That said, one of the holiest sites in Cairo, one of the major world centers of Sunni Islam, is the mosque of Sayyidna ("Our Saint") Husayn. It is off-limits to non-Muslims and houses an ornate shrine that contains Husayn's severed head, at least according to deeply-held tradition. In the same chamber as the shrine, a number of relics of the Prophet Muhammad are stored, but they are inaccessible to worshippers.

Confronted by Kharijite revolts and the rise of the Abbasids in the east, the Umayyads' hold on the distant Maghreb and *al-Andalus* was weakened by the middle of the eighth century. In 745, the Fihrids, aristocratic descendants of 'Uqba ibn Nafi, ruled the Maghreb independently of the caliphate, but only briefly due to a violent family dispute in 755. The leader of the Fihrids, 'Abd al-Rahman, was the great-grandson of 'Uqba and his father died in 741 while suppressing a Berber Kharijite revolt that shook the entire Maghreb.[33] During 'Abd al-Rahman's reign in Kairouan, he faced more revolts by Berber Kharijites and directed military campaigns against Sicily and Sardinia. After his assassination (by his own brother Ilyas), Berber Kharijites rose up and seized power.

Kairouan was ruled by Ibadi Berbers when the Abbasid caliphate, which toppled the Umayyads in 750, chose to reassert the caliph's authority in the Maghreb. Despite early allusions to Shia Islam, the Abbasids were a Sunni Muslim dynasty. And in 761, an Arab general came from Egypt and conquered Kairouan from the Ibadis under orders from the Abbasid caliph al-Mansur, the son of a Berber slave woman. In fact, al-Mansur's wife was from Kairouan and some amusing anecdotes exist about their union (she imposed monogamy on him).[34] The Abbasid victory at Kairouan forced the Ibadi governor, Ibn Rustum, to flee west where he settled in the Ibadi Berber stronghold of Tiaret (Tahert) in northern Algeria.[35] In Tiaret, Ibn Rustum was chosen as the new imam ("leader") or caliph of the Ibadis and a new Kharijite state emerged that enveloped much of the northern Maghreb at its peak. The Rustumids reigned from Tiaret until the early tenth century. Their rule is generally noted as one of prosperity, vibrant culture, quasi-democratic leadership, and tolerance of different religions.[36]

The chief rival of the Rustumids were the Sunni Aghlabids, a dynasty of powerful emirs (kings), who took power in Kairouan in 800 as vassals of the Abbasids. Despite numerous internal and external foes, the Aghlabids nevertheless fostered Sunni culture and undertook many building projects, including the renovation of the Mosque of 'Uqba. Under the Aghlabids, Kairouan became the foremost center of the Maliki legal school (*maddhab*) of Sunni Islam, surpassing

24 *The victory of Sunni Islam*

Cairo and Medina.[37] But the Aghlabids, along with the Rustumids, were destined to face their demise from a most unexpected foe.

In 893, an Arab Shia missionary arrived in the Maghreb from Yemen by invitation of Berbers he met during a pilgrimage to Mecca. The Berbers of the Kutama tribe in northeastern Algeria subsequently converted to Ismaili Shi'ism (distinct from the Twelver Shi'ism of Iran today) and organized into an army to fight the Sunni Aghlabids. Numerous battles against the Aghlabids took place over the ensuing years, culminating in 909 when the emirs were finally conquered. The Shia missionary, Abu 'Abdallah, taught that the sole legitimate leader (imam) of the Muslims was a direct descendent of 'Ali and Fatima (daughter of the Prophet Muhammad), specifically a man named 'Ubayd Allah. It was Abu 'Abdallah's job to prepare the way for 'Ubayd Allah as the divinely guided and infallible imam. However, 'Ubayd Allah and his son al-Qa'im were unable to reach Tunisia. They were imprisoned in the Kharijite-ruled Berber city of Sijilmasa in Morocco. Upon hearing the news, Abu 'Abdallah led his army of Kutama Berbers west, defeating the Kharijite Rustumids at Tiaret along the way.

'Ubayd Allah was proclaimed the true caliph near Kairouan at a former Aghlabid palace in Raqada in 910. He also claimed to be the long awaited Mahdi ("Guided One") who would usher in a new era of justice and peace in the world. 'Ubayd Allah's absorption of power from Abu 'Abdallah, who had fought for that power, created serious tensions, however. Thus, seeing his chief propagandist as a threat, the caliph had Abu 'Abdallah executed. As for the Sunni Muslims, such as the Maliki jurists of Kairouan, a policy of persecution and forced conversion was initiated. In one instance, two influential Sunni scholars in Kairouan, known for opposing Shia Islam, were flogged, killed, and dragged through the streets.[38] This was the birth of the Fatimid caliphate that ruled over North Africa, Sicily and parts of the Middle East, for some two and a half centuries.

The Fatimids were a unique Muslim dynasty for a number of reasons. First and foremost, being a Shia caliphate was a rarity in itself. The reign of the Fatimid caliphate also coincided with two other major caliphates, namely the Umayyad caliphate in Córdoba and the aforementioned Abbasid caliphate. There have been innumerable petty caliphs with pockets of followers throughout Islamic history, but there was never another time when three major rival claimants coincided in this manner. And unlike the other two, the Ismaili Shia Fatimids ruled over a populace that overwhelmingly did not share their creed. The Fatimid imams ruled over more Jews and Christians than they did fellow Ismailis. The fact that the Fatimids were able to maintain control of Sunni and Kharijite Muslims, Christians, Jews, and others, residing in the eclectic Maghreb for over two centuries is an impressive feat. And this apparent policy of internal toleration (heavy taxation aside) is one of several reasons why there are virtually no Ismailis in the Maghreb or Egypt today. North Africa is a bastion of traditional Sunni Islam, especially Cairo, which was ironically founded by the Fatimids as their royal capital in 969.

As we have already established, when the Fatimid dynasty began, the Muslims of the Maghreb were split between Sunnism (mainly Maliki) and

The victory of Sunni Islam 25

Kharijism in its Ibadi and Sufri forms.[39] Thus, despite 'Ubayd Allah's political claims, relatively few of his subjects (outside of certain Berber tribes) accepted them as a matter of creed. The potential for rebellion was always present. In recognition of this fact, 'Ubayd Allah built a heavily-fortified capital on the coast of Tunisia, away from the Sunni city of Kairouan, and called it *al-Mahdiyya* (Mahdia).

Elsewhere, the threat of revolt against the Fatimids was strong in northern Morocco. The venerable city of Fes was founded by the Idrisid dynasty on the fertile lands along the Jawhar River in 789. A large number of Arab migrants from Kairouan settled there in the early ninth century, adding to its distinctive culture. Among those migrants were members of the powerful Fihri clan, descendants of the famous Arab general 'Uqba ibn Nafi. In fact, two sisters of this illustrious aristocratic family, Fatima and Maryam al-Fihri, were responsible for the construction of the two preeminent mosques in Fes, namely al-Qarawayn and al-Andalus, in 859.[40] Built by Fatima and named after the holy city of Kairouan in Tunisia, the Qarawayn mosque was part of a complex of institutions that included a university. It remains one of the foremost centers of learning for Sunni Islam in the world today. Fes also held strong ties to Islamic Spain, or *al-Andalus*. Its Sunni Umayyad rulers, most notably Caliph 'Abd al-Rahman III, actively encouraged opposition there against the Fatimids.

As a port city, the impregnable al-Mahdiyya in Tunisia allowed the Fatimids to organize a powerful navy to defend their empire. Under 'Ubayd Allah's son and heir, al-Qa'im (who ruled for 12 years), the Fatimid navy became a dominant force and conquered much of the Mediterranean. Contemporary scholars even suspect that the Fatimids could have made major gains into mainland Europe, especially Italy, had the bloody rebellion of a Kharijite Berber, known as Abu Yazid, not pulled the Fatimids back to the Maghreb at a critical time.

Abu Yazid, known as the "Rider of the Donkey," lived in the Ibadi stronghold of Tiaret in Algeria when the Ismaili missionary Abu Abdullah led his army against the city. Thereafter, Abu Yazid fled from Fatimid rule to the Aurès Mountains, where other Berber rebels, like al-Kahina, found refuge before him. In 944, he led an army against the Fatimids in Algeria and Tunisia and conquered Kairouan, but failed to take al-Mahdiyya. Although a Kharijite, Abu Yazid initially had the support of many Sunnis. He even sent a delegation to 'Abd al-Rahman III in Spain offering his allegiance.[41] But his brutal, sometimes hypocritical, and destructive conduct ultimately undermined his support among the Sunnis.

The revolt of Abu Yazid was ultimately quelled in 947 by the Fatimid caliph al-Mansur (heir of al-Qa'im) with the help of the Zirids, a tribe of Ismaili Berbers. He was captured alive in the mountains of northern Algeria, but died of his wounds thereafter. His battered corpse was reportedly stuffed with straw and put on public display for mockery at al-Mahdiyya.[42] However, another report states that Abu Yazid's body was roasted and placed in a cage as a plaything for two monkeys.[43] Years later, when the Fatimids moved their capital eastward to Egypt, the loyal Zirids were appointed to rule the Maghreb as vassals.

26   *The victory of Sunni Islam*

In the late 1040s, the emir of the Zirids, al-Mu'izz ibn Badis, declared that the Maghreb was independent of the Fatimid caliphate. He even professed allegiance to the Sunni Abbasids. In this effort, the Maliki scholars of Kairouan, long opposed to Shia rule, encouraged the emir.[44] In 1016, nominally the first year of al-Mu'izz's reign (his aunt ruled on his behalf), Sunni rioting against Shia Muslims broke out, during which many thousands were killed. Some scholars have suggested that the riots (or the sentiment behind them) played a role in his later decision to secede.[45] Whatever the case, the Fatimid caliph in Cairo responded with a legendary military invasion from a tribe of Arab Bedouin, the Banu Hilal. The attack left al-Mu'izz hiding in al-Mahdiyya, and the Zirid dynasty never recovered.

The invasion of tens-of-thousands of Arab tribesmen from the Banu Hilal, along with their families, had a tremendous impact on the Maghreb. Centuries later, the great fourteenth century historian and sociologist, Ibn Khaldun, harshly compared the Banu Hilal to a cloud of locusts ravaging the countryside.[46] But their impact was more profound. While Berber language and culture survived in the mountains and countryside of Algeria and Morocco, it was lost to Arabization in Libya and Tunisia as a result. The story of the Bau Hilal's conquest also became a major Arabic epic that has been passed down to the modern era.

Although beaten by the Fatimids, the Zirids could take solace in the decline of the Ismailis. The western Maghreb fell from Fatimid influence by the latter half of the eleventh century. By the late 1070s, Yusuf bin Tashfin of the staunchly Sunni Almoravid dynasty conquered the cities of Fes and Tangier. Establishing a capital at Marrakesh, the Almoravid Empire, which acknowledged the Abbasid caliph as nominal suzerain, stretched from central Spain to Mauritania and parts of Mali at its peak. Fatimid power was therefore increasingly limited to Egypt, eastern Libya, and the coastal regions of the Middle East, particularly the three holy cities of Mecca, Medina, and Jerusalem. The Seljuk Turks, fierce champions of Sunni Islam, were coming from the east though. And the Crusaders were arriving from Europe. By the twelfth century, the Fatimid caliphate was reduced to Egypt, until 1171, when Salah ad-Din al-Ayyubi (Saladin) ended the dynasty and established a devoutly Sunni sultanate in Cairo, the Ayyubids.

When the Ottoman Turks, successors of the Seljuks and claimants to the Sunni caliphate, marched on the Maghreb in the sixteenth century, they found it dominated by peoples with Arab-Sunni identities, although distinctive Berber elements still remained (especially in Morocco and Algeria). There were also traces of Spanish Sunni Muslims, as well as Jews, who had fled the *Reconquista* of *al-Andalus*, still evident in the architecture of the region. And the once prominent Kharijites remained only in small quiet pockets, such as the Ibadis on the island of Djerba. The Maghreb was a firmly Sunni Muslim land now.

As champions of Sunni Islam, especially the Hanafi school (in contrast to the Maliki school that dominates the Maghreb), the Turks extolled the piety of the four "Rightly Guided Caliphs." Indeed, their arch-rival to the east, the Safavid Empire of Persia, professed Twelver Shia Islam as their state religion. This made identification with Sunni versus Shia Islam a matter of imperial allegiance. The arrival of the Ottoman Turks in the Maghreb thus reinforced and further entrenched the dominance of Sunni Islam in the region. It also came at a time when Catholic Europe, led by Portugal and Spain (now purged of Muslim kingdoms), launched military campaigns against the Maghreb, ensuring ongoing hostility between the two geo-cultural spheres.

The Maghreb was ruled by the Sunni kingdoms of the Wattasid, Hafsid and Zayyanid dynasties when the Spanish fleet began taking territory on the coast and constructing garrisons (*presidios*) at important ports, such as Oran and Tripoli.[47] These garrisons, which often extracted tribute from Muslim vassals, served as a pretext for the intervention of the Ottoman Turks in the name of Islam. Conflict with the Mamluk sultanate of Egypt (which had allied with the rival Safavids) resulted in Ottoman rule over Egypt from 1517 onwards as well.[48] This made action in the Maghreb all the more tenable. As part of the campaign in the Maghreb, allegiance was accepted by the Ottoman sultan from Khayr al-Din Barbarossa, known in the West as the fearsome Barbary pirate "Red Beard" (a name also held by his brother). His Ottoman-backed fleet, based in Algiers, inflicted many defeats on crusading Europeans in the Mediterranean Sea. Today, there are statues in tribute to Khayr al-Din, Admiral of the Ottoman fleet, in both Algiers and Istanbul (where he is also entombed).

The Ottomans solidified their reign in the Maghreb by the late sixteenth century, conquering Tripoli in 1551 and Tunis in 1574 (after holding it briefly in 1534). They built innumerable mosques with distinctly Ottoman minarets. The actual physical Ottoman presence in the Maghreb was limited largely to units of Turkish Janissaries, the elite fighting force of the empire, who were stationed in the cities (as well as the corsairs at the ports). The Ottoman garrisons generally remained separate from the Arabic and Berber speaking peoples of the countryside, although intermarriage and children did occur (called *kulughis*). Ottoman Algeria had some 12,000 Janissaries in the seventeenth century, and that number steadily declined over the eighteenth and nineteenth centuries.[49] But Ottoman rule in the Maghreb still remained marred by rebellions, mostly among its own soldiers, until the European powers, led by France, initiated their colonial occupations. In 1591, Ottoman troops in Tunisia revolted and installed a self-appointed leader from their ranks who was granted the title of *dey*, which is Turkish for maternal uncle.[50] Likewise, in 1671, the Janissary chief in Algiers, Agha 'Ali, was assassinated and replaced by an officer given the title of *dey*.[51] Although building projects and public works, including Sufi shrines, occurred during the Ottoman period, there was no attempt at "Turkization" of the Maghreb either. Despite Ottoman preference for the Hanafi school of Sunni Islam, not even the dominance of the Maliki school was disrupted among the populace. For most of the Arab and Berber population (i.e., the "sons of Tariq"), the Turks, albeit heavy-handed and troublesome at times, were protecting the Muslims of the Maghreb from further Crusader invasions from Europe.

28   *The victory of Sunni Islam*

Notes

1 See Kaegi (2010, 126–127).
2 Ibid., 124.
3 Ibid., 133.
4 See Abun-Nasr (1987, 29).
5 Ibid.
6 See Kaegi (2010, 243–244).
7 See Abun-Nasr (1987, 30).
8 See Kaegi (2010, 245).
9 M. Talbi, "Al-Kahina," in *Encyclopedia of Islam, Second Edition,* 2012. Accessed 22 March 2012.
10 See Abun-Nasr (1987, 31).
11 Ibid.
12 See Hillgarth (1986, 55).
13 See Ferreiro (1998, 137).
14 Ibid., 141.
15 See Watt and Cachia (2008, 8).
16 See Roth (1976, 145).
17 See Watt and Cachia (2008, 9).
18 Ibid., 12.
19 See Hitchcock (2008, 14).
20 See James (2009, 51–52).
21 Ibid., 52.
22 Ibid.
23 Ibid., 51.
24 Ibid.
25 Ibid., 56.
26 Ibid., 51.
27 Quoted in Roth (1976, 153).
28 Ibid.
29 See Livermore (2006, 100).
30 Ibid., 101.
31 Ibid., 101–102.
32 See Abun-Naser (1987, 37).
33 E. Lévi-Provençal, "Abdal-Rahmān b. Habīb b. Abī Ubayda (or Abda) al-Fihrī," in *Encyclopedia of Islam, Second Edition,* 2012. Accessed 22 March 2012.
34 See Bouhdiba (1998, 445).
35 Ibid., 392.
36 M. Talbi, "Rustamids or Rustumids," in *Encyclopedia of Islam, Second Edition*, 2012. Accessed 22 March 2012.
37 J. Schacht, "Aghlabids or Banu'l-Aghlab," in *Encyclopedia of Islam, Second Edition,* 2012. Accessed 22 March 2012.
38 See Abun-Naser (1987, 62).
39 M. Canard, "Fātimids," in *Encyclopedia of Islam, Second Edition*, 2012. Accessed 22 March 2012.
40 D. Eustache, "Idrīsids," in *Encyclopedia of Islam, Second Edition*, 2012. Accessed 22 March 2012.
41 See Abun-Nasr (1987, 66).
42 S. M. Stern, "Abū Yazīd Makhlad b. Kaydād al-Nukkārī," in *Encyclopedia of Islam, Second Edition*, 2012. Accessed 22 March 2012.
43 See Hallam (1966, 50).
44 See Abun-Nasr (1987, 68).
45 Ibid.

46 See Lowry and Stewart (2009, 79).
47 See Abun-Nasr (1987, 147).
48 Ibid., 148.
49 Ibid., 159.
50 Ibid., 160.
51 Ibid.

References

Abun-Nasr, Jamil M. 1987. *A History of the Maghrib in the Islamic Period*. New York: Cambridge University Press.

Bouhdiba, Abdelwahab, ed. 1998. *The Different Aspects of Islamic Culture, Volume 3: The Individual and Society in Islam*. New York: UNESCO Publishing.

Encyclopedia of Islam, Second Edition. 2012. Lieden: Brill.

Ferreiro, Alberto. 1998. *The Visigoths: Studies in Culture and Society*. Leiden: Brill.

Hallam, W. K. R. 1966. "The Bayajida Legend in Hausa Folklore." *The Journal of African History*, 7(1): 47–60.

Hillgarth, J. N. 1986. *Christianity and Paganism, 350–750: The Conversion of Western Europe*. Philadelphia: University of Pennsylvania Press.

Hitchcock, Richard. 2008. *Mozarabs in Medieval and Early Modern Spain: Identities and Influences*. New York: Ashgate.

James, David L. 2009. *Early Islamic Spain: The History of Ibn Al-Qutiya: A Study of the Unique Arabic Manuscript in the Bibliotheque Nationale de France, Paris*. New York: Routledge.

Kaegi, Walter E. 2010. *Muslim Expansion and Byzantine Collapse in North Africa*. Cambridge University Press.

Livermore, Harold. 2006. *The Twilight of the Goths: The Rise and Fall of the Kingdom of Toledo, c.565–711*. Bristol, UK: Intellect Books.

Lowry, Joseph E., and Devin J. Stewart. 2009. *Essays in Arabic Literary Biography: 1350–1850*. Weisbaden, DE: Harrassowitz Verlag.

Roth, Norman. 1976. "The Jews and the Muslim Conquest of Spain." *Jewish Social Studies*, 38(2): 145–158.

Watt, William Montgomery, and Pierre Cachia. 2008. *A History of Islamic Spain*. Piscataway, NJ: Aldine Transaction.

2 Occupation

Unless we see identity as a social construction and recognize the role of religion in such constructions, the emergence of Islamism in the post-colonial Maghreb will elude us. Islamism is not an anachronistic product of a seventh century text (i.e., the Qur'an) or simply the byproduct of zealous belief. Rather, there are numerous important historical factors and forces that played a part in the birth of Islamism in the twentieth century.[1] This book calls attention to the historical experience of European colonialism and its aftermath during the decades of post-colonial statehood. Too frequently, the trauma of colonialism is either unknown, dismissed, or softened in Western discourse. To emphasize the wide-ranging damage which colonialism had on the peoples examined in this book, this chapter concisely reviews its history in the Maghreb over the nineteenth and twentieth centuries. As historian Phillip Naylor aptly described it in his far-ranging study of North Africa, the European colonial occupation of the Maghreb was "unprecedented" and a "traumatic yet transformative transcultural event" in modern history.[2]

By the middle of the eighteenth century, the once mighty Ottoman Empire's control of the Maghreb had declined considerably. The French, under General Napoleon Bonaparte, took advantage and invaded Ottoman Egypt in 1798 at the port city of Alexandria, where they achieved sweeping victories. Contemporary historians generally identify Napoleon's invasion of Egypt, despite its short duration, as the onset of European colonialism in the Muslim world (although technically incorrect). The goal of the 1798 expedition into Egypt was to establish a trade route to India and deliver a major strategic blow to France's arch-rival, the British Empire. In that respect, the campaign was a failure. But the Egyptian campaign, despite lasting only three years, deeply disrupted the local Mamluk-Ottoman power structures and set a flurry of events into motion that shaped the future of the Maghreb.

When Napoleon secretly set sail for France in 1799, he left General Jean Baptiste Kléber in his stead in Cairo. Kléber led the French military to a resounding victory over the Ottoman Turks—still desperate to recover Egypt—at the Battle of Heliopolis on March 20, 1800, despite being vastly outnumbered. That victory complete, Kléber turned to the business of subduing a mass revolt in Cairo. The French spent a month crushing the rebellion and they committed great bloodshed

Occupation 31

and destruction in doing so.[3] At the time, it seemed that Kléber had succeeded and managed to reassert French control, much to the chagrin of the British (by then allied with the Ottomans). But on June 14, Kléber was assassinated.

The perpetrator was Sulayman al-Halabi, a 23-year-old Kurdish student from Ottoman-ruled Aleppo who had studied at al-Azhar University. As famously recounted by Egyptian playwright Alfred Farag, al-Halabi was part of a "second generation" of *'ulama* who refused any cooperation with the French. It was believed that the plot to assassinate Kléber was hatched by members of this younger cohort at al-Azhar.[4] After al-Halabi's arrest, the French military decapitated four of his colleagues for not alerting them to the plot. For his part, al-Halabi was forced to watch the decapitations. The French, thereafter, tortured him by burning his hand and arm to the bone (while he was alive), and later publicly impaled him on a wooden stake.[5] It reportedly took over four hours for him to die.[6] His corpse was subsequently decapitated, the flesh was removed from his head, and his skull was sent away to France for phrenological study at a medical college. Today, al-Halabi's skull is housed in the *Muséum national d'Histoire naturelle* in Paris for tourists and school children to view.

General 'Abdullah Jacques Menou, a French officer who had converted to Islam (largely to marry a local woman named Zubayda), was Kléber's successor as colonial administrator.[7] Historians have described him with unflattering terms such as inept, difficult, and widely disliked, as well as slovenly, fat and bald.[8] Much to the exasperation of French scholars at the time, Menou reportedly even slept with the priceless Rosetta Stone under his bed, adding to his popularity problems.[9] His troubled reign was short-lived though. In the summer of 1801, a coordinated British naval assault and Ottoman land invasion, led by an Albanian Ottoman regiment, forced Menou and the French to surrender and depart from Egypt. The Ottomans captured Cairo and the remaining French forces barricaded themselves in Alexandria, where Menou surrendered to the British. A power vacuum was left in the wake of the French and competing Mamluk and Ottoman factions struggled for power as the British bided their time. An Albanian Ottoman officer, Mehmet 'Ali (Muhammad 'Ali), emerged in control, ruling for decades thereafter. His descendants still ruled Egypt, driving it into terrible debt with mismanagement and ostentatious lifestyles, when it was invaded and colonized by the British in 1882.

Like Egypt, Europe's colonial occupation of the Maghreb began with the French. On April 27, 1827, the Ottoman *dey* of Algiers held a tense meeting with French consul Pierre Duval to discuss France's outstanding debts to Algiers stemming from the Napoleonic wars. The *dey* wanted answers but the French consul was arrogant and dismissive. Gravely insulted, the *dey* called Duval a "rascal" and struck him in the face with a fly swatter. This bizarre confrontation is generally known in the West as "the flywhisk incident." An international crisis subsequently ensued involving a naval blockade and pirates. It would end with the French invasion and conquest of Algiers three years later.

On March 2, 1830, King Charles X announced to the national assembly in Paris that France would invade Algeria, citing the need to avenge the grave

32   *Occupation*

insult of the fly swatter, rein in piracy, and reclaim Algeria for Christianity.[10] Indeed, the idea of reclaiming North Africa for the Church, lost to the Arab Muslims in the seventh century, had emerged as a vague but notable justification for colonial ambition in the region.[11] Some 37,000 French soldiers, carried in 84 naval vessels, soon landed on the beaches at Sidi-Ferruch, west of Algiers. Armed with superior modern firepower, they easily cut down an army of 35,000 Ottoman soldiers, armed mostly with muskets, swords and lances, on June 19.[12] In July, the French marched on the city of Algiers and the panicked *dey* accepted a hasty exile in Italy. With that, well over a century of brutal and bloody European occupation in Algeria began.

In Algiers, giving a taste of what was to come, the "civilized" French armies brought destruction, death, looting, and rape. And the barbarity of the French conquerors was not limited to the lowly infantry, but reached the highest offices of the military. For example, one French general, Nicolas Loverdo, was witnessed by his own men leaving Algiers with six mules loaded up with stolen goods.[13] And the treasury of the *dey* in Algiers held several hundred million francs when it was plundered, even though only 50 million reached the government back in France.[14] In the first two years of the French occupation of Algiers alone, the military destroyed over 400 buildings in the city and stripped them of marble columns, fountains, and other valued goods, for personal enrichment along the way.[15] Any homes not occupied by French officers had their doors and support beams used as firewood.[16] And by 1831, approximately 30,000 inhabitants of the city (out of a total population of approximately 40,000) had either died or fled into exile.[17] Even those families that managed to survive the devastation lost everything and were reduced to begging and working as impoverished day laborers or prostitutes, meaning slaves to the French colonial administration and the waves of European settlers yet to come.

Algiers was hardly the only coastal city to be decimated by the initial French invasion either. A town called Blida lies 60 kilometers southwest of Algiers. In November of 1830, when General Bertrand Clauzel and the French arrived in the town, they randomly slaughtered men, women, and children for over six hours.[18] Days later, Algerian resistance fighters launched an attack on the French soldiers stationed there. As punishment for this act of resistance, the French resumed their slaughter, killing 800 people in Blida as punishment for the death of 21 French soldiers.[19] Survivors scattered in terror and Blida was left decimated. As one French military reporter, writing for *Le Spectateur Militaire*, wrote at the time: "This unfortunate town can be considered no longer to exist."[20]

At this point in our discussion, it is worth noting that in 1830, the year that the French invaded Algiers and the surrounding coast, a merchant in the Algerian city of Tlemcen named 'Abd al-Qadir (not to be confused with Amir 'Abd al-Qadir) fled eastward to Cairo where he achieved financial success and later received the honorary title of Pasha from the Ottoman Sultan. Many decades later on November 4, 1904, a grandson of 'Abd al-Qadir was born in Cairo named 'Umar. A politically active lawyer in his youth, 'Umar would rise to become the third Supreme Guide (*Murshid*) of the Muslim Brotherhood in 1973. Indeed, 'Umar al-Tilmisani was the man who rebuilt the world's foremost Islamist movement (after Gamal 'Abdel-Nasser destroyed it) and guided the Muslim Brothers toward moderation and democratic participation by rejecting the revolutionary radicalism found among other Islamist factions at the time.[21] And among 'Umar's devoted students in the Muslim Brotherhood was a young 'Abdel Moneim Aboul Fotouh, who was later a prominent presidential candidate in Egypt's first free presidential election after the Arab Spring. He finished in fourth place in the elections, which were won by Mohamed Morsi of the Muslim Brotherhood.

In 1840, six years after Louise Philippe officially decreed the annexation of Algeria, Thomas-Robert Bugeaud was appointed governor-general. He controlled an army of over 100,000 French troops there, implementing the brutal tactic of *razzias* or raids against the indigenous population. As General Franciade-Fleurus Duvivier, who returned to France from Algeria in 1841, confessed at the time: "For eleven years, buildings have been overturned, crops burned, men, women and children massacred with an ever growing fury."[22] And still in Algeria, Lieutenant Colonel Lucian-Francois de Montagnac offered his insights about how to best "wage war on Arabs" through *razzias* and to "annihilate all who will not grovel at our [French] feet like dogs."[23] The French wanted to break the Algerian will to resist by extermination, leaving only those willing to serve as slaves, bow to the superiority of France, and serve European settlers, behind. As historian Benjamin C. Brower observed in his eye-opening study of French colonialism in Algeria:

> Terror became the army's most important weapon in this struggle: kidnapping, summary executions, outright murder, torture, and sexual assaults produced *metrus atrox*, the sense of 'terrible fear' that commanders thought would destroy existing social bonds and result in a docile population.[24]

The damage of *la mission civilisatrice* was evident in a myriad of ways. Defined for centuries by an informal system of social hierarchy organized loosely around wealth or prestige—what Ibn Khaldun described as *al-jah* system—Algerian civil society faced an unprecedented reversal as traditional landowning elites were marginalized by the military strength of the coast.[25]

To the west of Algeria, the Alaouite Sultanate of Morocco, already independent of the waning Ottomans, tried to maintain an insular policy of avoidance when it came to the Europeans. This even included banning exports to Europe and strongly discouraging imports.[26] But the French conquest of Algiers in 1830 forced a change in policy. The Sultan chose to dispatch his army to western Algeria to prevent further French expansion. The British, who captured Gibraltar (crossing point of Tariq) from Spain in 1704, had a vital strategic interest in keeping the French and Spanish out of Morocco as well. The potential for growing economic interests were playing a part too. English merchants in Gibraltar controlled a majority of Morocco's foreign trade in the 1830s.[27] But

34 Occupation

events in Algeria would soon spill over into Morocco, despite efforts to prevent it.

Amir 'Abd al-Qadir, the pious Sufi and Algerian Berber resistance leader (and national hero), fled from the French army into northern Morocco in 1843 after years of formidable organized resistance to the occupation. When the French tried to pursue him, the sultan of Morocco's army, led by his son, met them in battle to stop them. Following a French naval bombardment of Tangiers on August 6, the Battle of Isly broke out between Moroccan and French troops on August 14, 1844, near the strategic city of Oujda. The sultan's army was utterly defeated.

According to a French colonial report by Count Henri D'Ideville, former Prefect of Algiers, published in 1884, the victorious French Marshal at Isly, none other than Bugeaud, gave a rousing speech to his troops prior to the battle, declaring: "I have an army, [the sultan] has only a mob!"[28] D'Ideville further described the outcome of the battle at Isly as follows:

> We had killed or taken prisoners twelve or fifteen hundred Moors, without counting the dead and wounded who had been carried off by their comrades. We had taken more than a thousand tents, all the artillery, a great quantity of arms of all kinds, several standards, and an immense booty. We had only two hundred and fifty men killed and wounded.[29]

The sultan's son, he further wrote, was left "terrified by this bloody and shameful defeat."[30]

In June 1845 an infamous massacre occurred to the west of Isly in the Dahra mountains (between Algiers and Oran). One of the rebellious Berber tribes in the region, called the Ouled Riah, was pursued by French soldiers into the mountains. The tribe sought out some protection inside one of the many large caves in the mountains and refused to surrender to the French soldiers, who would have likely executed them on the spot. Colonel Aimable Jean Jacques Pélissier, commander of the French soldiers in pursuit, ordered a large fire to be built in the mouth of the cave. The fire was kept roaring throughout the night and by the next morning the smoke had "succeeded in asphyxiating nearly a thousand people [of the Ouled Riah], including men, women, and children."[31] After learning of the massacre, Governor-General Bugeaud wrote that this act was "necessary to strike terror into these turbulent and fanatical mountain people."[32] Pleased by his actions, Bugeaud granted Pélissier a promotion in rank. In 1849, in response to the siege of a military outpost in the district of Zaatasha near the city of Biskra, the Governor-General ordered 10,000 troops, led by Colonel Cribère, to capture the leader of the attack. According to historian 'Allal al-Fassi, 1000 resistance fighters were killed before Abu Zayyan was captured. The French gathered the remaining inhabitants of the oasis to observe his beheading. They also beheaded his three sons, the youngest of whom was 16. All four heads were sent to hang above the gates of Biskra. Thereafter a massacre ensued in the oasis, including 117 women who were killed with bayonets (haraab).[33]

Occupation 35

The crimes committed by the French were part of a 17 year campaign to "pacify" Algeria for France's "civilizing mission." The initial campaign of bloodshed, theft, and wanton destruction ostensibly ended with the surrender of Amir 'Abd al-Qadir, champion of the Algerian resistance. And soon thereafter Algeria was annexed by France. It was no longer a mere colony, but part of France itself. Meanwhile, 'Abd al-Qadir was sent into exile, never allowed to return. He later settled in Damascus, where US President Abraham Lincoln sent him a gift of two Colt pistols. Lincoln's gift came in recognition of 'Abd al-Qadir's protection of hundreds of Maronite Christians during a communal riot by members of the local Druze sect in Damascus in 1860.

The annexation of Algeria and surrender of 'Abd al-Qadir did not stop the brutality of the colonial occupation, nor the will to resist it. Much resistance remained elsewhere in the country, especially in the interior. Meanwhile, the aggressive work of "civilizing" and "modernizing" the country continued for the French administration. Early on, there was a Berber rebellion in the mountainous region of Kabylia east of Algiers. It was led, in part, by a charismatic young woman known as Lalla Fatma N'Soumer, who would later be compared to the legendary al-Kahina. The French occupied the Kabylia in 1847 when Fatma was a teen and she joined the growing resistance by her mid-twenties. Concerned by the growing number of rebels, the French marched an army of 35,000 soldiers into Kabylia in 1857. Fatma was captured during the assault and imprisoned by the French. She later died in their custody at the age of 33.

In 1855, a French scholar and diplomat, Arthur de Gobineau, published an influential study, *Essai sur l'inégalité des races humaines* ("An Essay on the Inequality of the Human Races"), which utilized the concept of race to explain the prosperity and decline of world civilizations. Decades later, Adolf Hitler would admire his work. Gobineau's essay argued that the "Aryan race," referring to the Germanic peoples of Western Europe, was the supreme race in every aspect (including beauty) so long as it was kept pure. Indeed, Gobineau believed that "mixing" of the races created chaos, and it played a direct role in the particular limits and characteristics of nations and the collapses of civilizations. A devout Christian, Gobineau also described the Bible as a "deep well of truth, whose riches we can only begin to appreciate when we go down into it with a fully enlightened mind."[34] Yet, he argued that even the exceptional and universal "light of the Christian faith," superior to all other religions, could not supplant the innate determining role of race in human history.[35] Regarding the Arabs, Gobineau wrote: "We harry and destroy the Arabs, but we do not succeed in changing them."[36] He also explained that the "French goodwill and conciliation" in Algiers at the time could never truly reach the Arabs or "other mixed races" in the Maghreb, because the latter is incapable of appreciating and understanding the white race by virtue of the blood in their veins.[37] And even the light of the Christian faith could not change these determining circumstances.

Elsewhere in Europe, the precursor to the modern academic study of religion was taking shape. "Mohammedanism" (or Mohametanism), as the Europeans erroneously called Islam, languished in the prejudicial minds of Western

36　*Occupation*

scholars, linguists, intellectual enthusiasts and travelers as a crude, backwards, Semitic religion, fundamentally contrary to the modern Aryan-Hellenic spirit of Western civilization. Forgotten were the advanced, sophisticated, and powerful Muslim civilizations of the last millennium, if they were ever acknowledged or known to Europeans at all. In their stead, Mohammedanism, seen as an archaic forgery created by an Arab prophet for his fellow Arabs, blossomed in the Western imagination, spilling into Western arts and literature, as an alien and exotic creature of lurid extremes. The Dutch scholar Abraham Kuenen, for instance, heaped scorn and countless faults on the primitive Arab religion of his imagination, pointing to the Prophet Muhammad as a figure baring "striking evidence of spiritual immaturity."[38] The Mohammedan peoples, including those of the Maghreb, were further regarded in the great halls of Europe as a tragic and revolting lot, beleaguered by irrational superstition, criminality, moral misguidance, and, of course, an inability to properly utilize their own resources. As Eugene Bodichon explained in *Considérations sur l'Algérie* (1845), the Arabs (including the Prophet) are

> enemies of other races, fickle, hot-headed, superstitious, religious, fanatical, lazy, proud, intransigent with others, selfish, given to sodomy, cheats, belligerent, undisciplined, with no lofty ideals nor any attachment to the place of their abode, and given to instinctive impulses rather than the reasoned thought.[39]

This fictitious construct of Western imaginations, so eager to justify imperial and racist ambitions, was a most useful psychological weapon for Europe, dehumanizing its vulnerable prey, as it unleashed slaughter and conquest on Muslims peoples from Morocco all the way to Indonesia.

In 1868 the first Archbishop of Algiers, Charles Martial Lavigerie, established a Roman Catholic missionary society, the Pères Blancs ("White Fathers"), intended to convert the "Mohammedan peoples" of Algeria—and later Tunisia— to Christianity. Delayed initially by the governor-general of Algeria, Lavigerie used an outbreak of disease and famine in Algeria during 1868 as a pretext to launch the society for assisting orphans and the ill.[40] He held an unapologetically hostile view of Islam, which he regarded as violent, primitive, and savage. Islam was furthermore reflective of the Arabs, and Lavigerie perpetuated the myth that the Berbers were racially superior to the Arabs, the heirs of North Africa's Christian past.[41] After shifting his work to Carthage in Tunisia, Lavigerie built a chapel devoted to the Crusading French king, Louis IX, and aspired to see a Christian empire reborn in the Maghreb.[42]

The "white man's burden" of "civilizing" the primitive Mohammedan (later Moslem) masses entailed many sinister projects and initiatives in the Maghreb. French psychiatry, still in its relative infancy as a medical science, treated colonial holdings in the Maghreb as a laboratory. As the enlightened Europeans saw it, the Maghreb was a mad world devoid of reason and inhabited by races, especially the Arabs, predisposed to criminality, sexual perversions (including

Occupation 37

sodomy), and above all pervasive violence. Obviously it was a perfect environment for French intellectuals to study. In fact, the informed assessment of the colonialists was that it was doubtful whether the natives of the Maghreb could be "civilized" at all. And this notion lent support to the idea that the Maghreb was a real danger and threat to Western civilization across the sea that had to be controlled, contained, and subjugated with brutal violence. As historian Richard C. Keller relates, "Psychiatrists in the Maghreb contributed significantly to the dehumanizing logic of colonial rule," and "brought a new degree of sophistication to colonial racism."[43]

Bloodshed, punitive measures, and enslavement, were insufficient for France's goal of transforming the troublesome indigenous Algerians into docile servants of Paris. It was impractical to pursue the extinction of the Arabs and Berbers there, although some certainly fantasized about the possibility of an Algeria without Algerians.[44] Indeed, the ethnic cleansing of the Americas by European colonialists was a model to be admired. However, it was not feasible in this instance, they concluded. Instead, the colonialists believed the minds of the surviving masses, particularly the youth, had to be corrected, despite their innate racial propensities of irrationality, superstition, and so forth that Europe's academies of scholars observed. And, of course, these people had to be liberated from the shackles of their "primitive religion" which weighed them down. Schools, hence, became tools of colonial power.

In the 1850s the French opened Arab-French schools for the children of indigenous elites to foster cultural assimilation in Algeria, including French language instruction.[45] "By targeting the children of Muslim elites," notes one historian, "colonial authorities expressed their belief that the values of French civilization would then trickle down to the popular classes, encouraging widespread assimilation with 'naturally' superior French values."[46] Few elites were willing to send their children to such places though. And in the late 1860s, these schools were reformed by the colonial administration to target the masses, including those most desperate for an improved lot in life. The colonial school system now encouraged "racial mixing" in the classroom, but many European settlers were averse to such a setting for their own children. And teachers in the colonial system were often so prejudiced in their attitudes towards Muslim children that they believed they were incapable of being educated. For instance, a 1905 issue of the colonial education system's monthly, *Bulletin de l'enseignement des indigenes*, states: "The native [Algerian] child … is literally a little savage who knows nothing of our language, our customs, our ways."[47] Even those Muslims who managed to ascend the colonial education system to serve as the Francophone "cultural mediators" among the indigenous population found harsh limits that they would never surmount. As British literary scholar Peter Dunwoodie has noted:

Barred by race from the upper echelons of the system they were to promote, the cultural and intellectual achievements of indigenous individuals [in Algeria] were assessed as mimicry, not mastery, thus displaying the ideological (racial) bias of the [French] republican ideal.[48]

38   *Occupation*

As further evidence of these limits, the 1870 Cremieux Decree granted full French citizenship to Algerian Jews, but Arab and Berber Muslims, despite Algeria being a province of France (in the eyes of Europe), would still not receive such status and remained as mere subjects without equal rights. As Jamal Abun-Nasr has noted:

> The Muslims in Algeria had no alternative but to attempt to live in a society whose political and economic structures were geared to serve the interests of the [European] settler community, and whose educational system was designed to submerge the Arab-Islamic identity.[49]

A massive uprising against these conditions in Algeria began in 1871. The resistance to the French had never fully abated despite years of bloody "pacification" campaigns, but this was a dramatic uptick in activity. In the land of Kabylia where Lalla Fatma once fought, over 250 tribes, consisting of a third of Algeria's population, revolted.[50] In the years prior to the uprising, terrible famine and pestilence had struck the area, adding further desperation to the dissent of these survivors. The revolt was led by Muhammad al-Muqrani, an aristocrat and military commander, and Shaykh Muhammad al-Haddad, a charismatic leader of the Rahmaniyya Sufi order (*tariqa*).[51] Together they raised an army (in the broadest sense of that word) of some 145,000 troops with 700,000 supporters.[52] The revolt took the French completely off guard, as they were still recovering from the Franco-Prussian war and facing internal conflict in France. Once a campaign to subdue the revolt was organized however, France's superior military quickly crushed the rebel tribes. Al-Muqrani was shot and killed in battle in May 1871. By the time it all ended in June 1872, unknown numbers, mostly starving peasants, had died in battle, and thousands more were executed by the French as punishment for their dissent. In addition, over 200 Kabyle Berbers were deported by French courts to forced labor camps in New Caledonia, a distant archipelago off the eastern coast of Australia. In total, the defeated Berber tribes were forced to pay over 36 million francs in indemnities and lost 574,000 hectares of their lands.[53] Kabyle folk songs would later lament: "1871 was our ruin, the year we became beggars."[54]

Still, the resistance continued. The revolutionary Paris Commune, established in 1871, created opportunities for new organizations to lobby peacefully for Algerian self-rule, including one led by the Algerian intellectual Sayyid Muhammad al-Badawi. Yet, armed uprisings continued in Oran and the Kabyle district, where yet another five-year insurgency was launched by the Muhraniyah tribes under the leadership of a Moroccan *shaykh*, Abi Umamah.[55] On July 18, 1873, the French colonial administration continued their campaign in turn by imposing the Warnier law, which declared that: "All rights, encumbrances or decisions of any kind based on Muslim law which are contrary to French law are hereby abolished."[56] The Warnier law facilitated the ongoing theft of lands traditionally held by Algerian Muslim tribes and families for the use of the colonial state and new European settlers. This law enabled so many abuses against Muslims that the colonial administration chose to suspend it in 1890.[57] But the confiscation of

Algerian land had rapidly accelerated nevertheless. By 1880 the French had taken 882,000 hectares of land (1 hectare = 2.47 acres) and transferred the land to the 195,000 European settlers living among the over two million indigenous Muslim Arabs and Berbers.[58]

In April of 1881, the French used the threat of ongoing cross-border raids into Algeria by Khroumir tribesmen as a pretext for the invasion of the small neighboring country of Tunisia. Both Britain and Italy had ambitions in Tunisia, but France's bold aggressive act resulted in the extension of French rule there as well. The *Bey* of Tunis had offered remuneration to the French for the tribe's damages and to send his own troops into the Khroumir's territory, but France insisted on punishing the tribesmen itself. When French forces crossed the border they advanced toward the northern port city of Bizerte, then turned eastward and not toward the Khroumir lands. Bizerte surrendered without bloodshed and within a week the French had captured the capital city of Tunis. An appeal from Tunis to the Ottoman Turks for help on May 3 failed to produce any support.[59] French soldiers camped in the vicinity of the palace in Tunis and military officials presented the *Bey* with the Bardo Treaty on May 12, which he was compelled to sign within hours.[60] France now had control of Tunisia's borders, finances, and foreign affairs as a protectorate. The *Bey* nominally retained sway in domestic affairs, especially in Tunis itself. But the French resident-general was the real ruler of the country now. On May 16, a London *Times* editorial harshly criticized the French conquest, stating:

> While foreign governments were being soothed by declarations that the sole object of the French expedition was to punish the Khroumirs, [the French General who led the invasion], beyond reasonable doubt, had in his pocket a cut and dried treaty, prepared in Paris, to be forced upon the Bey at the point of the bayonet.[61]

The Italians, in particular, were furious over the French conquest of Tunisia. Their outrage was not out of any concern over injustice or the rights of the indigenous Muslim peoples of Tunisia, but rather because they wished to control Tunisia themselves. Italy henceforth turned attention toward the conquest of Libya. At the turn of the century, the power of the Sanussi Sufi order (*tariqa*) in Libya, where its first center was established in 1843, was considerable and threatened Ottoman sovereignty there. Indeed, Egypt had been lost first to the largely autonomous Ottoman officer Mehmet 'Ali and then to the British Empire. Algeria and Tunisia were lost to France. Libya (as the three provinces of Tripolitania, Fezzan, and Cyrenaica) was the last nominal Ottoman outpost in North Africa. Hence, the Ottomans fiercely tried to retain it and stomp out the rebellion, until September of 1911, when Italy's Prime Minister declared war on the Ottoman Empire. The Ottoman Turks offered diplomatic solutions from the start, but all offers were rejected. Italy's goal, rooted in the same ambitions as the French and British, was the conquest of Libya and their own taste of colonial rule in the Maghreb.

40   *Occupation*

On October 3, the Italians invaded Libya by sea, landing at Tripoli, Benghazi, and other coastal cities, pushing the vastly outnumbered Turkish troops inland.[62] Ottoman officers from outside of Libya were forced to covertly enter the country to join the resistance. Mustafa Kemal, later known as Atatürk (the arch-secularist founder of the Turkish republic), slipped into British Egypt masquerading as an Arab Bedouin and found a sympathetic Egyptian who helped him cross into Libya.[63] Despite prior tensions and revolts, the Italian invasion fostered pan-Islamic sentiment in Libya and unity between Turks and Arabs, including thousands from the Sanussi Sufi order. It was certainly not a perfect union, but the combined inland resistance succeeded in fending off the Italian expansion from the coast. However, the vulnerability of the Ottoman Empire ("sick man of Europe") at the moment, struggling to retain its last territories in North Africa, inspired nationalists in the empire's few remaining Balkan lands to declare independence, resulting in the First Balkan War. Outmatched, the Ottomans sustained heavy losses and were forced to sign treatises with regional European powers. One of the provisions that the Ottoman sultan accepted in 1912 relinquished all claims to Libya, and Ottoman troops were soon withdrawn.[64] The resistance to the Italian occupation was thereafter left to the Arabs and the Sanussis in particular.

In 1912 'Omar al-Mukhtar, a village Qur'an teacher, organized a popular guerilla resistance to the Libyan occupation in the wake of the Ottoman defeat. He led an army of outgunned Libyan rebels as a champion of the people until he was finally captured and hanged by the Italians in 1931. He was 70 years old, and the Italians took photographs with the old man for posterity before killing him. 'Omar al-Mukhtar's story was later depicted for Western audiences in the film *Lion of the Desert* (1981), directed and produced by Moustapha Akkad. It starred Anthony Quinn as al-Mukhtar.

Meanwhile, a dispute with Spain developed in Morocco after the death of the Alaouite sultan. Successive Moroccan sultans struggled to preserve the country's independence from the European powers and hastily attempted to modernize their armies with imported European weaponry and military advisers. It was a futile effort. In fact, one young sultan, 'Abd al-'Aziz, who reigned from 1894 until 1908, had an infatuation with Europe and its customs. As a result, the sultan quickly alienated his own people and religious leaders and a revolt against his reign ensued. The most formidable threat to 'Abd al-'Aziz came from his own brother, 'Abd al-Hafiz, who defeated him in battle. The French, meanwhile, had already exchanged concessions with colonial rivals in the Maghreb (i.e., Britain and Italy). France would take full control of Morocco, except for the territories already occupied by Spain. When 'Abd al-Hafiz ascended to the sultanate in 1908, it took only three years for instability and internal revolts to drive him into the arms of the French. On March 30, 1912, Sultan 'Abd al-Hafiz signed the Treaty of Fez, which established Morocco as a French protectorate under the control of a resident-general, Hubert Lyautey. The French quickly deposed 'Abd al-Hafiz in favor of a brother of their choosing, Yusuf.

During Yusuf's ceremonial reign, a major Berber uprising against the Spanish and French broke out in the northern mountainous territory of the Rif. The leader of the revolt was Muhammad ibn 'Abd al-Karim al-Khattabi ('Abd el-Krim) who studied at the venerable Qarawiyyin in Fes from 1904 to 1906 and later served as *qadi* (religious judge) in Melilla.[65] An austere religious nationalist and master of guerilla warfare in mountainous terrain, 'Abd el-Krim united the Rifian Berber tribes. Together they inflicted heavy losses on the Spanish at the Battle of Anual in July of 1921, and 'Abd el-Krim declared independence for the Rif. Beginning in February of 1923, it would be free from colonial rule as the Republic of Rif. The victory of the Rifians rattled the Spanish and French, driving them into a coalition to contain the Berber threat. Meanwhile, chemical weapons, specifically mustard gas, were being developed in Spain with the assistance of German chemists. At the time (still prior to World War II), Europe's colonial powers made a distinction between proper treatment of fellow Europeans and colonial subjects who resisted European hegemony, thus the Spanish (with full French knowledge) did not hesitate to secretly deploy horrific aerial bombardments and chemical warfare against civilian men, women, and children in Morocco.[66] Elsewhere, the British were already deploying chemical weapons (phosgene and mustard gas) against Arabs in Iraq and Afghans of the northwest frontier of British India. In fact, Winston Churchill defended the tactic by stating: "I am strongly in favor of using poison gas against uncivilized tribes."[67] Likewise, Italy under Benito Mussolini deployed chemical weapons against the Libyan populace in air raids during the 1920s. Years of Spanish mustard gas attacks against the Berbers led to the collapse of the Republic of the Rif and ultimately the surrender of 'Abd el-Krim. He was sent into exile for 20 years before escaping the French in 1947 and taking refuge in Cairo.

The fall of Morocco to the French meant that Europe's conquest and occupation of the Maghreb was now complete. However, unlike the Americas or Australia—where European migration and colonization permanently entrenched colonial projects—the peoples of the Maghreb would never relent in their resistance. European settlers had reached 6 to 10 percent of the populations of France's colonies in the Maghreb by the end, while Italian settlers peaked at 16 percent in Libya.[68] By 1940, 400,000 hectares of Algerian farm lands were devoted to wine production—a substance explicitly forbidden in the Qur'an.[69] And by the 1950s, European settlers had taken 23 percent of Algeria's best farm lands, 21 percent of Tunisia's, and a modest 8 percent of Morocco's.[70] The privileged existence of the colonialists was not to last. In the wake of the great changes wrought by World War II, independence was finally achieved in the Maghreb, beginning in Libya (1951), Morocco (1956), Tunisia (1956), and lastly Algeria (1962) with much bloodshed. For the indigenous peoples of the Maghreb, however, the trauma of those decades continued to shape their collective future. As many as three million in Algeria, one million in Libya, and lesser but still horrifying numbers of people in Tunisia and Morocco died as a result of European colonialism.[71] The wide range of other crimes, including the theft of lands and property, as well as rape, torture, and other abuses, committed by the colonialists cannot be overlooked. And still others in the Maghreb were traitors and collaborators with the occupation forces. Some of the collaborators

42   *Occupation*

sought to share power with the colonialists, while others wanted to reap some economic benefits, or, more admirably, advance the modernization of their country.[72] The *harkis* of Algeria are the best known of these collaborators. Those that did not flee the country with the Europeans at independence were the target of harsh reprisals and mob violence.

In the Maghreb, the survivors of European colonialism had not completely lost their identities, but they had emerged battered, broken, and profoundly different than before. "The social institutions of colonialism were by far more destructive than the military and political institutions," exclaimed historian 'Allal al-Fassi to a gathering of Moroccan *'ulama* in 1959. "Western experiences have become—or rather have been made—a standard according to which things and ideas of the East [Orient] should be evaluated," he continued. "This is intellectual slavery, which, for many Islamic thinkers, is even worse than the Crusades."[73] Indeed, things had changed dramatically since the days of the Ottomans. Yet, the peoples of the Maghreb had retained their languages, even if they spoke French, Spanish, English or Italian now too. Most importantly, they had not forgotten their Islam, even if nationalism and Marxism were integral parts of their societies too. In the chapters to follow, we will explore how the physical departure of the colonial occupation forces—including two million residents in the first ten years—still left behind many things, especially in the realm of political ideologies.[74] The immediate period of post-colonial statehood was not characterized by a rapid reassertion of Arab-Muslim identities, but by fierce European-inspired nationalism and authoritarianism that spoke the language of power and progress. It exploited the fears of a population concerned about being conquered by outsiders (including Zionists) yet again. Religion was used by post-colonial states as needed, and also brutally suppressed when contrary to the interests of the ruling elites. In one of the most radical instances (outside of the Maghreb), the Egyptian writer Sayyid Qutb came to conclude that independence and the rule of fellow Muslims was not enough. Indeed, he argued, these rulers were not actual Muslims at all. Rather, they were hypocrites and apostates, imitating European laws and political systems while forsaking Islam. For his views, articulated most famously in the small book *Milestones*, Qutb was hanged by Nasser's government and his body discarded in the desert. A year later, Nasser's Egypt was shocked and humiliated by a devastating military defeat at the hands of the Israelis in the Six-Day War. The defeat, some Islamists would say, was a sign from God and a call to return to Islam.

Notes

1 Jeffry R. Halverson has previously written about one important factor, namely the conditions that existed in the field of Islamic theology (*kalam*) when Islamism emerged. For this factor, see Halverson (2010). For additional studies of Islamism discussing other factors, see R. Hrair Dekmejian, *Islam in Revolution: Fundamentalism in the Arab World*, 2d ed. (Syracuse, NY: Syracuse University Press, 1995); Gilles Kepel, *Jihad: The Trail of Political Islam* (New York: I. B. Tauris & Co Ltd, 2006); Olivier Roy, *The Failure of Political Islam* (Cambridge, MA: Harvard University Press, 1998).

Occupation 43

2 See Naylor (2009, 165).
3 See McGregor (2006, 47).
4 See Faraj (1965, 144).
5 See Jedamski (2009, 5).
6 Pascale Ghazaleh, "Digging up the Garden," in *Al-Ahram Weekly Online*, Issue no. 486 (June 15–21, 2000). Accessed April 27, 2012. http://weekly.ahram.org.eg/2000/486/feat2.htm.
7 See du Villiers, *et al.* (2003, 205).
8 See McGregor (2007, 37).
9 See Strathern (2007, 414).
10 See Evans (2011, 9).
11 See Keller (2007, 24).
12 See Evans (2011, 7).
13 See Brower (2011, 15).
14 Ibid.
15 Ibid.
16 See Bennoune (1988, 36).
17 Ibid.
18 See Brower (2011, 16).
19 Ibid.
20 Quoted and translated in Brower (2011, 16).
21 See Halverson (2010).
22 Quoted in Welch (2003, 237).
23 Quoted in Brower (2011, 21).
24 See Brower (2011, 22).
25 See Ghalim (1998).
26 See Abun-Nasr (1987
27 Ibid., 298.
28 See D'Ideville (1884, 123).
29 Ibid., 125.
30 Ibid.
31 See Brower (2011, 23).
32 Ibid.
33 See al-Fassi (1948, 6).
34 See Gobineau (1915, xii).
35 Ibid., 67.
36 Ibid., 177.
37 Ibid., 171.
38 Quoted in Masuzawa (2005, 194).
39 Quoted in Lorcin (1999, 667).
40 See Tejirian and Spector Simon (2012, 119).
41 Ibid., 155.
42 Ibid., 119.
43 See Keller (2007, 4).
44 See Brower (2011, 23–24).
45 See Rogers (2005, 237).
46 Ibid.
47 Quoted in Colonna (1997, 348
48 See Dunwoodie (1998, 24).
49 See Abun-Nasr (1987, 268).
50 See Ferro (1997, 196).
51 See al-Fassi (1948, 9).
52 See Von Sivers (1990, 49).
53 See Beinin (2001, 57); Reudy (2005, 79).

44 *Occupation*

54 See Ferro (1997, 197).
55 See al-Fassi (1948, 10).
56 Quoted in Dunwoodie (1998, 17).
57 See Oliver and Sanderson (1985, 163).
58 See Beinin (2001, 57).
59 See Ling (1960, 408).
60 Ibid., 409.
61 Quoted in Ling (1881, 411).
62 See Simons (1993, 114).
63 Ibid.
64 Ibid., 115.
65 See Abun-Nasr (1987, 378–379).
66 See Balfour (2002, 124).
67 Quoted in Balfour (2002, 127).
68 See Brown (1973, 174).
69 See Naylor (2009, 156).
70 See Brown (1973, 175).
71 See Burke III (2000, 21).
72 See Balfour (2002, 3).
73 See al-Fassi (1973, 155).
74 See Etienne (1966, 50).

References

Abun-Nasr, Jamil M. 1987. *A History of the Maghrib in the Islamic Period.* New York: Cambridge University Press.

al-Fassi, 'Allal. 1948. *Al-Ḥarakat al-istiqlaliyah fi al-Maghrib al-'Arabi.* Ṭanjah: 'Abd al-Salam Jasus.

al-Fassi, 'Allal. 1973. "Mission of the Islamic 'Ulema." In *Man, State, and Society in the Contemporary Maghrib.* Translated by Hassan Abdin Mohammed, edited by Ira William Zartman. New York: Praeger, 151–158.

Balfour, Sebastian. 2002. *Deadly Embrace: Morocco and the Road to the Spanish Civil War.* New York: Oxford University Press.

Beinin, Joel. 2001. *Workers and Peasants in the Modern Middle East.* Cambridge, UK: Cambridge University Press.

Bennoune, Mahfoud. 1988. *The Making of Contemporary Algeria, 1830–1987.* New York: Cambridge University Press.

Brower, Benjamin. 2011. A *Desert Named Peace: The Violence of France's Empire in the Algerian Sahara, 1844–1902.* New York: Columbia University Press.

Brown, L. Carl. 1973. "The Many Faces of Colonial Rule in French North Africa." *Revue de l'Occident Musulman et de la Méditerranée*, no. 13–14, 171–191.

Burke III, Edmund. 2000. "Theorizing the Histories of Colonialism and Nationalism in the Arab Maghrib." In *Beyond Colonialism and Nationalism in the Maghrib*, edited by Ali Abdullatif Ahmida, 17–34. New York: Palgrave, 2000.

Colonna, Fanny. 1997. "Educating Conformity in French Colonial Algeria." In *Tensions of Empire: Colonial Cultures in a Bourgeois World*, translated by Barbara Harshav, edited by Frederick Cooper and Laura Stoler. Berkeley, CA: University of California Press, 346–372.

D'Ideville, Henri. 1884. *Marshal Bugeaud: From His Private Correspondence and Original Documents, 1784–1849.* Translated by Charlotte M. Yonge. London: Hurst and Blackett Publishers.

Dunwoodie, Peter. 1998. *Writing French Algeria*. New York: Oxford University Press.

Etienne, Bruno. 1966. "Succession d'Etat et Conditions des Habitant." In *Annuaire de l'Afrique du Nord*, 25–50. Paris: Editions du Centre National de la Recherches Scientfique.

Evans, Martin. 2011. *Algeria: France's Undeclared War*. New York: Oxford University Press.

Faraj, Alfrid. 1965. *Sulayman al-Halabi*. Cairo: Dar al-Hilal.

Ferro, Marc. 1997. *Colonization: A Global History*. Translated by K. D. Prithipaul. London: Routledge.

Ghalim, Muhammad. 1998. "Madinat fi azmah: Mustighanim al-ahtilal al-Faransi 1830–1833." *Insaniyat* 5. Accessed March 29, 2017. http://insaniyat.revues.org/12322.

Gobineau, Arthur de. 1915. *The Inequality of Human Races*. Translated by Adrian Collins. New York: G. P. Putnam's Sons.

Halverson, Jeffry R. 2010. *Theology and Creed in Sunni Islam: The Muslim Brotherhood, Ash'arism and Political Sunnism*. New York: Palgrave Macmillan.

Jedamski, Doris, ed. 2009. *Chewing Over the West: Occidental Narratives in Non-Western Readings*. New York: Rodopi.

Keller, Richard C. 2007. *Colonial Madness: Psychiatry in French North Africa*. Chicago: University of Chicago Press.

Ling, Dwight L. 1960. "The French Invasion of Tunisia, 1881." *Historian* 22(4): 396–412.

Lorcin, Patricia M. E. 1999. "Imperialism, Colonial Identity, and Race in Algeria, 1830–1870: The Role of the French Medical Corps," *Isis* 90(4): 653–679.

Masuzawa, Tomoko. 2005. *The Invention of World Religions*. Chicago: The University of Chicago Press.

McGregor, Andrew. 2006. *A Military History of Modern Egypt: From the Ottoman Conquest to the Ramadan War*. Westport, CT: Praeger.

Naylor, Phillip. 2009. *North Africa: A History from Antiquity to the Present*. Austin, TX: University of Texas Press.

Oliver, Roland, and G. N. Sanderson, eds. 1985. *The Cambridge History of Africa: From c. 1050 to c. 1600, Volume 6*. New York: Cambridge University Press.

Reudy, John. 2005. *Modern Algeria, Second Edition: The Origin and Development of a Nation*. Bloomington, IN: Indiana University Press.

Rogers, Rebecca. 2005. *From the Salon to the Schoolroom: Educating Bourgeois Girls in Nineteenth Century France*. University Park, PA: The Pennsylvania State University Press.

Simons, Geoffrey L. 1993. *Libya: The Struggle for Survival*. New York: St. Martin's Press.

Strathern, Paul. 2007. *Napoleon in Egypt*. New York: Random House.

Tejirian, Eleanor H., and Reeva Spector Simon. 2012. *Conflict, Conquest, and Conversion: Two Thousand Years of Christian Missions in the Middle East*. New York: Columbia University Press.

Villiers, T. E. du, T. M. Villiers and Alain Pigeard. 2003. *L'expédition D'egypte: Journal D'un Jeune Savant Engagé Dans L'état-Major De Bonaparte, 1798–1801*. Paris: Cosmopole.

Von Sivers, Peter. 1990. "Rural Uprisings as Political Movements in Colonial Algeria, 1851–1914." In *Islam, Politics, and Social Movements*, edited by Edmund Burke and Ira A. Lapidus. Berkeley, CA: University of California Press, 39–59.

Welch, Cheryl B. 2003. "Colonial Violence and Rhetoric of Evasion: Tocqueville on Algeria," *Political Theory* 31(2): 235–264.

3 Algeria

Algeria was famously the last of the Maghreb states to achieve independence from colonial rule. In turn, the armed struggle against the French occupation profoundly shaped Algerian society and culture. The War of Independence, beginning in 1954, ended in 1962. After enormous destruction and bloodshed, the French relinquished control of the country (which they considered part of France) and Algerian leftist revolutionaries assembled a new nation-state in their wake. The leftist orientation of the Algerians who ruled the new state was part of a global revolutionary trend steeped in the political tensions of the Cold War era. It was the age of Che Guevara, who visited Morocco and Egypt during an official international tour on behalf of Cuba in the summer of 1959; the age of Nasserism and Ba'athism in the *Mashriq* (Arab East); and the age of Mao Zedong and his disastrous "Great Leap Forward" in China, wherein many millions of people perished. The passing of this generation would ultimately yield to deeper cultural trends and conceptions of identity engrained in Algerian society for centuries, albeit hardly untouched by the events and traumas of modern history. Indeed, even the socialist revolutionaries of Algeria wrangled with the idea of how best to pair Islam with the revolutionary state socialism they aspired to implement. As Phillip Naylor put it, "the principal problem was existential," and the country's post-colonial leadership struggled to create an "authentic national identity."[1] Their failure to do so would ultimately foster the Maghreb's first Islamist victory in the voting booth, many years before the Arab Spring.

In October of 1954, two years after Egypt's "Free Officer" revolution, a gathering of Algerian Muslim nationalists met and agreed on a date for their own revolution. It would be November 1. Calling their movement the National Liberation Front (French acronym FLN), they formed a united militant anti-colonial front against the French army and their allies, most notably the one million European settlers or *pied-noirs* in Algeria. Initially, the FLN had only a few thousand guerilla fighters. Using hit-and-run attacks, the FLN was met with brutal French reprisals that killed Muslims by a ratio of no less than ten-to-one. But things would soon change.

By the spring of 1956, both Tunisia and Morocco had achieved independence from France. These two neighboring states thereafter became FLN training, recruiting, and organizing grounds. In September, the FLN sent operatives into the *qasba* of Algiers and started the infamous year-long "Battle of Algiers." The FLN operations in the capital were backed by Abane Ramdane, a Kebylia Berber and member of the FLN's governing council. Ramdane, a friend of Frantz Fanon, was later murdered by his own FLN comrades in December of 1957. His charismatic personality and alleged "Berberist" ideas were a threat to the vanguard of the revolutionary movement. But his efforts to bring the fight to the French and bring international attention to Algeria's struggle succeeded.

The personalities of the FLN would become a topic of intense interest for intellectuals and artists across the newly decolonized Arab world. In Egypt, Gamal 'Abdel-Nasser's *Sawt al-Arab* ("Voice of the Arabs") broadcast news of the struggle. Interviews and profiles of FLN members appeared in daily newspapers and magazines. In 1959, Studio Misr released *Jamila al-Jaza'iriyya*, or *Jamila the Algerian*, one of the definitive cultural productions of the Pan-Arabist movement. Directed by Youssef Chahine and co-written by 'Ali al-Zarqani and 'Abd al-Rahman al-Sharqawi, both Soviet-trained writers in the vanguard of the Arab literary boom, the film depicted the life of Djamila Bouhired, a young revolutionary who would go on to become one of the most celebrated figures in modern Arab history. Like Gillo Pontecorvo's 1965 film *The Battle of Algiers*, *Jamila al-Jaza'iriyya* framed the struggle for independence through the lens of urban warfare. Crucially, however, the film locates the roots of the struggle outside the coastal capitals. It takes audiences to the countryside where young men from otherwise tranquil villages are shown being recruited and sent to join the Allied front in Europe. The narrative closely reflects the ideology of the FLN.

In a 1962 interview, Ahmed Ben Bella described the "peasant population" as the "decisive force in the country, the backbone of the army in every region, in every village, in the country, and in the *bled*."[2] From at least the time of Muhammad 'Ali ("Friend of the Peasants" or *sadiq al-fellahin*),[3] this sentiment dominated nationalist discourse. Nasser famously mandated that half of his revolutionary parliament come from the *fellahin*. And artists from the time of Husayn Haykal, who wrote his novel *Zaynab* (1914) under the penname "Masri Fellaha" ("Egyptian peasant"), to 'Abd al-Rahman al-Sharqawi, with his revolutionary masterpiece *al-Ard* (1956), sought to mitigate the politics of the postcolonial city via *ahlam al-quriyya*—"dreams of the village."[4] Comparable perhaps only to Mohammed Dib's monumental *Sayf Afriqi* (1959)—a romantic depiction of cultural resistance to French occupation surrounding the construction of a railway in the countryside—Chahine's film situated the Algerian struggle within the greater, pan-Arab cosmology of revolution. Gillo Pontecorvo's film, on the other hand, brought the cause to a global audience.

Shot almost entirely in the *qasba* of Algiers and in collaboration with actual FLN members, the film was banned in France for years. Among the personalities featured in the film was "El-Hadi Jafar" played by Saadi Yacef. Yacef was not an actor, but the FLN's military commander in Algiers in 1957, before he was captured and imprisoned. The French counter-offensive, which netted Yacef, was carried out by a paratroop regiment under General Jacques Massu. The character of "Colonel Matheiu" in the film is based largely on Massu. *The Battle of*

48 *Algeria*

Algiers vividly depicts the brutal tactics used by both sides in the conflict. The French instituted arbitrary arrests, checkpoints and mass searches, military assaults, and the systematic use of torture as an interrogation aid.[5] Executions of Muslim rebels, as opposed to those simply shot, blown up, or beaten to death in the streets, were carried out by guillotine. Several thousand Muslims in Algiers were killed in all. Meanwhile, the FLN used bombings and assassinations in cafés, restaurants, and offices, targeting French policemen, soldiers, and civilian officials.[6] The FLN was responsible for the death of many hundreds, including fellow Algerian Muslims that they deemed to be traitors, morally corrupt, or simply collateral damage.

With the city of Algiers seemingly pacified by the summer of 1957, the French completed work on the Morice Line—a barrier of electrified fences, barbed wire, and mine fields along the Tunisian and Moroccan borders to cut off support to the FLN. The French army then turned toward suspected FLN out-posts in Tunisia and bombarded the village of Sakiet Sidi Youssef in the Kef governorate on February 8, 1958, killing 69 civilians and wounding 130.[7] "We have heard of the horrors inflicted on the Algerian people by the French forces, now we have seen these horrors in Tunisia," the Secretary of Defense of Tunisia declared at a memorial service for the victims.[8] Elsewhere, an editorial in the Tunisian newspaper *L'Action* urged President Habib Bourguiba to abandon the West and "follow the path taken by Nasser" in Egypt, so that Tunisia will "no longer be a victim of aggression and calumny."[9]

By the end of 1958, France was confident that the rebellion in Algeria was fading and would pose no further threat to its remaining dominion. The French army in Algeria now consisted of hundreds-of-thousands of soldiers. The Muslims would accept their fate as French subjects, they imagined. And indeed the French began to revise their administration of Algeria with the mindset that "French Algeria" was a firm reality of the future. But the FLN survived. And guerilla attacks resumed. Morocco expressed their support for the independence movement and backed the creation of an Algerian government in exile. Tunisia, enraged by the Sidi Youssef incident, did the same.[10] Having been prompted to intervene in the wake of the cross border attack, American attention toward the question of Algeria intensified as well. Despite failure on the battlefield, momen-tum was clearly moving in favor of the FLN and the political situation in Paris was in total disarray. Infuriated, the European settlers or *pied-noirs* stormed gov-ernment offices in Algiers. They declared a provisional administration under Massu and General Raoul Salan, later a leader of the extremist group OAS, or the Organization of the Secret Army. Back in Paris, General Charles de Gaulle rose to power once again during the crisis.

In Algeria, De Gaulle's efforts to resolve the bloody conflict and integrate the Muslims into French society were rebuffed by the FLN. Instead, the rebels responded by creating a Provisional Government of the Algerian Republic (GPRA) in Cairo (later in Tunis) in September of 1958. Every Arab state except Lebanon recognized the GPRA, followed by the Communist states of China, North Korea, and North Vietnam.[11] Within a year, even De Gaulle began to speak of Algerian self-determination, much to the ire of the *pied-noirs* who had helped bring him to power.[12] This occurred despite the fact that FLN forces had dwindled to less than 15,000 (broken into small scattered cells) by the summer of 1961, its leaders were exiled in Tunis and Cairo, or imprisoned, and French forces were half-a-million strong, with testing of France's first nuclear weapons underway in the Sahara.[13]

In fact, the forces that Paris feared most were not the Muslim rebels of the FLN but their own military commanders and settlers in Algeria, who fiercely opposed any negotiation over the "Algerian question."[14] The formation of the fascist OAS by French military commanders, including Raoul Salan, represented the most dangerous challenge to Paris. The OAS network of supporters and fighters extended throughout Algeria, France, and even Spain. It had a modest but broad coalition of forces, including active and former French soldiers, resistance fighters and supporters of the pro-Nazi Vichy regime, disillusioned Gaullists, neo-fascists, and a variety of other conservatives.[15] Seeking to prevent a negotiated settlement with Algerian Muslim nationalists, the OAS used terror as their tactic of choice, inspired by the Zionist Haganah in Palestine.[16] From April of 1961 onwards, the OAS launched guerilla attacks on French officials, Muslims (hoping to spark an ethno-religious war), and even resorted to a scorched earth policy to leave nothing behind for an independent Algeria.[17] Attacks often took the form of machine-gunning or bombings of cafés and crowds of pedestrians, believing that "any dead Arab will do."[18] In Algeria, over a period of less than a year, the OAS killed 2360 people and wounded 5418.[19] When France sent in Special Forces to fight the threat, the OAS militants ironically received the same treatment (including torture) previously reserved for the FLN. Meanwhile, hundreds of thousands of Europeans began to flee from Algeria. And feeling particularly betrayed by De Gaulle, the OAS carried out several plots to assassinate him, including a nearly successful attempt in a suburb of Paris in 1962, which was later the subject of the 1971 book and 1973 film *The Day of the Jackal*.

It was ultimately the international furor and diplomatic pressures and tensions that were advancing the cause of Algerian independence, rather than the guns and bombs of the FLN. As historian Matthew Connelly has argued "what the Algerians call 'the Revolution' was distinctly diplomatic in nature," and "its most decisive struggles occurred in the international arena."[20] And Algeria's independence ultimately transformed international politics far beyond the Maghreb. The FLN never achieved military victory, yet won the struggle for freedom from occupation. Rather, as Connelly writes: "This was the first time a subject people who lacked the means to control any of the territory they claimed declared their independence and won the recognition that finally made independence possible. Their example inspired the African National Congress [in South Africa], the Palestine Liberation Organization, and many other such movements."[21] While exact numbers are impossible to determine, Algerians came to adopt the figure that "one million martyrs" had lost their lives in the War of Independence and it remains a common national refrain of pride and passion to this day.[22]

50 *Algeria*

A final cease-fire (The Évian Accords) between the French government and the FLN's GPRA in Tunis (as the sole representative of Algeria's Muslims) was concluded and signed at Évian on March 18, 1962. Among the articles of the agreement was the stipulation that a national referendum over the question of Algerian independence would be held and France would accept the results. On July 1, the referendum was held in Algeria and out of over six million votes cast, 97 percent voted for independence; two days later De Gaulle officially recognized Algerian independence.[23] A mass exodus of Europeans from Algeria immediately ensued, despite assurances about their rights made in the Évian accords, leaving the new state of Algeria almost exclusively Muslim and Arab-Berber. Many *pied-noirs* even set fire to possessions they were leaving behind rather than let the Muslims have them.[24]

Along with independence came freedom for FLN leaders and fighters from colonial prisons and exile. Among them was Ahmed Ben Bella, imprisoned since 1956, who declared of the Algerian nation after his release: "*Nous sommes des Arabes!*"[25] But despite the euphoria of independence, Ben Bella and his supporters condemned the GPRA. The concessions that they granted to the French in the Accords were unacceptable to him and his more militant supporters. There were also tensions between exiled FLN leaders in Tunisia and Morocco and those in the interior of Algeria who had been largely cut-off from them. Meanwhile, Kabylia Berbers, who had long been the most Westernized in the country, affirmed a distinct identity that took separatist overtones.[26] Bloodshed and guerrilla fighting between different Muslim factions soon followed. The GPRA collapsed and an FLN cadre led by Ben Bella emerged from the rubble in power, while their opponents were imprisoned, exiled, or executed.

The worst outbreak of violence, however, was directed at Algerian Muslims who had fought for the French—the *harkis*. For the small percentage of *harkis* who were permitted to migrate to France, the French government failed to honor their service and placed them in squalid internment camps fitted with barbed wire and guard towers for years.[27] Meanwhile, the *harkis* in Algeria, abandoned by their French allies, were forced by the FLN to clear the perilous mine fields of the Morice Line. Others were tortured, mutilated, or simply executed in cold blood. Reports of *harkis* being dismembered and having their body parts displayed in local markets were not uncommon.[28] Sometimes entire families were massacred, including children.[29] In total, estimates of the numbers of Algerians killed amidst the post-independence reprisals range from 30,000 to 150,000.[30]

In 1963 Ahmed Ben Bella was chosen as president of the independent republic of Algeria. He was backed by Houari Boumediene, a senior FLN military commander during the War of Independence. But as Ben Bella solidified his power, Algeria lapsed into poverty. It survived only by virtue of international aid packages, including funds from France (as an expression of French "magnanimity"). Ben Bella's attempts to socialize the new state were disastrous and he grew increasingly authoritarian and detached from the realities (and comrades) around him. In 1964, the commander of the armed forces, Colonel Mohamed Chaabani, rebelled against Ben Bella, repudiating him for authoritarianism and subordinating

Algeria's Muslim identity.[31] The rebellion was suppressed however, and Chaabani was court-martialed and executed. Thereafter, when Ben Bella tried to purge supporters of Houari Boumediene from his cabinet, Boumediene led a military coup on June 19, 1965, and installed himself as president.[32] Ben Bella was placed under house arrest; he was set free and exiled only after Boumediene's death.

Ben Bella escaped no less than three assassination attempts during his lifetime. He was the son of a farmer and a decorated World War II veteran, who joined the FLN in the 1940s before fleeing to Cairo. He was later captured and imprisoned in Algiers in 1956 before regaining his freedom upon independence. Adequately characterized as a Marxist revolutionary, Ben Bella was influenced by the ideas of Mirza Sultan-Galiev, a Tatar Bolshevik who sought to synthesize Marxism and Islam, but who was ultimately executed under Stalin's orders in 1940.[33] Ben Bella held an affinity for Nasserism and Ba'athism too. And he was later a supporter of Saddam Hussein during both Gulf Wars. In a 2001 interview Ben Bella explained the place of Islam in his leftist worldview, by stating: "The West tried hard and long to obliterate our Arab and Islamic culture. We Algerians are only too aware of this historical fact. That is why being a Muslim is an essential, a sacrosanct, component of our identity."[34]

Ben Bella's successor, Houari Boumediene, was the child of a peasant farmer who spoke no French and proudly retained his Arab-Muslim identity.[35] Born as Mohammed Ben Brahim Boukharouba in northeastern Algeria, Boumediene was educated in an Islamic school in Constantine as a teenager. When conscripted into the French army, he fled to Cairo where he joined the FLN and studied at the prestigious Islamic seminary of al-Azhar. It was there that he also chose his *nom de guerre*, Haouri Boumediene, in reference to the patron saint (*wali*) of Tlemcen, Algeria. He kept this name throughout the rest of his life. Boumediene was also the only member of the FLN leadership to have significant formal training in Islamic studies.[36] His opponents would, at times, cite his religious training as something contrary to the Marxist orientation of the revolution and its goals. Nevertheless, when he assumed power, Boumediene declared that his rule, as well as a newly founded Council of the Revolution, was a corrective coup to mend the distortions of Ben Bella; it was not, he asserted, a rejection of socialism.[37] He would survive no less than two assassination attempts in the first three years of his reign. And indeed, the coup in Algiers had made many of Algeria's allies uneasy. Nasser even requested that Algeria place Ben Bella under the custody of Egypt, much to Boumediene's outrage.[38] Castro's Cuba nearly broke all diplomatic ties with Algeria.

Boumediene exhibited isolationism and only modest skills in the international arena during his reign. His attention and energies were devoted mostly to matters within Algeria's own borders. In one of his most notable moves, he nationalized Algeria's oil industry in 1971 and took control of all French-owned assets.[39] It was a bold move on Boumediene's part in more ways than one. After all, when Iranian Prime Minister Mossadegh nationalized Iran's oil industry (previously the domain of what is now British Petroleum or BP), a coup plot in 1953 known as Operation Ajax was carried out by American and British intelligence to overthrow him. The

52 Algeria

coup succeeded and the authoritarian monarch, Mohammad Reza Pahlavi, reigned with the blessing of the Western powers (and their corporations) until the 1979 Islamic Revolution. Boumediene managed to escape such a fate.

Boumediene's socialist regime undertook rapid industrialization and radical reform of national agricultural production. However, these ambitious initiatives failed to prosper, largely due to mismanagement and corruption. Algeria was also undergoing a population boom at the time, which placed considerable pressure on the country's developing infrastructure. This period was furthermore marked by significant Soviet influence, especially through military aid and arms, despite the fact that Algeria assumed leadership of the Non-Aligned Movement (NAM) at the historic Fourth Summit at Algiers in 1973.[40] For a time after the summit, Algiers was the capital of the Third World, much as Cairo had been a decade before.[41] And at the United Nations, Boumediene echoed the central message of the Algerian-led NAM, stating that the existing economic order was "as unfair and as antiquated as the colonial order from which it gathers its origin and its substance."[42]

In 1974, the prominent Algerian *shaykh* 'Abdellatif Soltani, who had trained at al-Zaytouna in Tunis, released a book in Morocco denouncing the Boumediene regime for its socialist orientation and deviating from true Islamic principles in favor of foreign ideologies and customs.[43] The book, *al-Mazdakiyya hiyya 'Asal al-Ishtarakiyya* ("Mazdakism is the Source of Socialism"), was banned in Algeria and it is considered one of the primary ideological texts of Algerian Islamism.[44] Soltani was a former member of the *Jam'iyya al-'Ulama al-Musulmin al-Jaza'rin* (Association of Muslim 'Ulama or AMU) established by the reformist scholar 'Abdelhamid Ben Badis in 1931. Despite adopting an apolitical stance, the AMU of Ben Badis had attracted the ire of the French colonialists because of its emphasis on Islamic and Arabic language instruction, undermining French attempts to erase Algeria's Arab-Muslim identity.[45] In the immediate years following independence, the group's presence was limited in respect to the various Marxist and socialist currents gripping universities and public debate at the time, but the AMU still caught the attention of the regime. The president of the organization, Mohamed Bashir al-Ibrahimi, was sentenced to house arrest for suggesting the country was at "risk of civil war" for failing to recognize the country's "Arabo-Islamic" origins.[46] Recognizing the influence of the country's religious establishment the regime sought to compromise with the leadership of the AMU, settling on the doctrine of "Islamic socialism."[47] For Soltani, however, Islamic socialism was an impossibility:

> This is why the socialist regime—true communism in its flesh and blood—must impose its governance, especially with Muslims (*shu'ub Islamiyya*). Muslims will not allow themselves to be deprived of their religion.... When an official declares that the people have chosen socialism he does so shamelessly. For he has consulted along the way not a single person. Nor do the people have the right to express themselves. If they did their voice would be one of rejection, refusal, and indignation.[48]

To illustrate the historical proportions of his indignation, Soltani framed his critique of socialism around the figure of a mythical tyrant ("Mazdak") from fifth-century Persia—"land of the barbarians" (*bilad al-'ajim*).[49] Even in this land of pagans, Soltani writes, Mazdak was the "devil incarnate."[50] His creed "al-Mazdakiyya" promised security and reform by "obligating all of his followers to abide by his principles.... Such that there existed no difference between them, no unique devotion between brothers, no distinction between the sacred and the profane."[51] This critique—of the perceived propensity in socialism to neutralize differences—became particularly pronounced in Soltani's commentary on the appearance of women in public whom he believed were imitating European styles too closely.[52] Additionally, his well-known attack on writers Fadila Mrabet and Kateb Yassine, who promulgated a distinctly European vision of Algeria and criticized conservative values associated with Islam, assumed the guise of a greater critique of socialism as an imported and ultimately destructive cultural trend.[53] In addition to his writings, Soltani worked as an educator and an imam in Algerian mosques where he taught young Algerians who later became leaders of the Islamic Salvation Front (FIS). He was put under house arrest in 1981. And his death and burial three years later became the impetus for the "largest Islamist mobilization" of the movement's clandestine years, according to Burgat and Dowell.[54]

In 1976, after the state was adequately consolidated, Boumediene introduced a new constitution (national charter) to replace the one suspended during the 1965 coup. It affirmed the socialist nature of the state and a one-party system (the FLN), while also stipulating that Islam was the state religion and Arabic the official language. Gestures to Algeria's Muslim identity were implemented as well, such as changing the weekend to Thursday and Friday instead of the standard Western weekend.[55] In the early eighties came the first domestic national newspaper published in Arabic, *Al-Khabr*, which quickly surpassed the French *Le Matin* in terms of circulation, printing 200,000 copies a day.[56] Boumediene was subsequently elected as president after leaving the post vacant since the coup. But in December of 1978, Boumediene died suddenly of a rare blood disease. His death left the state in political turmoil until FLN military veteran and former minister of defense, Chadli Bendjedid, was chosen to succeed him.[57]

The ascent of Bendjedid to power, considered a political moderate, had a significant impact on the future of Algeria. He oversaw a revival of French-Algerian relations through *rapprochement* with socialist French president François Mitterrand.[58] He also liberalized Algeria's economy (as Sadat had done after Nasser in Egypt). The *Washington Post* reported in January of 1984 that Bendjedid "has jettisoned much of the austere economic planning and radical foreign policies of his predecessor" and "set his country on a pragmatic course designed to give Algerians a taste of some of the good things in life."[59] But the shift away from the socialist state of Boumediene brought with it an end to subsidies on basic goods. Oil prices had dropped too, depriving the underdeveloped state of much needed revenue. Under these conditions, the

54 Algeria

authoritarian FLN's grip on society was met with a feverish response known as the 1988 October riots.

During the 1988 uprising, hundreds of Algerian youths, protesting economic conditions and social injustice, died in bloody clashes with state security forces. In Algiers, the police withdrew in favor of the heavy-handed military, which deployed tanks and machine guns against the protestors. At the time, nearly 60 percent of the population was under 20 years of age.[60] As Fouad Ajami wrote afterwards:

> For the young urban poor and the half-educated, the legend of the ruling party [FLN] and its *combattants* summoning the Algerian nation back from the world of the dead in the struggle against France is like a tale of *A Thousand and One Nights*; it is not their tale of their world.[61]

Once that uprising was suppressed with alarming bloodshed, the moderate Bendjedid enacted a series of reforms in an attempt to bring stability to the fragile state. Algeria's constitution was amended to permit party pluralism for the first time and opened the door to Islamist political parties.

In March of 1989, the Islamic Salvation Front (FIS) was established at a popular mosque in a suburb of Algiers. Soon thereafter, mosque after mosque became a part of the FIS's political network. Muslim preachers were enlisted for the cause, which included the administration of social services that rivaled or surpassed the state. At the head of the FIS movement were two men, Abbassi Madani and 'Ali Belhadj. The senior of the two, Madani was previously a member of the FLN. He was born in Sidi Okba in 1931, later moved to Biskra, and fought as a young man at the onset of the War of Independence. But he was soon arrested by the French and imprisoned until after independence in 1962. After the war, he returned to his studies and attained a degree in philosophy before embarking on doctoral studies in educational sciences in London.[62] Then back in his homeland, 20 years after independence, Madani (along with Soltani) led one of Algeria's first Islamist protests at the University of Algiers demanding the application of *shari'a*.[63] He also drafted a petition alongside Shaykh Ahmed Sahnoun, a former AMU leader, calling for such things as a ban on alcohol, greater Arabization, and other Islamic stipulations.[64] For these acts, he was arrested and imprisoned by the FLN until 1984.

From the time of its founding, the FIS was an amalgam of Algerian Islamist trends. On one side was Madani—older, educated and worldly—who represented the moderate reformist trend and the thinking of Soltani and Malik Bennabi. On the other side was the charismatic and fiery Belhadj. He represented the radical revolutionary trend and the thinking of Sayyid Qutb and Mustafa Bouyali, a former FLN fighter whose followers formed the Algerian Islamic Armed Movement in 1982 (also known as the Bouyali Group). Bouyali was killed by state security forces in 1987, but his name would be invoked in the cause of violent *jihad* for decades to come. For example, reporters for *Al-Quds al-'Arabi* drew a direct ideological line connecting Bouyali and *Jund al-Khilafa*

("Soldiers of the Caliphate") when the group declared allegiance to the Islamic State (IS) in 2014.[65] When Belhadj was arrested in 1982, it was for his affiliation with the Bouyali Group.

Born in Tunis in 1956 to Algerian refugees, 'Ali Belhadj's father died while fighting the French in the early years of the War of Independence.[66] His mother died years later, leaving him in the care of relatives. Belhadj later moved to Algiers where he emerged as a popular preacher in its depressed suburbs in the late 1970s while still in his twenties. Contrary to the dominant Maliki school of Sunni Islam in the Maghreb, Belhadj and other Bouyali followers aligned with the Hanbali-Salafi trend more recently introduced to the region. After his imprisonment, lasting until 1987, he returned to preaching his Salafi message in Algiers. Belhadj exhibited an intense hatred for the Western world in his sermons, denouncing virtually anything "Western," including democracy, as an insidious infidel innovation.

When the FIS was founded, Madani and Belhadj portrayed the movement as the true heir of the revolution that began in 1954. Their narrative of Algerian independence characterized 1954 as an Islamic uprising that was later co-opted by socialists and distorted by foreign influence. The independent Algerian state that emerged under the FLN in 1962 did not reflect Algerian aspirations or identity, they argued, but rather the ongoing trauma and contamination of European colonialism. The original principles of the November 1954 revolution had been betrayed by French-trained Algerians; people who even built monuments like the Riadh El-Feth monument constructed in 1982 that encouraged idolatry (*shirk*) rather than submission to God.[67] The FIS claimed it would cleanse the country of these ongoing colonial forces. As Belhadj declared at the time: "If my father and his brothers [in Islam] have expelled France, *physically*, with its oppression from Algeria, I, with my brothers [in Islam], intend to devote myself, with the arms of faith, to banish it *intellectually* and *ideologically*, to break with its supporters who have sucked its venomous milk."[68]

While Belhadj rejected democracy outright as a "Western" concept, the senior Madani's viewpoint on democracy won out over any internal objections within the FIS. He championed what he saw as a distinctly Islamic model of democracy, while also criticizing liberal and socialist democracies for what he saw as their inherent contradictions and injustices.[69] In an Islamic democracy, he argued, *shari'a* balances the rights and duties of the individual with those of society, making it the best model, especially for a society faced with a historical crisis.[70] The differences evident between Madani and Belhadj did not derail their combined efforts under the banner of the FIS either. They were driven by their shared goal of an Islamic state in Algeria based on *shari'a*.[71] And so long as democratic channels for the achievement of greater Islamization of Algeria remained open, the radical factions were willing to restrain their ranks. The FIS victories in the municipal elections of 1990 validated the FIS strategy. But while the outward approach was democratic, the internal governing of the FIS was not. Indeed, Madani exerted near absolute control with little patience for dissenting views, even from Belhadj.

56 *Algeria*

Madani's leadership over the FIS executive council (*majlis al-shura*) faced its greatest challenge in June of 1991. After the FIS victories in municipal elections, the FLN regime implemented election reforms that redrew voting districts to hinder further success (i.e., gerrymandering). Madani called on the FIS to strike in protest, but he was opposed by Belhadj and others in the council. "We spoke a double language—one for the mosques and another among ourselves, and Abbassi [Madani] disregarded us whenever he liked," recalled one council member.[72] A three-day strike was ordered by Madani and he refused to end it once it began.[73] The strategy was disastrous. Several members of the council resigned–"Abbassi is a danger for the FIS, a danger for Islam," one member declared.[74] And the military and FLN used this "danger" as a pretext to carry out arrests of FIS members, including Madani and Belhadj.

In their absence, leadership of the FIS ultimately fell to a moderate FIS leader (an engineer by trade) named 'Abdelkader Hachani. Under the new leader, the FIS continued their popular campaign for national parliamentary elections. Their resounding first round victory in December, despite efforts by the regime to hinder their success, deeply unsettled the FLN. The military, which formed the backbone of the state, chose to act, as much to preserve its own interests as that of the FLN regime. Hachani was arrested in January of 1992 along with thousands of others and remained imprisoned until 1997. He was mysteriously assassinated two years later in Algiers. Meanwhile, the elections were canceled. And President Bendjedid was forced to resign with an announcement over state television on the evening of January 11, 1992. In his place, the military installed an exiled FLN founding member, Mohammed Boudiaf, as president. Boudiaf's tenure then ended suddenly when he was assassinated by a bodyguard just five months later.

During the elections, the Kabylia Berber region was one of the few where the Islamists of the FIS failed to dominate. In addition to the Islamists, the process of democratization had opened the door to reassertions of minority identities too. FLN leaders believed that the Berberist movement was a natural ally against the Islamists because their particular vision of a unified society based on Islam as a single source of identity clashed visibly with the Berberists' call for greater recognition of minority identities.[75] To gain the Berberists as allies, the Algerian regime began making concessions, such as introducing Berber (*Tamazight*) language instruction into schools. In 1994, Prime Minister Mokdad Sifi gave a public speech affirming Berber elements of Algeria's identity and called for greater integration of Berber language into everyday life.[76] The Islamists and some pan-Arabists, however, saw the Berber movement as a product of French neo-colonialism. Similar tensions were evident in Morocco at the time.

A direct result of the military's cancelation of Algeria's experiment with democracy was the outbreak of civil war. The most radical factions among the Islamists, once nominally restrained by the success of the FIS, and the state security forces, now seemed bent on purging one another from the country with bloodshed. In 1994, groups of pro-FIS guerrillas united as the Islamic Salvation Army (French acronym AIS) to fight against the military. The strength of the

Algeria 57

AIS was concentrated in the borderlands of Algeria, away from the capital. Meanwhile, the north-central region of the country around Algiers was the domain of a far more extreme faction known as the Armed Islamic Group (French acronym GIA).

Formed principally by supporters of the Bouyali group, many of whom were released after the 1989 amnesty, the GIA derived its name from the *Gama'a Islamiyya* in Egypt and began its operations against the state in 1991.[77] In 1994 the GIA attacked and killed 140 pro-FIS Islamists, including leaders such as Mohammed al-Sa'id and 'Abd al-Razzak Radjam.[78] A year later, the GIA sent fighters across into Tunisia where they killed seven police officers. But when Antar Zouabri (aka Abou Talha) became *amir* of the GIA in 1996, an epidemic of civilian massacres ensued, often carried out with machetes, swords, and knives. Some people were even burned alive.[79] The GIA guerrillas, proponents of *takfir* (excommunication of other Muslims), quickly grew infamous for their indiscriminant violence, including beheadings.[80] Among the GIA's favorite targets were foreign nationals (e.g., French Trappist monks) and Algerian journalists who wrote in French. By 1998, more than 150 journalists in Algeria had been killed as part of the GIA's campaign to purge the country. Anyone accused of being an advocate of *al-taghout*, or "the false god" of power, was a legitimate target.[81] Zouabri explained: "In our war, there is no neutrality, except for those who are with us, all others are renegades."[82] The horrific violence committed by the extremists of the GIA horrified Algerians and the international community. Schoolgirls were killed for not covering their hair.[83] Popular Berber singers from the Kabylia region, such as Cheb Hasni, were kidnapped and killed for being "enemies of God" and "symbols of deprivation and debauchery in the Kabylia region."[84] Seldom has there been anything akin to the GIA in all of Islamic history, save perhaps the Qarmatians and the Islamic State organization.

Meanwhile, in a speech in October 1994, retired general and head of the High State Council Liamine Zeroual declared that he would achieve "total eradication" of the Islamist guerrillas.[85] The GIA was furthermore condemned by the rival and pro-FIS AIS too. The GIA considered democracy to be an infidel religion and something completely antithetical to Islam. Therefore anyone who supported or participated in democratic elections (e.g., the FIS) was an apostate (*murtad*) to be killed. The GIA would strive to eliminate all surviving activists and organizers of the FIS and AIS once and for all.[86] As a result, Algeria was torn apart in all directions by war. And amidst the violence, some were participating for economic reasons, indulging in piracy and looting. Historian Luis Martinez has described the GIA's *jihad* in Algeria as a "lucrative business" willing to accept dubious fighters who were rejected elsewhere.[87]

In 1995, new elections were held by Zeroual to legitimize his rule. Two years later, as the civil war raged on, a new pro-military political party was formed called the National Rally for Democracy (RND). The new party marched onto future electoral victories and the FLN filled the role of an opposition party. That same year, political scientist John P. Entelis noted that "should [open] elections be held in the near future, a relegalized FIS would win, as it was about to when

58 *Algeria*

the military halted the December 1991 legislative elections."[88] Nevertheless, the military and its allies maintained control. The regime was steadily shifting the popular mood against all Islamists, portraying them as part of the bloody and indiscriminant "jihad" of the GIA.[89] The FIS/AIS soon declared a ceasefire.

In 1998 a regional *amir* of the GIA named Hassan Hattab parted ways with Zouabri. His splinter group rejected the disturbing excesses and deviations of the Zouabri GIA in the war. Indeed, countless grisly acts had been committed in shocking violation of Islamic legal norms. This new Algerian Islamist faction received support from Osama Bin Laden and called itself the Salafist Group for Preaching and Combat (French acronym GSPC).[90] The GSPC, initially more selective in their attacks, later gave their allegiance to the global al-Qaeda network and became known as al-Qaeda in the Islamic Maghreb (AQIM). It would act as the official franchise of al-Qaeda in North Africa. A renewed wave of attacks by AQIM, centered on Algiers, would begin in 2007. The group continues to operate today under their veteran *amir* since 2004, 'Abdelmalek Droukdel (aka Abu Musab 'Abdel-Wadoud).

The AIS, meanwhile, disbanded in 1999 after a nearly two year ceasefire, the same year that FLN official 'Abdelaziz Bouteflika, born to Algerian refugees in the Moroccan border city of Oujda, became president of Algeria. Bouteflika ran unopposed in the election and succeeded Zeroual. The regime under Bouteflika quickly issued the controversial Civil Concord Initiative, which promised amnesty or light prison sentences to all Islamist guerillas who surrendered by January 13, 2000.[91] Some 8000 AIS fighters accepted the offer and received amnesty. It is widely claimed by media and government outlets that 100,000 people were killed in the civil war by that time. And the GIA, GSPC, and other small hardline splinter groups, which rejected the amnesty offer, continued to fight the regime.

With the amnesty deadline passed, the regime mobilized to eliminate the remaining Islamist guerillas fighting in the countryside. The terror attacks in the United States on September 11, 2001, quickly created dramatically closer ties between Bouteflika's regime and the United States. The Bush administration was eager to learn from the Algerian experience with Islamist terrorism and offered its substantial resources to help Bouteflika eradicate the remaining Islamist factions.[92] By 2002, the GIA was weakened. Although a shadow of its former self, sporadic bloodshed still continued. That same year, the FLN returned to power in a new round of national elections. The two leaders of the FIS, Abassi Madani and 'Ali Belhadj, were released from prison in June 2003, but banned from participating in political life.[93] The following year, 'Abdelaziz Bouteflika was reelected to a second term as president by winning 85 percent of the vote. Save for the ongoing activity of AQIM, the violence of the civil war was largely behind Algeria. And as a further step forward, Bouteflika proposed the Charter for Peace and National Reconciliation in 2005, which controversially granted amnesty for any alleged crimes committed during the civil war, including those committed by the state security forces.[94] The charter was overwhelmingly (some say fraudulently) passed and implemented in 2006. Under Algerian law, a person

Algeria 59

may criticize the Holy Qur'an, but not the charter, a text seemingly above Islam's most sacred text.[95]

In January of 2011, as the Arab Spring toppled the regime of neighboring Tunisia, protestors took to the streets and demanded that Bouteflika step down from power. Violent demonstrations and clashes with state security forces shook Algerian cities. 'Ali Belhadj was arrested in Algiers for participating in demonstrations, and Abbassi Madani fled the country to Qatar. But by mid-February, major opposition parties had organized a protest movement in Algiers.[96] As an eventual concession, the state of emergency in place since the election crisis and start of the civil war in 1992 was lifted on February 24, 2011. But Bouteflika and the longstanding FLN regime survived. In contrast to the uprisings elsewhere in the Maghreb, the protests in Algeria were led by secular-leftist parties. This fact "clearly alienated many Algerians, particularly the young," argues historian Michael Willis, and these parties had, furthermore, "openly applauded and supported the abandonment of the electoral process in 1992" when the Islamists were poised for victory.[97] An arguably even greater factor, however, was the ongoing impact of the decade-long civil war.

The horrific violence and devastation of the country in the conflict with Islamist guerillas undoubtedly left many in Algeria uninterested in reliving the events of 1992 and the tragedy of the ensuing years again. Meanwhile, the small Movement of Society for Peace (MSP), the Algerian branch of the moderate Muslim Brotherhood (which rose to power in Tunisia and Egypt), was already an existing part of the status quo, and unrelated to the FIS. Therefore, the MSP represented no change. They were not an outlawed and persecuted movement like the Muslim Brothers in Egypt and had no legitimacy as an independent political alternative.[98] In national elections held on May 10, 2012, subsequently declared "not credible" by a national monitoring commission, Bouteflika's FLN took 208 of the national assembly's 462 seats, followed by Prime Minister Ahmed Ouyahia's RND with 68 seats, and the MSP's Green Algeria Alliance, which predicted victory ahead of the vote, with only 49 seats.[99] It is within this context that the prime minister of Algeria, Ahmed Ouyahia, addressed a rally in Algiers in May of 2012, and declared that the Arab Spring was "a disaster" and "a plague," and insisted that Algeria did not need lessons from countries like Tunisia, Libya, or Egypt, because "our spring is Algerian, our revolution is November 1, 1954."[100]

Notes

1 See Naylor (2009, 218).
2 Maria Antonietta Macciocchi. 1973. "Man, State, and Society in the Contemporary Maghreb." In *Man, State, and Society in the Contemporary Maghrib*, edited by I. W. Zartman, 124. New York: Praeger.
3 See Awad (1994, 269).
4 See al-Hawwi (1980, 54–56).
5 Matthew S. Gordon, "Algiers, Battle of (1956–1957)." In *Encyclopedia of the Modern Middle East and North Africa*, edited by Philip Mattar, 141. New York: Macmillan.
6 Ibid.

60   *Algeria*

7 See Abun-Nasr (1987, 343–347).
8 "Tunisians moving to expel French: Influential newspaper bids Bourguiba abandon his pro-Western policy." *New York Times* (February 10, 1958): 3.
9 Ibid.
10 For more on the American and British efforts to respond to the incident in Tunisia, see Barei (2012).
11 See Connelly (2002, 194).
12 John D. Ruedy. 2004. "Algerian War of Independence." In *Encyclopedia of the Modern Middle East and North Africa*, edited by Philip Mattar, 139. New York: Macmillan.
13 See Connelly (2002, 3).
14 Ibid., 3–4.
15 See Engene (2004, 121).
16 See Evans (2012, 304–305).
17 See Engene (2004, 353).
18 See Evans (2012, 304).
19 See Horne (2006, 531).
20 See Connelly (2002, 4).
21 Ibid., 5.
22 See al-Jarah, (2000, 14).
23 See Horne (2006, 531).
24 Ibid., 532.
25 See Maddy-Weitzman (2011, 69).
26 Ibid., 43–44.
27 See Nightingale (2012, 391).
28 See Evans (2012, 326).
29 See Horne (2006, 537).
30 Ibid., 538.
31 See Naylor (2009, 218).
32 Ibid., 219.
33 See Benningsen and Wimbush (1980, 112).
34 Gamal Nkrumah. 2001. "Ahmed Ben Bella: Plus Ca Change." *Al-Ahram Weekly Online*, no. 533 (10–16 May). http://weekly.ahram.org.eg/2001/533/profile.htm.
35 See Evans and Phillips (2007, 65).
36 Ellen Laipson. 1990. "Haouri Boumediene." *Political Leaders of the Contemporary Middle East and North Africa: A Biographical Dictionary*, edited by Bernard Reich, 112. New York: Greenwood Press.
37 Ibid., 115.
38 See Ottaway and Ottaway (1970, 230).
39 See Laipson (1990, 116).
40 Ibid., 118.
41 See Malley (1996, 145).
42 Ibid., 145.
43 See Roberts (2003, 15); Stone (1997, 153).
44 See Stone (1997, 153).
45 See Willis (2012, 27).
46 See Burgat and Dowell (1993, 250).
47 Ibid.
48 See Soltani (1974, 170).
49 Ibid., 14.
50 Ibid., 12.
51 Ibid., 11.
52 See Burgat and Dowell (1993, 251).
53 Ibid., 253.

Algeria 61

54 Emad Eldin Shahin, "Soltani, Abdellatif [1904–1983]." *Encyclopedia of the Modern Middle East and North Africa, Second Edition*, Vol. 4, edited by Philip Mattar, 2078. New York: Macmillan Reference USA.
55 See Naylor (2009, 220).
56 Nouri al-Jarah. 1998. *"Al-Azma fi sanatha al-a'ashaara: al-Hayat tatajawwal ala mudaar 31 yuman fi al-Jizaa'ir,"* *Al-Hayat* (May 5). Accessed May 3, 2017. http://daharchives.alhayat.com/issue_archive/Hayat84.html.
57 See Bourgoin (1998, 403).
58 See Bonora-Waisman (2003, 5).
59 Jonathan C. Randal. 1984. "Algerian President Bendjedid Charts a Pragmatic Course: Without Fanfare, Algeria Jettisons Radical Policies." *Washington Post*, January 30: A13.
60 See Burgat and Dowell (1993, 269).
61 Fouad Ajami. 1990. "The Battle of Algiers." *The New Republic, 203* (July 9): 12.
62 See Burgat and Dowell (1993, 275).
63 Giles Kepel. 1995. "Islamists versus the State in Egypt and Algeria," *Daedalus*, 124(3): 121.
64 See Burgat and Dowell (1993, 263).
65 Kamal Zayit. 2014. "Al-jama'at al-masallah fi Jazaa'ir min 'Bouyali' ila 'jund al-khilafa'," *Al-Quds al-Arabi* (October 11). www.alquds.co.uk/?p=233522.
66 See Esposito and Voll (1996, 158).
67 See Evans (2012, 357).
68 Quoted in Kepel, 121.
69 See Esposito and Voll (1996, 158–159).
70 Ibid., 159.
71 John P. Entelis. 1997. "Political Islam in the Maghreb: The Nonviolent Dimension." In *Islam, Democracy, and the State in North Africa.* Bloomington, IN: Indiana University Press, 61.
72 Judith Miller. 1996. *God has Ninety-Nine Names: Reporting from a Militant Middle East.* New York: Touchstone, 196.
73 Ibid.
74 Quoted in Burgat and Dowell (1993, 269).
75 See Willis (2012, 217).
76 Ibid., 216–217.
77 See al-Jarah (2000, 83).
78 See Wiktorowicz (2001, 68).
79 Ibid., 69.
80 Zayit, "Al-jama'at al-masallah fi Jazaa'ir min 'Bouyali' ila 'jund al-khilafa'."
81 Al-Jarah. 1998. *"Al-Azma fi sanatha al-a'ashaara: al-Hayat tatajawwal ala mudaar 31 yuman fi al-Jizaa'ir."*
82 Quoted in Lauren Vriens. 2009. "Armed Islamic Group (Algeria, Islamists)." *Council on Foreign Relations* (May 27). Accessed May 3, 2017. www.cfr.org/algeria/armed-islamic-group-algeria-islamists/p9154.
83 See Wiktorowicz (2001, 70).
84 Ibid.
85 See Martinez (2000, 116).
86 Ibid.
87 Ibid., 138.
88 Entelis, *Islam, Democracy, and the State in North Africa*, 57.
89 See Wiktorowicz (2001, 75).
90 Ibid., 76–77.
91 Ibid., 65.
92 See Willis (2012, 319).
93 Ibid., 188.

62 *Algeria*

94 Ibid., 112.
95 Rachid Tlemcani. 2008. "Algeria under Bouteflika: Civil Strife and National Reconciliation." Carnegie Paper No. 7, February. Washington, DC: Carnegie Endowment for International Peace, 10.
96 See Willis (2012, 153).
97 Ibid.
98 Agence-France Presse (AFP). 2012. "Vote Confirms Algeria as Arab Spring Exception: Analysts." *Al-Arabiya* (May 12). Accessed May 3, 2017. http://english.alara biya.net/articles/2012/05/12/213647.html.
99 Agence-France Presse (AFP). 2012. "Algeria's elections not credible: monitoring commission." *Al-Arabiya* (June 2). Accessed May 3, 2017. http://english.alarabiya. net/articles/2012/06/02/218127.html.
100 Quoted in Brian Whitaker. 2012. "Algerian Prime Minister calls Arab Spring a 'Plague'." *Guardian UK* (May 9). Accessed May 3, 2017. www.guardian.co.uk/ world/2012/may/09/algerian-prime-minister-arab-spring.

References

Abun-Nasr, Jamil M. 1987. *A History of the Maghrib in the Islamic Period*. New York, NY: Cambridge University Press.

al-Hawwi, Ḥakima. 1980. "Najib Mahfuẓ l-il-Watan al-Arabi: Ana ra'id al-Mudarasat al-Ḥaditha fi al-Sh'ir b-il-Manaz'a," *Al-Waṭan al-'Arabi* 172: 54–56.

al-Jarah, Nouri. 2000. *Al-Firdaus al-dami: 31 yuman fi al-Jaza'ra*. Beirut: Riad el-Rayyes.

Awad, Luwis. 1994. *Tarikh al-fakir al-Masri al-hadith*. Cairo: Dar al-Hilal.

Barei, Geoffrey. 2012. "The Sakiet Sidi Youssef incident of 1958 in Tunisia and the Anglo-American 'Good Offices' mission." *The Journal of North African Studies* 17(2): 355–371.

Benningsen, Alexandre A., and S. Enders Wimbush. 1980. *Muslim National Communism in the Soviet Union: A Revolutionary Strategy for the Colonial World*. Chicago: University of Chicago Press.

Bonora-Waisman, Camille. 2003. *France and the Algerian Conflict: Issues in Democracy and Political Stability, 1988–1995*. Burlington, VT: Ashgate.

Bourgoin, Suzan Michele. 1998. "Chadli Bendjedid." In *Encyclopedia of World Biography*, Vol. 3. Toronto: Cengage Gale.

Burgat, Francois, and William Dowell. 1993. *The Islamic Movement in North Africa*. Austin, TX: University of Texas Press.

Connelly, Matthew. 2002. *A Diplomatic Revolution: Algeria's Fight for Independence and the Origins of the Post Cold-War Era*. New York: Oxford University Press.

Engene, Jan Oskar. 2004. *Terrorism in Western Europe: Explaining the Trends since 1950*. Northampton, MA: Edward Elgar Publishing.

Esposito, John L., and John O. Voll. 1996. *Islam and Democracy*. New York: Oxford University Press.

Evans, Martin. 2012. *Algeria: France's Undeclared War*. New York: Oxford University Press.

Evans, Martin, and John Phillips. 2007. *Algeria: Anger of the Dispossessed*. New Haven: Yale University Press.

Gordon, Matthew S. 2004. "Algiers, Battle of (1956–1957)." In *Encyclopedia of the Modern Middle East and North Africa*, edited by Philip Mattar. New York: Macmillan, 140–142.

Horne, Alistair. 2006. *A Savage War of Peace: Algeria 1954–1962*. New York: New York Review Books.

Maddy-Weitzman, Bruce. 2011. *The Berber Identity Movement and the Challenge to North States*. Austin, TX: University of Texas Press.

Malley, Robert. 1996. *The Call from Algeria: Third Worldism, Revolution, and the Turn to Islam*. Berkeley: University of California Press.

Martinez, Luis. 2000. *The Algerian Civil War: 1990–1998*. Translated by Jonathan Derrick. New York: Columbia University Press.

Mattar, Philip, ed. 2004. *Encyclopedia of the Modern Middle East and North Africa*. New York: Macmillan.

Naylor, Phillip. 2009. *North Africa: A History from Antiquity to the Present*. Austin: University of Texas Press.

Nightingale, Carl H. 2012. *Segregation: A Global History of Divided Cities.* Chicago: University of Chicago Press.

Ottaway, David, and Marina Ottaway. 1970. *Algeria: The Politics of the Algerian Revolution.* Berkeley: University of California Press.

Reich, Bernard, ed. 1990. *Political Leaders of the Contemporary Middle East and North Africa: A Biographical Dictionary*. New York: Greenwood Press.

Roberts, Hugh. 2003. *The Battlefield: Algeria 1988–2002, Studies in a Broken Polity*. New York: Verso.

Soltani, Abdellatif. 1974. *al-Mazdaqiyya hiyya 'asal al-Ishterakiyya.* Casablanca: Aljaza'ir: Jami'a al-haquq mahfuza l-il-mu'lif.

Stone, Martin. 1997. *The Agony of Algeria*. New York: Columbia University Press.

Willis, Michael J. 2012. *Politics and Power in the Maghreb: Algeria, Tunisia, and Morocco from Independence to the Arab Spring*. New York: Columbia University Press.

Wiktorowicz, Quintan. 2001. "Centrifugal Tendencies in the Algerian Civil War." *Arab Studies Quarterly* 23(3): 65–82.

4 Tunisia

In 2011 the "Jasmine Revolution" in the small state of Tunisia (population 11 million) began the Arab Spring, reshaping world politics. The revolt started in the central city of Sidi Bouzid, where a young street merchant set himself on fire in an act of protest against government repression and corruption on December 17, 2010. In a series of rapidly unfolding events, massive demonstrations across the country toppled the secular ruling party, the Constitutional Democratic Rally (French acronym RCD). Political exiles quickly returned, including Rachid al-Ghannouchi, the leader of the country's foremost Islamist group Ennahdha ("The Renaissance"). When al-Ghannouchi arrived at the Tunis-Carthage International airport there were thousands of people waiting to celebrate his return after 22 years in exile. He had spent years participating in debates about the compatibility of Islam and democracy. After the Arab Spring, he would put his views to the test when Ennahdha competed in Tunisia's first free elections in October 2011.

"We had to see how the people would receive us," said future Tunisian prime minister 'Ali Laraayedh, noting that the RCD regime of Zine al-Abidine Ben 'Ali had disparaged Ennahdha for years.[1] Much of Ennahdha had become clandestine and dispersed throughout the country, while leaders like al-Ghannouchi lived in exile. Only now were they reconstituted as a public social movement. When the first round of the historic elections approached, Ennahdha laid out a broad political platform that promised "economic liberalism and social conservatism."[2] There were many skeptics, however. Youssef Seddik, a Sorbonne-trained philosopher and columnist for *Le Temps*, perceived a new and dangerous populism in Ennahdha's rhetoric that threatened Tunisia's liberal values. "It began with the return from exile—a *hijra*," Seddik wrote. "Then, like a metastasis [al-Ghannouchi's influence] spread quickly, affecting all parts of the body, including words, dress, and comportment."[3] In the end, Ennahdha failed to win an outright majority in Tunisia's election. But with a diverse slate of parties splitting the vote, the country's foremost Islamist movement emerged as the victors.

The victory of the Islamists in Tunisia was the latest twist in a long saga that began with a group of activists led by Habib Bourguiba. In 1932, agitating for independence from France, Bourguiba and his colleagues founded a radical political newspaper, *L'Action Tunisienne*, defending Tunisia's culture and customs from French reproach.[4] *L'Action* inspired the nascent independence

Tunisia 65

movement, sparking protests against the French nationwide and elevating Bourguiba to the leadership of the Destour (Constitution) Party. His popularity created dissention in the ranks however, and Bourguiba and his supporters soon established a new movement known as the Neo-Destour in 1934.

Bourguiba came from a military family with humble beginnings on the coast, but attended elite schools in Tunis that exposed him to French culture and ideas. He subsequently studied law and politics at the Sorbonne in Paris, where he took part in the city's cosmopolitan culture and even married a French war widow.[5] After he founded the Neo-Destour in 1934, organized protest campaigns against France spread across Tunisia and his arrest soon followed. At the start of World War II, Bourguiba was in prison, and when France entered the war in 1939 they transferred Bourguiba to a facility in France. When the Germans captured France in 1940, they transferred Bourguiba into the custody of Fascist Italy, which ruled Libya.

After the end of the war, a freed Bourguiba slipped away to Cairo to lobby for Tunisian independence and seek support from other independent nations, including the United States. When he returned to Tunisia, the Neo-Destour still faced harsh repression and Bourguiba was exiled once again. Things began to change in 1954, however, when socialist Pierre Mendès-France became the new prime minister of France. Negotiations between the Neo-Destour and France commenced, and Bourguiba returned to participate. When an agreement was reached, a faction of the Neo-Destour led by Salah Ben Youssef rejected it and withdrew to form an armed resistance in the south. The deal proceeded though and Ben Youssef was later assassinated in Germany in 1961.

Elsewhere in Tunisia, Rachid al-Ghannouchi was just a teenager in the coastal governorate of Gabés. His father was a village *imam* (without formal training) and educated his son in the study of the Qur'an.[6] In contrast, al-Ghannouchi's maternal uncle was a modern, educated Nasserist, who spoke with pride about Gamal 'Abdel-Nasser's struggle against Western imperialism.[7] His uncle's ideas would have a lasting influence on him. Indeed, Nasser would capture the attention of young Arabs everywhere. In 1952, Nasser and the "Free Officers" of Egypt overthrew the Ottoman-rooted monarchy and declared independence from British rule. He subsequently established an authoritarian regime that articulated a brand of Pan-Arab socialism and courted the support of the Soviet Union during the Cold War. In doing so, Nasser became the hero of the Arab world until the disaster of the Six-Day War in 1967.

On March 20, 1956, when al-Ghannouchi was 14 years old, Tunisia declared its independence from France. Shortly thereafter Tunisia became a republic with Bourguiba as the country's first president. The great hero of Tunisia's independence struggle now became an autocrat, and pursued a platform comparable to Mustafa Kemal Atatürk's in the Republic of Turkey. Abandoning his earlier ideas, Bourguiba now steered Tunisia toward emulating the European states in order to modernize and achieve economic development. This meant removing Islam from public life. Similar to the system developed in Turkey, religion and the state were not truly separated. Rather, the state firmly controlled the practice of religion and kept it out of public life, by force if necessary. As Franck Frégosi

66 *Tunisia*

described it: "The unique policy toward Islam followed by Habib Bourguiba was an *alchimie subtile* that combined elements of anticlericalism and religious modernism with a stage of symbolic power and ongoing religious instrumentalization."[8] As part of this complex relationship, Bourguiba abolished *shari'a*, reformed al-Zaytouna in Tunis, nationalized religious endowments, and personally discouraged religious practice, such as fasting and wearing the *hijab*.[9] In addition, he ridiculed several traditional Muslim beliefs and moral taboos.[10] In one of his most notable reform efforts, Bourguiba issued the *majallat al-ahwal al-shakhsiyya* (Personal Status Code). It was the most progressive women's rights platform in the Arab world. The code outlawed forced marriages and polygamy, legalized adoption, and granted equal entitlement to divorce, among other reforms.[11] It became a major flashpoint in Tunisia's politics for decades, and remained so in the aftermath of the Arab Spring.

Although Tunisia was now independent, al-Ghannouchi's coastal hometown of Gabès retained a good deal of its French colonial character.[12] Many young men in Gabès abandoned prayer (*salah*), including al-Ghannouchi, and occupied their time with other activities like football (soccer).[13] Reflecting on his youth, al-Ghannouchi would later explain that he had yet to understand that Islam was a comprehensive system of life capable of responding to change, like the challenges of modernity.[14] Still, al-Ghannouchi obeyed his devout father and left to pursue studies at al-Zaytouna in Tunis in 1959.

Al-Ghannouchi's years at al-Zaytouna were marked by a critical transitional period in the country's history. The traditional Islam of Tunisia's Sunni religious establishment seemed to have little relevance to the rapidly changing world around him and his peers. Hmida Ennaifer was also enrolled in al-Zaytouna at this time, and later explained that it was precisely this crisis they would ultimately seek to mitigate. "We worked on the idea of identity," Ennaifer recalled. "Tunisian identity, Arab identity, and Islamic identity, but which Islam?"[15]

In 1964, after working as a teacher for two years, al-Ghannouchi left for Cairo, eager to immerse himself in the Nasserist movement and to continue his studies. With a "head full of dreams," he enrolled at Cairo University, but found that the circumstances there did not meet his expectations.[16] He stayed for only a few months. "Bourguiba practiced repression in the name of national unity," al-Ghannouchi would later write, "while Nasser did it in the name of liberating Palestine and uniting the Arabs."[17] Facing deportation with other Tunisian dissidents, al-Ghannouchi fled Nasser's Egypt for Syria in search of his Arabist ideals. He initially considered relocating to Albania, compelled by the country's anti-Western communist system, but was persuaded by other Tunisians to contact the Syrian embassy and received a visa to study in Damascus.[18]

Only a few years removed from its union with Nasser's Egypt (1958–1961), Syria was governed by a Ba'athist regime in Damascus who took power in a coup d'état in 1963. At the time of al-Ghannouchi's stay, Syria was home to a range of activist currents, and the state had yet to adopt the authoritarianism that later characterized the Assad regime. On the campus of Damascus University, al-Ghannouchi found himself in the middle of a struggle between secularists and

Tunisia 67

Islamists.[19] The leaders of the Islamists were the Syrian *Ikhwan* (Muslim Brotherhood), an alliance of Islamists established in the 1940s by the anti-colonial activist and al-Azhar-educated scholar Mustafa as-Siba'i. The secularists took inspiration from figures like Sati al-Husri and Michel Aflaq. These factions debated a range of pressing issues, including Palestine and the worldwide struggle against Western imperialism. According to Hmida Ennaifer, it was there at Damascus University that al-Ghannouchi abandoned indefinitely the idea of Nasserism and Pan-Arabism as a liberation ideology, and turned his attention fully to Islamism.

Leaving during the summer of 1965, al-Ghannouchi travelled throughout Europe, staying in youth hostels with international students and doing odd jobs.[20] The experience reportedly confirmed his existing negative impressions of the West.[21] Like the Egyptian Islamist Sayyid Qutb, al-Ghannouchi saw the secular-nationalistic West as materialistic and devoid of anything more than a superficial religiosity or ethical worldview. These impressions shaped his study of Arab nationalism and its European influences. Syrian Arabist trends, like other ideologies of the Arab East (*Mashreq*), often had Marxist and other European elements. Al-Ghannouchi would come to see these ideologies as "another commodity imported from nineteenth century European thought, impregnated with the problems and customs of foreign societies that underwent their own course of development."[22] Rather, he was seeking an ideological framework that was true to the Maghreb's own historical, cultural, and intellectual heritage.

According to al-Ghannouchi's own account, June 15, 1966, was the night in Syria that he converted to Islamism. The traditional Islam of his upbringing in Tunisia was no longer "true Islam," because Islam was a comprehensive approach to life, society, and the world. "That very night I shed two things off of me: secular nationalism and traditional Islam," he later recalled.[23] In an interview with Azzam Tamimi in London, al-Ghannouchi described his conversion in almost mystical terms. "On that night I was reborn," he said. "My heart was filled with the light of God, and my mind with the determination to review and reflect on all that which I had previously conceived."[24] Al-Ghannouchi's account is reminiscent of the conversion described by the late Muslim Brotherhood leader 'Umar al-Tilmisani, who had been a nationalist (Wafdist) during his youth in Egypt. Recounting his conversion to Islamism in 1933, al-Tilmisani wrote: "The latent religious passion in my heart broke out within me."[25]

The subsequent outbreak of the Six-Day War was a disaster for the Arab states, particularly Egypt and Syria. The Arab defeat delivered a crushing blow to the Nasserists and the Ba'athists. Some Islamists even saw God's hand in the defeat. As the Egyptian Islamist and al-Qaeda ideologue, Ayman al-Zawahiri, would later write: "The direct influence of the 1967 defeat was that a large number of people, especially youths, returned to their original identity: that of members of an Islamic civilization."[26] Notably, al-Ghannouchi claims that he converted to Islamism prior to the Six-Day War.

In 1968, al-Ghannouchi completed his studies in Damascus and began associating with Salafi groups. The Salafi movement calls for a revival of Sunni Islam

68 Tunisia

by returning to the pure way of the pious ancestors (*al-salaf al-salih*), which refers to the first three generations of Muslims. After its initial independence in the early twentieth century, the Salafi movement increasingly blurred with Wahhabism, the eighteenth-century puritanical sect that dominates Saudi Arabia. Al-Ghannouchi carried his interest in the Salafi approach to Islam with him to Paris, where he intended to study at the Sorbonne and reconnected with Hmida Enneifer. There in Paris, al-Ghannouchi also began meeting with a local branch of the Sunni revivalist group, the *Tablighi Jamaat*.

The *Tabligh*, one of the world's largest Islamic movements, was founded by a Sunni reformist, Muhammad Ilyas, in British India in 1926. It stresses personal outreach to Muslim communities to encourage greater devotion, orthodox piety, and strongly eschews politics. And most of its adherents and missionaries are South Asian. Thus, the *Tabligh* group in Paris that al-Ghannouchi met was formed by Pakistanis in the 1960s who recruited North African laborers.[27] "Living with the *Tabligh* community," al-Ghannouchi recalled, "provided me with immunity and protection from fierce winds and added a new dimension to my molding."[28]

The *Tabligh* provided al-Ghannouchi with a supportive and conservative social environment to practice Islam, while other migrants felt the pull of liberal Parisian culture. His involvement with the *Tabligh* concerned his family however, and his elder brother came to Paris to take him home after only one year. During the return journey, al-Ghannouchi met with Malik Bennabi in Algeria. Bennabi's writings on the decline of Muslim societies appealed to al-Ghannouchi and explained the harmony of reason (*'aql*) and revelation, asserting that "neither may exist without the other."[29] Bennabi was also critical of the Egyptian Islamist Sayyid Qutb, whose ideas al-Ghannouchi had studied alongside many others.[30] And it was Bennabi's influence in the early 1970s that led al-Ghannouchi to ultimately realize the inadequacy of Salafi and *Tabligh* approaches to the problems facing Tunisia.[31]

After his return home to Tunisia, al-Ghannouchi taught philosophy at the Lycée al-Mansoura, near Kairouan, for two years. A colleague of al-Ghannouchi's at al-Mansoura, the aforementioned Youssef Seddik, noted their parallel but divergent interests at the time—Seddik worked on philosophy, but al-Ghannouchi focused on Islamic philosophy.[32] Bourguiba's educational reforms were well established when Seddik and al-Ghannouchi joined in the *vaste cours du lycée*.[33] Al-Ghannouchi's area of focus, Islamic philosophy, reflected an effort to reintegrate Zaytouna instructional methodologies into a new, bicultural hybrid secondary system based on Sadiki College, a Franco-Arab institution where Bourguiba and several other Neo-Destour elites were educated. But as L. Carl Brown observed in a report for the Institute of Current World Affairs in 1960, despite "official publications" that noted the "need to re-integrate Islamic philosophy into independent Tunisia's educational system," instructors like al-Ghannouchi were instructed to critically examine religion.[34] The report notes:

> The methods to be relied upon in teaching Islamic thought should be those
> employed in what is today called the study of religious thought from the

Tunisia 69

sociological point of view (*sociologie religieuse*). This is the method that attempts to go beyond the investigation of any given Weltanschauung (*'aqliyya*) to discover the substantive factors that determined its various viewpoints just as they determined the solutions and the problems arising from that very Weltanschauung in any given age. This [method] in short, calls not for simply receiving and believing but for thought, investigation, and criticism.[35]

During this period al-Ghannouchi met a young Islamist lawyer, 'Abdelfattah Mourou. Born to a merchant family in Tunis, Mourou studied at Sadiki College and the University of Tunis.[36] Together, along with Hmida Ennaifer (recently returned from Paris), al-Ghannouchi and Mourou formed an Islamist association called *al-Jama'a al-Islamiyya*, or the Islamic Group.[37] In 1981 the group would become the *Harakat al-Ittijah al-Islami*, or the Movement of the Islamic Tendency (French acronym MTI), and still later the *Harakat al-Nahda* or Ennahdha in 1988. But in the early 1970s, the Islamic Group began its existence by challenging the traditionalism of the Tunisian religious establishment and criticizing the perceived laxity of the people from a Salafi perspective.[38] "We started in the lycées and mosques ... then we developed in the universities and institutions until forty years later we arrived in power," al-Ghannouchi later recalled.[39] The Islamic Group recognized early on the importance of reaching the youth. However, there was a dearth of material for the group to disseminate and attract students into the movement. To remedy the situation, the group turned to the Muslim Brotherhood in Egypt. "We went to Cairo, but it seemed incredible," Ennaifer later recalled. "They had no opinion on the crisis in Vietnam, the economic crisis in Egypt ... 'Hassan al-Banna, Hassan al-Banna,' was their only response."[40] Yet, despite the perceived shortcomings, the Islamic Group integrated the Muslim Brotherhood's ideology and literature into their platform and outreach initiatives.[41] Ennaifer, in particular, would grow increasingly critical of the Muslim Brotherhood and the ideas of its founder, al-Banna, who was assassinated in 1949.

In a graduate thesis completed in Tunis, later published as *al-Qadar 'inda Ibn Taymiyya*, al-Ghannouchi expressed his interest in reviving Islam through direct engagement with the Qur'an and abandoning the traditional practice of *taqlid* (imitation of historical precedents). Beginning with a critical defense of *al-'aqliyya* (rationality), this work became a blueprint for al-Ghannouchi's subsequent critique of traditional adherence to established precedents in the Maliki school of law (i.e., *al-taqlid al-madhabi*) and the "Sufist education policy and 'Ashari belief system that bound the country's political and religious establishment."[42] Through his study of Ibn Taymiyya, an unconventional choice for a Tunisian, al-Ghannouchi asserted:

Al-'aqlaniyya, we learn from Ibn Taymiyya, was a project born in the shadow of Western hegemony (*al-himna al-gharbiyya*). It is an alternative way between moderation (*i'tidal*) and excess (*ghuluw*). An integral part of

70 *Tunisia*

the project to banish from the lands of our *umma* the bipolarity of Western liberalism and socialism.[43]

This type of rationalism underscored al-Ghannouchi's early intellectual project. In a 1994 interview with the newspaper *Al-Shira*, al-Ghannouchi explained how he saw this approach as a means to "identify reality" and harness realism as a method of critique and ultimately resistance.[44] The "balance" between the two polarities stemmed from a common reading of Ibn Taymiyya's *fatwa* regarding the caliphal successors of the Prophet Muhammad (*khilafat al-nubuwwa*) and the subsequent role of *mulk*, or kingship, in administering the *umma*.

In *Longing for the Lost Caliphate*, Mona Hassan describes this dynamic by stating: "As for Ibn Taymiyya's middle path, achieving an exemplary caliphate, one that realistically embraces the guidance of the Prophet and his righteous successors, is the ideal of Islamic governance."[45] Ibn Taymiyya was attempting to mitigate two extremes. On one side was the faction that included the Kharijites, "who deem *khilafat al-nubuwwa* to be obligatory under all conditions," and on the other side was the worldly faction of oppressors and libertines (e.g., Umayyad caliphs) who would "declare the absolute permissibility of *mulk*, or worldly rule, without holding it to the standard of the religious caliphs."[46] The modern-day interpretations, Hassan suggests, would be "religious extremism" on one hand and "excessive secularism" on the other. Al-Ghannouchi describes a similar framework in his study of Ibn Taymiyya. But whereas the latter explored the bipolarities of the "*khilafat al-nubuwwa* and the *mulk*," it was the eighteenth century revitalizer of Ibn Taymiyya, Muhammad bin 'Abd al-Wahhab (d. 1792), whose mission of *jihad* and *ijtihad* defined the modern parameters of Ibn Taymiyya's message of religious renewal for the young al-Ghannouchi.

> Just as in the West in the age of Renaissance, the Muslim world was stirred by a great awakening. Muhammad bin 'Abd al-Wahhab's message of *jihad* and *ijtihad* inspired an unbroken movement—from India and Pakistan (Dehlawi and Mawdudi) to Egypt (al-Afghani, 'Abduh, Rashid Rida, and al-Banna), Sudan (the Mahdiyya movement), North Africa (the Sannusi and Jama'iyya al-'Ulama' movements), and the movement of Khayr al-Din al-Tunisi, 'Abd al-'Aziz al-Thalabi, Muhiyi al-Din al-Qalabi, and 'Allal al-Fassi—to push the *umma* towards *jihad* against its enemies, to abandon the guise of tradition (*taqlid*) and to unite its divisions around the mystical origins (*al-minab 'a al-safiyya*) of Islam and Islamic thought.[47]

Alongside this religiously inspired movement (*harakat al-aslahiyya al-diniyya*), al-Ghannouchi notes that this period of awakening, or *nahdha*, produced a literary renaissance to reclaim the elegance and fluidity of Arabic and to break from the cultural conformities of "Turkification."[48] Though still early in his career as a scholar and activist, al-Ghannouchi sought to identify not simply the historical grounds of a modern religious identity movement, but the veritable

Tunisia 71

foundation of Arab modernity. However, this concept ran contrary to the views of Arab nationalists like Bourguiba.

Once the Neo-Destour consolidated power, the Tunisian regime assumed authoritarian form and accorded great power to the presidency. At the meeting of the Destour Congress at Monastir in 1974, Bourguiba was declared President for Life.[49] Government policy was a matter decided by Bourguiba and a select cadre of Neo-Destour insiders. It was not the subject of national debate. As Clement H. Moore observed: "Bourguiba's speeches before the national assembly were designed to publicize decisions he had already made rather than to defend a point of view."[50] Meanwhile, the regime actively cultivated a cult of personality around Bourguiba, making his birthday a national holiday, naming streets for him, building statues in his image and a golden-domed mausoleum in Monastir with the words "liberator of women, builder of modern Tunisia" above the door.[51] The firm grip of the Neo-Destour and Bourguiba loyalists made Tunisia into an autocratic one-party state devoid of substantive political opposition.

For al-Ghannouchi and his Islamic Group colleagues, the *Mujahid al-Akbar*, as Bourguiba was known in Tunisia, succeeded in ending the physical, military occupation of the country, but Western cultural and intellectual colonialism in Tunisia was continuing unabated. As al-Ghannouchi later recalled:

> The independence achieved from the French in 1956 was not a real victory … it turned out to be a continuation of the process of destruction in the form of an intensive campaign to culturally annex Tunisia to France as fast as possible.[52]

And as Ennaifer noted, regarding the crisis of identity felt in the country: "Those who joined the Islamists' ranks were those who found nothing to be attached to—right or left; they were uprooted."[53]

During this period, communism continued to make inroads in Tunisia, despite Bourguiba's active repression of the far-left and banning of the Communist Party.[54] Not only was communism an atheist ideology, but it was also perceived by the Islamists as yet another Western import that undermined Tunisian culture and identity. To help curb the growth of communist revolutionary sentiment, Bourguiba's regime strategically tolerated the doings of religious activists like al-Ghannouchi and the Islamic Group. Anwar Sadat pursued a similar strategy in Egypt with the Muslim Brotherhood under 'Umar al-Tilmisani. However, a confrontation in 1978 between the Bourguiba regime and Tunisia's foremost labor organization, the Tunisian General Labor Union (French acronym UGTT), altered al-Ghannouchi's relationship with the postcolonial state.

The 1970s were plagued by socioeconomic unrest in Tunisia. In October, 1977, a labor strike at a state textile plant in the town of Ksar Hellal grew into a three-day uprising.[55] Three months later, in 1978, came "Black Thursday," the first general strike in Tunisia since independence. Thousands of workers, led by the aforementioned UGTT, took to the streets and attacked state facilities until

72   *Tunisia*

authorities violently suppressed them, killing between 200 and 500 people.[56] The clash shocked al-Ghannouchi and led him to reconsider his existing ideas. As he later explained:

> It was thanks to the Left that we realized that the socioeconomic conflict was no less important than the ideological conflict; that is between Communism and Islam. It was the Left that opened our eyes to the conflict between the exploited, destitute, and impoverished majority and a small minority that in collaboration with the state exploited the entire population.[57]

The labor struggle led al-Ghannouchi to revisit his understanding of Islam and the movement's nominal cooperation with the regime against the communists. The Islamic Group subsequently attempted to appeal to the workers that the Leftists held sway over. They urged members to join labor unions, and mosques became suddenly centers for socioeconomic activism, increasing animosity from the regime. As al-Ghannouchi later recalled: "[We] supported and joined the workers and students and sought to restore the role of the mosque as a center of cultural and educational activities."[58]

During this period Ennaifer and Slaheddine al-Jourchi parted ways with al-Ghannouchi and Mourou over differing views on *al-'aqlaniyya* and Ghannouchi's integration of the Muslim Brotherhood's ideology into the Tunisian Islamist movement. They formed the new Progressive Islamists group, also known (borrowing from Egyptian usage) as the Islamic Left (*al-yasar al-Islami*). Enneifer had been second-in-command in the Islamic Group after al-Ghannouchi.[59] Thus, their departure was significant but the new faction failed to garner a large following. The Progressive Islamists would remain small and intellectual in orientation. Both Ennaifer and al-Jourchi held a range of academic and government posts in the ensuing years and avoided open confrontation with the Bourguiba and Ben 'Ali regimes.

Islamism as a whole came under new scrutiny after the events of 1979. The Western-backed Pahlavi regime of Iran fell after 50 years and the Islamic Republic of Iran emerged in its place. Al-Ghannouchi and other Islamists around the world viewed the events with great interest. "The Iranian revolution gave a new dimension to Islamic culture," he later said. "Like Marx's call to unite workers of the world," Khomeini's appeal to the "disinherited of the earth" represented a "movement of the streets" (*harakat al-shara'a*) that "gave meaning to the common man" (*al-insan al-'adi*).[60] Reflecting on the fall of the Pahlavi regime, al-Ghannouchi published a piece in the Islamic Group's journal *Al-Ma'arifa* on February 12, 1979, stating:

> Islam is not simply a spiritual call. It is a creed (*aqida*) and devotional service (*'abada*). It is a political system (*nizam siyasi*) and a complete society (*ijtima 'i shamil*). There is no difference between the material (*al-madi*) and the spiritual (*al-ruhi*). And that is why the Imam al-Khomeini is

Tunisia 73

at once a spiritual leader for the Iranian nation as well as the leader of its great revolution.[61]

Seeing Islam as a "populist ideology," al-Ghannouchi treated the Iranian revolution as an expression of a broader global uprising against the "tyranny" of Western hegemony. Al-Ghannouchi even went so far as to assert the harmony of the ideas of the Muslim Brotherhood's founding ideologue, Hassan al-Banna, with Iran's Ayatollah Ruhollah Khomeini, despite the clear sectarian differences.[62]

Later that same year, al-Ghannouchi travelled to Sudan, which was in the midst of its own Islamist uprising. A national reconciliation initiative under President Ja'afar al-Numayri allowed the return of exiled Islamist ideologue Hassan al-Turabi, who was subsequently appointed as Sudan's minister of justice. Al-Ghannouchi now met with al-Turabi in Khartoum and found that Sudanese women actively participated in Islamist movement there, interacted with male members, expressed their opinions, and possessed equal rights and responsibilities.[63] Al-Ghannouchi's religious conservatism and the perception that active roles for women in public life were "Western" led him to assert staunchly patriarchal positions for the Islamic Group. However, back in Tunis, al-Ghannouchi now announced a change in his views on women in the movement, and called for greater equality, encouraged higher education for women, and called for training female leaders in the group.[64] Thus, during the 1980s, the role of women in the movement changed dramatically and the number of women in the group reportedly doubled in a span of one year.[65]

With the platform of the movement evolving and membership growing, Bourguiba's crackdown on the Islamists became increasingly intense. On December 5, 1980, Tunisian police discovered the existence of the Islamic Group, which had existed largely clandestinely since 1973. According to Walid Bennani, a deputy member of Ennahdha, the incident compelled the group towards greater legalization. After changing their name to the *Harakat al-Ittijah al-Islami*, the group gathered at Sousse in April of 1981 and decided to pursue open activities and register as a political party.[66] As al-Ghannouchi later noted, this became the impetus for MTI to rebrand itself as a "democratic Islamic movement." During the MTI's first public press conference in 1981, al-Ghannouchi described the political objectives of the group as pluralistic and said their aim was "the renewal (*ijtihad*) of Islam" and to "purge the country of Western influence." The group's petitions for legalization were met with hostility, however, and during the summer of 1981, Bourguiba's regime arrested and sentenced many of its members to years in prison.[67] Al-Ghannouchi was among those who were arrested. But as he later wrote in the preface to his most influential work, *al-Hurrayat al-'ama fi al-dawla al-Islamiyya* (Public Liberties in the Islamic State), the three-year sentence was a veritable "fellowship" (*minha*) from the "travails of quotidian life."[68]

Drawing on a broad range of sources, including Ibn Khaldun, Emmanuel Kant, Sayyid Qutb and Muhammad Husayn Haykal, the goal of al-Ghannouchi's *al-Hurrayat al-'ama* was to challenge preconceived linkages between Western

74 *Tunisia*

society and universal values, such as human rights and democracy. Pushing back against Islamic thinkers like Muhammad 'Abduh and Rashid Rida, who saw in Islamic civilization a counterpoint to Western-style democracy, al-Ghannouchi argues that the "project of Islam" (*al-mashru'a al-Islami*) and democracy "do not necessarily contradict one another."[69] Indeed, the very premise for al-Ghannouchi is an impossibility since the Islam he envisions entails "a comprehensive system of life."

> So long as man is social by nature, Islam will remain a comprehensive system of life and the Islamic state, thereby, a singular mode for creating a social environment that allows as many of its members as possible to live in spiritual and material accordance with the innate laws of God. The Islamic state is only a political medium for achieving the ideals of Islam, for creating a nation (*umma*) that stands for the good, and the just, and that affirms the truth while exposing falsehoods wherever they may dwell.[70]

From this vantage point, Islam is the beginning and end of social existence. As expressions of human value in the context of social existence, ideals such as "freedom," "human rights" and "democracy," are already Islamic for al-Ghannouchi. For example, he writes:

> Freedom is in Islam, in its culture and its civilized experience. As a fundamental value, it serves as the basis for the valorization and condition of martyrdom, Islamic beliefs, and civilized society. Before the believer confirms his acknowledgment of the existence of God and the truth of Muhammad's message, he affirms himself as a free, rational being. The 'I' in the moment of consciousness and freedom decides: '*I* testify that there is no god but Allah and *I* bear witness that Muhammad is the Messenger of God.'[71]

In the "Islamic state," al-Ghannouchi, like Hassan al-Banna before him, sought to identify in political Islam not simply an ideological alternative to secularism, but a new language, "a comprehensive system," for understanding the world free of any influence perceived to be outside of Islamic thought. Written while behind bars and later published in exile, al-Ghannouchi's manifesto would remain undeniably utopist. To be certain, though, his movement was gaining ground.

Among the few who eluded arrest during the 1981 crackdown was Hamadi Jebali, who later served as prime minister of Tunisia from 2011 to 2013. In a broadcast via *Qana al-Sha'ab al-Hurra* ("The Free Peoples Network"), Jebali vowed to continue the struggle against the regime. "We organized by sector," he later recalled, noting that every sphere of Tunisian society would be part of the movement.[72] As pressure on the Bourguiba regime mounted, uprisings and clashes with security forces grew in number, including the infamous Tunisian bread riots in January of 1984 that claimed the lives of over 100 people.

Freed from prison in 1984, al-Ghannouchi led the MTI into active dialogue with Prime Minister Mohammad Mzali. On July 30, 1984, Mourou visited Mzali

Tunisia 75

at his home and an official meeting was held with al-Ghannouchi and Mourou at the government palace in October 1985.[73] But after the removal of Mzali in July of 1986, Bourguiba appointed a Western-educated military officer, Zine al-Abidine Ben 'Ali, as his new prime minster to monitor security threats. At the time concerns about Bourguiba's health, particularly his mental health, were high. Now prone to fits of paranoia, Bourguiba reportedly perceived Iranian-backed Islamist plots against him and believed Iran was funding protests in Tunisia. He shuttered the Iranian embassy in Tunis and sent assurances to the United States that Tunisia would protect its "national achievements."[74] Having praised the Iranian revolution previously in the pages of *Al-Ma'arifa*, al-Ghannouchi was a primary target of the regime's latest crackdown (despite no material ties to Shia Iran). He was arrested, tried in a security court, and sentenced to life imprisonment for allegedly plotting against the state.[75]

Bourguiba's days in power were now numbered. Following months of conflict between Islamists and the state, a tightly organized military coup was carried out by Prime Minister Ben 'Ali on November 7, 1987. Bourguiba was declared medically unfit to continue as president, marking the first change in leadership since Tunisia's independence from France. Ben 'Ali, the new president, was from the coastal town of Hammam Sousse and studied at military academies in France and the United States.[76] When he assumed power, the autocratic RCD regime remained in place. However, ideological shifts were occurring throughout the region. Like Sadat's rapprochement with the religious right after the death of Nasser, Ben 'Ali spoke of reconciliation, economic reforms and a new political culture.[77] The new president took a different approach to Islam and even began his first public speech as president with the *basmala*; a common practice in Muslim countries that Bourguiba had abandoned.[78]

Ben 'Ali issued new concessions to the Islamists, including an *Eid al-Fitr* pardon that released al-Ghannouchi and other MTI prisoners in 1988.[79] Those that had escaped imprisonment in 1987, such as Mourou and Jebali, returned from exile.[80] On the first anniversary of his presidency, Ben 'Ali announced his National Pact (*al-mithaq al-watani*), which acknowledged Tunisia's Islamic heritage and bonds to the Arab world, especially the Maghreb states.[81] The personality cult around Habib Bourguiba ended, and Islamic symbols and language were reintroduced into the public life.[82] Ben 'Ali also undertook the lesser pilgrimage to Mecca (*umra*), modernized al-Zaytouna, and declared before the congress of the RCD: "It is incumbent for the state and it alone to ensure the vitality and influence of Islam."[83]

Eager to capitalize on Ben 'Ali's gestures, al-Ghannouchi and his colleagues prepared for a new era of Tunisian politics. However, according to Tunisia's constitution, political parties could not reference religion in their names. To circumvent this obstacle, the group changed its name to Ennahdha, but Ben 'Ali was still reluctant to allow their participation. According to Hédi Baccouche, Tunisia's prime minister from 1987 to 1989, Ben 'Ali contacted al-Ghannouchi to gauge his evolving position on the Personal Status Code in particular. He also insisted the group remove any reference to Islam from its platform.[84] Ennahdha

76 *Tunisia*

did not receive legal recognition, and the group's candidates were obliged to run as independents.[85] In the elections of 1989, Ben 'Ali and the RCD party won 80 percent of the vote and every seat (141) in the lower house of parliament, while Ennahdha's candidates took 14.6 percent.[86] The election results were perceived as fraudulent, but Ennahdha proved itself as a formidable threat to the RCD's monopoly on power.[87] After the election, Baccouche and Hamed Karoui, Ben 'Ali's prime minister from 1989 to1999, argued in favor of legalizing the Islamist party, but Ben 'Ali chose a different tact.[88]

Rejecting Ennahdha's efforts to pursue legal democratic channels, the brief period of reconciliation with the state now ended. Al-Ghannouchi fled into exile, where he remained for over two decades. Government crackdowns against political dissidents and violence erupted nationwide. In 1991 student protests escalated into an arson attack on an RCD office in Bab Souika, resulting in the death of one guard and the hospitalization of another. Meanwhile, the regime accused Ennahdha of infiltrating the Tunisian military in a coup plot to create an "Islamic state." Hundreds were arrested and the regime's war on Islamists, supported by neighboring Algeria's own war, peaked.

As al-Ghannouchi lived in exile, Mourou remained in Tunisia and distanced himself from any militancy in Ennahdha, whether real or concocted by the regime. Although he may have had ideological differences with al-Ghannouchi, his break with Ennahdha was attributed largely to intense pressure from the state. Specifically, Mourou was reportedly subjected to severe interrogations and threats against his family by state security forces.[89] After he publically broke from Ennahdha and decided to form his own party, the Ben 'Ali regime silenced him with accusations of sexual indiscretions.[90] Mourou subsequently withdrew from public life and practiced law quietly until the events of the Arab Spring.

Away in London, al-Ghannouchi's role as an ideologue and political philosopher became more pronounced. His vision for the future of Tunisia became a distinctly intellectual enterprise. He now grappled on a deeper level with issues like the status of non-Muslims in an "Islamic state" or the rights of women under an Islamic government. Among the most contentious issues in Islamist thought, these topics were amplified further by the open environment and cynical voices surrounding al-Ghannouchi in London.

In his book *al-Mar'a bayn al-Qur'an wa Waqa' al-Muslimin*, published during his exile, al-Ghannouchi addressed the status of women under his ideological platform. "The decline" of humanity into its current state and its failure to cultivate a virtuous society, he explained, is "apparent in the color [or complexion] of the family's upbringing in which the woman forms its backbone."[91] This decline is "firmly rooted in the woman's sense of her Self, that depends on establishing [or proving] her personhood to others."[92] At the heart of the problem lies the erroneous idea that "the finer sex was not created except for amusement, and that they do not have a weapon in the battle of life except their body, and should learn how to focus on mastering ornamentation and refinement and pleasantness."[93] Social transformation, therefore, requires a change in attitudes toward women. "The real transformation of society," he wrote, "must pass through the family and thus its core element: the woman."[94]

The status of women is among the most embattled components of Islamist thought. As Nikki Keddie noted, Islamists "see Western practices toward and views on women as part of a Western Christian and Jewish cultural offensive, accompanying political and economic offensives, and turn to their own traditions as a cultural alternative."[95] Women thus become referents for society as a whole and a representation of its character and values. In the Iranian revolution, women donned cloaks and headscarves in public as an act of defiance of the pro-Western regime and as an affirmation of a Muslim identity.

In the early 1990s al-Ghannouchi published an article in *al-Sahifa al-Wahda al-Tunisiyya*, the newspaper of the Popular Unity Party (*Hizb al-Wahdha al-Sha'biyya*)—one of only two legal opposition parties in Tunisia at the time. In it, he wrote that the "great jihad" against the "devastating invasion" (*al-mudammira al-ghrazu*) of Western culture on Tunisia was not only material but intellectual. Summoning the diverse lineage of "Shaykh Rashid Rida, Hassan al-Banna, Sayyid Qutb, Abu al-A'la al-Mawdudi and Malek Bennabi," and citing verse 110 of *Surat al-'Imran*,[96] he argued that the Islamic resistance had yet to fully realize a "Qur'anic method" (*al-minhaj al-Qur'ani*) to pursue the necessary intellectual reform.[97] The Islamist movement, he argued, needed a new approach to undertaking the challenge of broad political and social reform. In doing so, the movement could legitimize participation in a secular system, and indeed, he argued, it was necessary to do so for the eventual restitution of full Islamic governance.[98]

To support his argument, al-Ghannouchi recalled several Islamic narratives, including the Prophet Yusuf's service to the ruler of Egypt, the early Muslim migration to the Christian kingdom of Abyssinia, and the eighth-century reign of Caliph 'Umar ibn 'Abdul-'Aziz who governed in a corrupted Umayyad system. Even if a government is not based on *shari'a*, a system based on *shura* (community consultation) or the authority of the community (*umma*) is sufficient in al-Ghannouchi's view, especially if it prevents "the evils of dictatorship, foreign domination, or local anarchy."[99] In another later treatise, al-Ghannouchi further wrote that Ennahdha accepts "that the popular will is the source of political legitimacy and believe[s] in pluralism and in the alternation of power through free elections."[100] But true to his Islamist views, he also noted that "a conflict between Islamic culture and aspects of the incoming Western culture does exist, whether in Tunisia or in other parts of the Arab and Muslim world."[101]

Tensions between the Western-oriented state and the Muslim populace of Tunisia, especially beyond the capital, remained readily apparent beneath the surface. Beyond the regime-approved Islam with its state-appointed preachers and Friday sermons in official mosques, the private observance of Islam, the study of the Qur'an and other Islamic literature continued in homes and quiet meetings. Furthermore, as Rikke Hostrup Haugbolle and Francesco Cavatorta found, Ben 'Ali's economic liberalization in the 1990s and 2000s fostered a materialistic consumer culture that pulled many back to religion, albeit outside

78 *Tunisia*

of official regime-controlled settings. In one example, six young men founded the Riadh Ennasr Qur'an association in a suburb of Tunis in 2007, which had 1800 participants by 2010 (most of them women).[102] Thus, the sudden ground-swell of support for Ennahdha's platform after the revolution was not limited simply to Ennahdha members or close sympathizers, but rather a broader spectrum of the population that identified with al-Ghannouchi's values and conception of Tunisian identity.

In the ensuing days after Mohamed Bouazizi's 2011 death by self-immolation, protests grew nationwide. And more national martyrs soon emerged. Video footage of protests and clashes spread across the region, shared via social media sites (e.g., YouTube, Facebook, Twitter), and broadcast by satellite television channels like *Al-Jazeera*.[103] Organized labor soon joined, and hundreds protested in Tunis, decrying unemployment and economic injustices, especially the corruption and cronyism of the Ben 'Ali regime. As the regime's security forces struggled to crackdown on protestors, lawyers joined the demonstrations and condemned their brutality. The regime carried out sweeps against bloggers and activists. Yet, the protests kept growing. Shocked, the Ben 'Ali regime finally conceded and announced major concessions on January 13. The next day, Ben 'Ali fled to Saudi Arabia.

In Tunisia, the military struggled to maintain control, and an interim unity government was established. It consisted of several Ben 'Ali loyalists, which provoked only further protests. Gradually, changes in the interim government met protestors' demands and won the support of the unions and other opposition groups. The interim government also later agreed to recognize all banned political parties and grant a general amnesty for all exiles and political prisoners.[104] This amnesty law opened the door for al-Ghannouchi's return and the public reemergence of Ennahdha.

On January 30, 2011, al-Ghannouchi boarded a plane in London and stated: "When I return home today, I am returning to the Arab world as a whole."[105] A crowd of supporters awaited him in Tunis, reportedly as many as five or six thousand people, and cheered in celebration when he emerged at the gate.[106] Critics, warning of the "Islamist threat," immediately drew comparisons to Ayatollah Khomeini's return to Iran via plane from exile in Paris in 1979 after the overthrow of the Shah. Shortly after al-Ghannouchi's return, in an interview with the *Associated Press*, he responded directly to those comparisons by stating: "Some Western media portray me like [Ayatollah Ruhollah] Khomeini, but that is not me."[107]

When the first free elections in Tunisia's history were held to select the 217 members of the constituent assembly that would draft a new national constitution, Ennahdha came in first with 40 percent of the seats. As the results were announced, a young female Ennahdha supporter named Zeinab Omri told *Reuters*: "This result shows very clearly that the Tunisian people is [*sic*] a people attached to its Islamic identity."[108] Falling short of an outright majority, Ennahdha soon entered into a ruling coalition with two secular-left parties, the Congress for the Republic (or Al-Mottamar) and Ettakatol. Together the ruling coalition was known as the Troika. The secretary-general of Ennahdha, Hamadi Jebali, was appointed as prime minister in December 2011. In a remarkable reversal of fortunes, Ennahdha suddenly held the future of Tunisia in its hands.

The subsequent debate over a new constitution to replace the Bourguiba-era constitution ratified in 1959 exposed significant divisions in Tunisia's post-Arab Spring political scene. Opposition to Ennahdha appeared on all sides, including from far-right Salafis who opposed democracy as an infidel concept that compromised strict monotheism (*tawhid*) and divine sovereignty (*hakimiyya*). Liberal secularists, in contrast, saw Ennahdha as no different from the Salafis. In their view, Ennahdha would eliminate individual freedom, especially for women, and implement strict *shari'a* laws that would criminalize alcohol consumption, immodest dress, and artistic expression. To support their claims, secularists pointed to a leaked video posted on YouTube that showed al-Ghannouchi telling a Salafi activist to "be patient." In reference to the Islamists of Algeria, who entered into a bloody-civil war with the military in the early 1990s, he said: "We don't want to go down their path." Al-Ghannouchi further added: "Today we have more than a mosque, we have a Ministry of Religious Affairs. We have more than a single store, we have a state."[109] Despite these fears, however, the draft constitution, made public by the Arabic Tunisian daily *Al-Chourouk* in August of 2012, contained no reference to *shari'a*. The document was markedly secular compared to the Islamist constitutions drafted elsewhere, such as the Muslim Brotherhood-backed constitution in Egypt. The prologue of the draft constitution made only references to the "values of the Arab-Islamic identity" and the "strengthening of our [Tunisia's] cultural and civilizational bonds to the *umma*."

The articles of the draft constitution that reaffirmed Tunisia's Arab-Muslim identity were not enough for the Salafists. Indeed, as debates and negotiations between Ennahdha and secular-leftists ensued and continued into 2013, an extremist Salafi group affiliated with al-Qaeda, called Ansar al-Shari'a in Tunisia (AST), emerged. They held impassioned public rallies, well-publicized charitable activities, and launched attacks against "enemies of Islam" and "un-Islamic" behavior, such as the sale of alcohol. Led by Sayf Allah Ben Hassine (also known as Abu 'Ayyad al-Tunisi), a former student of Palestinian-Jordanian Salafi-Jihadi ideologue Abu Qatada and veteran of the Afghanistan conflict, the AST had several thousand supporters, making it a relatively small but active and vocal group. Rejecting Ennahdha's methods and questioning their commitment to "true Islam," AST and other hardline Salafis initially avoided direct confrontation with the Ennahdha-led Troika. However, this changed on September 14, 2012, when angry protests outside of the US Embassy in Tunis, decrying an insulting anti-Muslim film made in the United States, turned into a sudden flurry of violent rioting, looting and arson.

Amidst the Troika's ensuing crackdown on hardline Salafists, during which approximately 100 activists were arrested, Ennahdha called for the arrest of AST's leader Abu 'Ayyad, who fled westward into rural Algeria. From hiding, Abu 'Ayyad declared that the Ennahdha government was un-Islamic and a

80 *Tunisia*

puppet of the Americans.[110] In November, a group of armed Salafists attacked two military posts in the northeastern city of Manouba. One Salafist was killed. Then in December 2012, the interior minister, a member of Ennahdha, announced that state security forces had arrested al-Qaeda in the Islamic Maghreb (AQIM) operatives at a camp near Kasserine, along the Algerian border. The operatives had formed a terrorist cell in Tunisia called the Army of 'Uqba ibn Nafi in Tunisia. The weapons in the cell's possession reportedly came from Libya, where access to arms and munitions had become widespread during the fall of longtime dictator Mu'ammar al-Gaddafi during the Arab Spring.

Notes

1 Quoted in *Ennahdha, un histoire Tunisienne* (2014).
2 Ibid.
3 Youssef Seddik. 2013. "Figures d'une Revolution qui n'a pu devenir..." *Le Temps*, January 24: 26.
4 See Perkins (2004, 91).
5 See Hopwood and Terry (1992, 25–26).
6 See Tamimi (2001, 4).
7 Ibid., 6.
8 Franck Frégosi and Malika Zeghal. 2005. *Religion et Politique au Maghreb: Exemples Tunisien et Marocain, Policy Paper* 11, 9. Paris: Ifri.
9 See Tamimi (2001, 10).
10 See al-Ghannouchi (2000, 98).
11 See Curtiss, 1998, 34–36).
12 See Tamimi (2001, 7).
13 Ibid.
14 Ibid., 8.
15 Quoted in *Ennahdha, un histoire Tunisienne* (2014).
16 See Burgat and Dowell (1993, 187).
17 See al-Ghannouchi (2000, 101).
18 See Burgat and Dowell (1993, 187).
19 See Tamimi (2001, 17).
20 Ibid., 19.
21 Ibid.
22 Ibid., 21.
23 Quoted in Tamimi (2001, 22).
24 Ibid.
25 Quoted in Halverson (2010, 98).
26 Quoted in Montasser al-Zayyat (2004, 23).
27 See Tamimi (2001, 24).
28 Ibid., 25.
29 Ibid., 31.
30 Ibid., 31–32.
31 Ibid., 32–33.
32 Youssef Seddik. 2012. "'Le moine' et le philosophie, ma rencontre avec R. Ghannouchi." *Le Temps*, April 19.
33 Ibid.
34 Quoted in Brown (1973, 377).
35 Ibid., 378.

Tunisia 81

36 See Shahin (1998, 68).
37 See Hamdi (2000, 18).
38 See Tamimi (2001, 40–41).
39 Quoted in *Ennahdha, un histoire Tunisienne* (2014).
40 Ibid.
41 Ibid.
42 See al-Ghannouchi (2005, 23).
43 Ibid., 21.
44 Quoted in "Tunisia's Islamists are Different than Those in Algeria," *al-Shira* (October 1994). Accessed 1 April 2017. http://collectiondevelopment.library.cornell.edu/mideast/ghanush.htm.
45 See Hassan (2016, 112).
46 Ibid.
47 See al-Ghannouchi (2005, 19).
48 Ibid.
49 See Allani (2009, 259).
50 See Moore (1965, 81).
51 Ibid.; See also Anon. 2000. "Habib Bourguiba." *The Economist*, 355(8166): 94.
52 See al-Ghannouchi (2000, 108).
53 Quoted in Hamdi (2000, 10).
54 See Allani (2009, 259).
55 See Alexander (2010, 47).
56 Ibid.; See also Tamimi (2001, 50).
57 Ibid., 51.
58 See al-Ghannouchi (2000, 109).
59 See Allani (2009, 262).
60 Quoted in *Ennahdha, un histoire Tunisienne* (2014).
61 Rachid al-Ghannouchi. 1979. "al-Thawra Iraniyya Thawra Islamiyya." *al-Maarifa* 3.2, February 12.
62 See Allani (2009, 259).
63 See Tamimi (2001, 57).
64 Ibid.
65 Ibid., 58.
66 See Allani (2009, 260).
67 See *Ennahdha, un histoire Tunisienne* (2014).
68 See al-Ghannouchi (1993, 17).
69 Ibid., 14.
70 Ibid., 93.
71 Ibid., 319.
72 Quoted in *Ennahdha, un histoire Tunisienne* (2014).
73 See Allani (2009, 262).
74 See Boroweic (1998, 43).
75 Ibid., 43–44.
76 See Habeeb (1990, 79).
77 See Boroweic (1998, 62).
78 See McCarthy (2014, 741).
79 See Boroweic (1998, 64).
80 See McCarthy (2014, 742).
81 See Perkins (2004, 187).
82 See Burgat and Dowell (1993, 230).
83 See Leveau (1993, 107).
84 Quoted in *Ennahdha, un histoire Tunisienne* (2014).
85 See Burgat and Dowell (1993, 237).
86 See Boroweic (1998, 45).

82 *Tunisia*

87 See Tamimi (2001, 70).
88 Quoted in *Ennahdha, un histoire Tunisienne* (2014).
89 See Burgat and Dowell (1993, 244).
90 Ibid.
91 See al-Ghannouchi (2000, 65).
92 Ibid., 65.
93 Ibid.
94 Ibid., 66.
95 See Keddie and Baron (1991, 2).
96 The verse reads:

> Of all the communities raised among men you are the best, enjoining the good, forbidding the wrong, and believing in God. If the people of the Book had come to believe it was best for them; but only some believe it was best for them.

97 See al-Ghannouchi (1984, 183–189).
98 See al-Ghannouchi (2007, 272).
99 Ibid., 273.
100 See al-Ghannouchi (2000, 101).
101 Ibid.
102 See Cavatorta and Hostrup Haugbolle (2013, 53).
103 Robert Mackey. 2011. "Video that Set-Off Tunisia's Uprising." *New York Times* (January 22). Accessed November 22. 2011. http://thelede.blogs.nytimes.com/2011/01/22/video-that-triggered-tunisias-uprising/.
104 David D. Kirkpatrick. 2011. "Tunisia Takes Step Toward Allowing Exiles to Return." *New York Times* (January 20). Accessed November 27, 2011. www.nytimes.com/2011/01/21/world/africa/21tunis.html.
105 Quoted in "Tunisia's Exiled Leader Returns to Rapturous Welcome." *Dawn.com* (January 31). Accessed November 27, 2011. http://dawn.com/2011/01/31/tunisias-exiled-leader-returns-to-rapturous-welcome/.
106 Cecily Hilleary. 2011. "Return of Islamic Leader Worries some Tunisian Women." *Voice of America* (February 3). Accessed November 27, 2011. www.voanews.com/content/article/134523.html.
107 Quoted in Molly Hennessy-Fiske. 2011. "Tunisia: Returned Exile Insists 'I'm no Khomeini.'" *Los Angeles Times* (January 30). Accessed November 27, 2011. http://latimesblogs.latimes.com/babylonbeyond/2011/01/tunisia-returned-exile-insists-im-no-khomeini.html.
108 Tarek Amara and Andrew Hammond. 2011. "Islamists Claim Win in Tunisia's Arab Spring Vote." *Reuters* (October 24). Accessed March 28, 2017. www.reuters.com/article/us-tunisia-election-idUSTRE79L28820111024.
109 The video can be found at: www.youtube.com/watch?v=Qu2TXVzQXQ4.
110 Houda Trabelsi. 2012. "Tunisia takes action against Salafists." *Magharebia.com* (November 1). Accessed 26 December, 2012. www.magharebia.com/cocoon/awi/xhtml1/en_GB/features/awi/features/2012/11/01/feature-01.

References

Alexander, Christopher. 2010. *Tunisia: Stability and Reform in the Modern Maghreb.* New York: Routledge.
al-Ghannouchi, Rachid. 1984. *Maqalat.* Paris: Dar al-Qayrwan.
al-Ghannouchi, Rachid. 1993. *al-Huriyyat al-'Ama fi al-Dawla al-Islamiyya.* Beirut: Merkaz Darasat al-Wahda al-'Arabiyya.
al-Ghannouchi, Rachid. 2000. *al-Mar'a bayn al-Qur'an wa Waqa al-Muslimin.* London: Maghreb Center for Research and Translation.

Tunisia 83

al-Ghannouchi, Rachid. 2000. "Secularism in the Arab Maghreb." In *Islam and Secularism in the Middle East*, edited by Azzam Tamimi and John L. Esposito, 93–123. London: Hurst & Company.

al-Ghannouchi, Rachid. 2005. *Al-Qadir 'anda Ibn Taymiyya*. Saudi Arabia: al-Markaz al-Raya.

al-Ghannouchi, Rachid. 2007. "The Participation of Islamists in a Non-Islamic Government." In *Islam in Transition, Muslim Perspectives: Second Edition*, edited by J. J. Donohue and John L. Esposito, 271–278. New York: Oxford University Press.

al-Zayyat, Montasser. 2004. *The Road to al-Qaeda*. New York: Pluto Press.

Allani, Alaya. 2009. "The Islamists in Tunisia between Confrontation and Participation: 1980–2008." *The Journal of North African Studies*, 14(2): 257–272.

Boroweic, Andre. 1998. *Modern Tunisia: A Democratic Apprenticeship*. Santa Barbara, CA: Praeger.

Brown, L. Carl. 1973. "Tunisia: Education, 'Cultural Unity,' and the Future." In *Man, State, and Society in the Contemporary Maghrib*, edited by Ira William Zartman, 367–377. New York: Praeger.

Burgat, Francois, and William Dowell. 1993. *The Islamic Movement in North Africa*. Austin: University of Texas Press.

Cavatorta, Francesco, and Rikke Hostrup Haugbolle. 2013. "Beyond Ghannouchi: Islamism and Social Change in Tunisia." In *The Arab Revolts: Dispatches on Militant Democracy in the Middle East*, edited by David McMurray and Amanda Ufheil-Somers. Bloomington, IN: Indiana University Press.

Curtiss, Richard H. 1996. "Women's rights: An Affair of State for Tunisia." In *Arab Women: Between Defiance and Restraint*, edited by Suha Sabbagh, 33–40. Northampton, MA: Olive Branch Press.

Ennahdha, un histoire Tunisienne. 2014. Directed by Christophe Cotteret. ARTE.

Habeeb, William Mark. 1990. "Zine El Abidine Ben Ali." In *Political Leaders of the Contemporary Middle East and North Africa: A Biographical Dictionary*, edited by Bernard Reich, 78–83. Westport, CT: Greenwood Press.

Halverson, Jeffry R. 2010. *Theology and Creed in Sunni Islam: The Muslim Brotherhood, Ash'arism, and Political Sunnism*. New York: Palgrave Macmillan.

Hamdi, Mohamed E. 2000. *The Politicisation of Islam: Essays on Democratic Governance*. Boulder, CO: Westview Press.

Hassan, Mona. 2016. *Longing for the Lost Caliphate*. Princeton, N.J: Princeton University Press.

Hopwood, Derek, and Sue Mi Terry. 1992. *Habib Bourguiba of Tunisia: The Tragedy of Longevity*. New York: Palgrave Macmillan.

Keddie, Nikki R., and Beth Baron. 1991. *Women in Middle Eastern History: Shifting Boundaries in Sex and Gender*. Hartford, CT: Yale University Press.

Leveau, Rémy. 1993. *Le Sabre et le Turban: L'Avenir du Maghreb*. Paris: Francois Bourrin.

McCarthy, Rory. 2014. "Re-Thinking Secularism in Post-Independence Tunisia." *The Journal of North African Studies*, 19(5): 733–750.

Moore, Clement H. 1965. *Tunisia since Independence: The Dynamics of One-Party Government*. Berkeley: University of California Press.

Perkins, Kenneth. 2004. *A History of Modern Tunisia*. New York: Cambridge University Press.

Shahin, Emad Eldin. 1998. *Political Ascent: Contemporary Islamic Movements in North Africa*. Boulder, CO: Westview Press.

Tamimi, Azzam. 2001. *Rachid Ghannouchi: A Democrat within Islamism*. New York: Oxford University Press.

5 Libya

Nowhere was the tension of the Arab Spring more acute than Libya, where the shadow of the Arab world's longest standing dictator, Mu'ammar al-Gaddafi, loomed large over the region-wide unrest. Across Libya's western border with Tunisia, opportunists and marketers in the country's bustling post-revolutionary cities were ready to seize the moment. Stores and street kiosks were awash in revolutionary paraphernalia, including silk-screened images of Alberto Korda's iconic image of Che Guevara, *Guerrillero Heroico*, and Libyan anti-colonial resistance leader 'Omar al-Mukhtar. The black, red, and green flag of the Libyan rebels was everywhere.

Libya's capital and largest city, Tripoli, sits less than 100 miles from the Tunisian border. As the uprising in Libya escalated into a bloody and protracted conflict, many thousands fled to Tunisia, while still others left for Egypt or further abroad to Europe and elsewhere. In the wake of the country's tumultuous first ever general elections in 2012, two rival governments formed in the East and the West of Libya. From the political vacuum, as one scholar on the ground estimated, there emerged some 300 armed militia groups, nearly 125,000 fighters in all.[1] In November 2014, a consortium of Libyan militias in the coastal city of Durna even pledged allegiance to the self-declared "caliph" of the Islamic State in Iraq and Syria (ISIS). One of the leading figures behind the alliance was a Tunisian and the founder of *Ansar al-Shari'a*, which was responsible for attacking the US consulate in Benghazi two years prior.[2] By all accounts, five years after the fall of al-Gaddafi, the modern state of Libya appeared to be dissolving. As history shows, however, its uniformity has always been tenuous.

It was only during World War II that Libya emerged from three former Ottoman provinces—Cyrenaica, Tripolitania, and Fezzan—relinquished to the Allies from Italy in 1947. This was an unusual start compared to the surrounding states. As André Martel observed in the *Annuaire de l'Afrique du Nord* in 1966, no other country in the Maghreb was created in such a fashion, requiring neither bilateral agreement nor armed insurgency.[3] Two years later, the United Nations General Assembly overwhelmingly passed a resolution (only one vote was against it) approving independence for Libya, effective before the start of 1952. Thereafter, Libya declared its independence on December 24, 1951, and a constitutional monarchy was established under King Idris I, the chief of the Sanussi

Libya 85

Sufi order (*tariqa*) and reigning Emir of Cyrenaica and (nominally) Tripolitania. His flag, resurgent in 2011, was black, red, and green: three colors for three distinct provinces.

The new postcolonial monarch Idris was born during Ottoman rule in an oasis border town in Cyrenaica. He was the grandson and heir of the Algerian founder of the Sanussi order, Sayyid Muhammad ibn 'Ali al-Sanussi, also known as the Grand Sanussi. Before settling in the isolation of eastern Libya, the Grand Sanussi studied in Fes and in Cairo at al-Azhar, later founding a Sanussi *zawiyya* (or religious center) in Mecca. In Ottoman Libya, he established a new *zawiyya* in the mountains and quickly attracted followers from the rural tribes of the region. His teachings reflected the Sufism of the nineteenth century Moroccan *shaykh*, Sidi Ahmed ibn Idris al-Fasi, which emphasized ascetic emulation of the Prophet Muhammad (as the bearer of *nur* or divine light), and the popular reformist trends of the time that urged a return to the "true Islam" of the original sources, free from historical accretions.[4] By the turn of the twentieth century, the Sanussi order dominated "spiritually and economically" a veritable empire extending from Cyrenaica to Chad and the Western Sahara.[5]

As the grandson of the Grand Sanussi, Idris was his spiritual heir and the grand master (*murshid*) of the Sanussi brotherhood (*ikhwan*), enjoying all the influence and authority that this inherited role entailed. During the onset of Italian colonialism, the Sanussi brotherhood under Idris put up a formidable struggle against the foreign invasion. In fact, this struggle against occupation forced Idris into exile in Cairo where the League of Arab States was marshalling resources to press the case for Syrian and Libyan independence before the United Nations.[6] During World War II, Idris (again in Cairo) rallied Sanussi guerillas to aid the British against the Italians. His support for the Allies ultimately benefited Libya's independence effort.

The Italians defeated, Idris became the first (and only) king of an ostensibly unified Libya. The kingdom's National Assembly, comprised mostly of tribal elders, began to draft a national constitution. The charter established Libya as a federalist monarchy with Islam as the state religion. And after much haggling and negotiation, the charter was ratified in Benghazi in October 1951. At the time, Libya had a small population of only one million people, most of whom were desperately poor. The Italian colonial administration had excluded Libyans from virtually the entire professional class of society, leaving a nation without doctors, scholars, bureaucrats or administrators.[7] Literacy rates were abysmal. According to Lisa Anderson, the country's leading export quickly became scrap metal collected from the debris left behind by the war.[8] Arms traffic from Cairo flowed across the territory towards anti-Bourguiba Youssefists in Tunisia and Fellahin fighters in Algeria.[9] In addition, hundreds of thousands of Libyans had died in the struggle against the colonial occupation, and the country's rich oil reserves were not yet developed. Reflecting this reality, the king's administration was simple and powers were delegated to tribal allies and prominent families in different regions.[10] Unfortunately, when parliamentary elections were held in February 1952, wherein only men over the age of 21 could vote, tensions flared

86 *Libya*

and they were marred by violence and factional distrust.[11] Differences between the three Libyan provinces were tense. When the electoral results appeared to favor the king's interests, accusations of tampering and fraud resulted in riots that were brutally suppressed. All political parties in Libya were subsequently banned and King Idris was quick to secure military and economic aid arrangements with powerful Western patrons, namely Britain and the United States.[12]

Ten years prior to these events, a boy named Mu'ammar Muhammad al-Gaddafi was born in a small village south of Sirte in the western province of Tripolitania. His father was an illiterate tent-dwelling goat herder of Arabized Berber stock.[13] The al-Gaddafi (*al-Qaddhafi*) tribe, like the Sanussis or the Alaouites of Morrocco, claimed direct descent from the Prophet Muhammad. This gave the tribe a degree of prestige and pride. But from his simple rural upbringing, disrupted by colonialism and war, Mu'ammar came to idolize Egypt's Gamal 'Abdel-Nasser and to see the military as his path forward in life. Indeed, it is reported that young Mu'ammar often memorized Nasser's speeches and recited them for classmates.[14] He was about ten years old when Libya's independence was achieved, which preceded Egypt's revolution by less than a year. Initially sent to a religious school in Sirte, he later studied at a school in the southwestern desert city of Sabha (in Fezzan), where he ran afoul of the royal family's tribal allies.[15] Fleeing to the coastal city of Misrata thereafter, al-Gaddafi later relocated to Benghazi, where he enrolled and graduated from the military academy in 1965.[16] After a brief stint abroad in Britain, he returned to Libya and studied in Benghazi while actively seeking out like-minded people who wanted radical change in their country.

After the humiliation of the 1967 Six-Day War, popular hostility toward the old (but pious) king and his pro-Western policies grew. The rise of Pan-Arab sentiment and Muslim bonds to Palestine aside, the Libyan government had done almost nothing to support the Arab states in the conflict. This was not the sole source of the population's enmity though. The king was unapologetically biased toward his home province of Cyrenaica (over Tripolitania and Fezzan), prone to reclusiveness, and averse to the day-to-day business of governance.[17] Oil was discovered in 1959 too and the king's government worked to avert any provincial obstacles to its development by abolishing the hard-fought federalist system of the constitution.[18] The oil industry, in turn, brought intense foreign interest and investment in Libya. With it, the economy suddenly boomed. But the enormous new wealth from Libya's oil reached very few. Thanks to the oil industry, Libya was no longer the poorest country on earth, but its wealth was pent up in the woefully underdeveloped and inexperienced institutions of a nascent state bureaucracy. Corrupt tribal elders and royal officials took advantage and amassed great personal fortunes. Rural peoples, in particular, who were desperate for a better life, flooded into the coastal cities, but were left wanting in squalid shanty towns. Conditions were ripe for revolutionaries to take action.

While King Idris was abroad in Turkey for medical treatment on September 1, 1969, a group of Libyan military officers led by Captain (later "Colonel") Mu'ammar al-Gaddafi carried out a sudden and mostly bloodless coup. The officers abolished the Sanussi monarchy of the short-lived Libyan kingdom and declared the country to be an Arab republic. Al-Gaddafi was quick to emphasize his humble origins to the Libyan people, stating "we are not rich people; the parents of the majority of us are still living in huts."[19] A new constitution was produced by the officers soon thereafter in December 1969. Meanwhile, members of the royal family, prominent officials, senior military officers and others deemed loyal to the monarchy were arrested and subjected to televised trials.[20] King Idris (condemned to death in absentia) lived out the rest of his life as an exile and died in Cairo in 1983. Al-Gaddafi openly modeled his revolutionary "Free Officers" after those of Nasser, who overthrew Egypt's monarchy in July 1952 and established the Republic of Egypt. In his 1975 masterpiece, *al-Tariq ila Ramadan* ("The Road to Ramadan"), Egyptian journalist and confidant of Nasser, Mohamed Hassanein Haykal, recounts that Egyptian officials determined the identity of those behind the September Coup in Libya because of their slogan, which was captured in a broadcast from *Al-Ahram*'s radio monitor in Tripoli. The phrase *hurriyya, ishtirakiyya, wahda* ("Freedom, Socialism, Unity"), distinguished the revolutionaries from the Ba'athists of Iraq and Syria, whose axiom followed in reverse order: "Unity, Socialism, Freedom." The Libyan version signaled direct alignment with Nasser who held the order of the slogan to be specific. As Haykal wrote, Nasser's point of view was that "you cannot have unity unless you are free, so that freedom must come first."[21] However, al-Gaddafi's political program would prove to be very different than Nasser's.

The new Libyan Arab Republic, as outlined in the articles of the 1969 constitution, was governed by a Revolutionary Command Council (RCC), as Egypt was after its revolution. It adopted a new red, white, and black flag for a time, similar to that of the Republic of Egypt. Yet, when Nasser delivered his famous 1969 speech in Tripoli, extolling "Libiyya huriyya, Libiyya 'arabiyya" ("Free Libya, Arab Libya"), it was clear that it was al-Gaddafi alone who would speak "on behalf" of the people, their "freedom" and their "attachment to Arab unity." More profoundly still, as Nasser exclaimed, Libya's "dear revolutionary brother" was more than a political leader. With a rhetorical twist of no slight religious import, Nasser proclaimed that al-Gaddafi would speak for the "feelings" (*masha'ir*) of the Libyan people. In addition to being their political and military voice, it appeared that al-Gaddafi, like Nasser, was to become the nation's spiritual voice as well.[22]

The RCC consisted of 12 military officers led by al-Gaddafi as chairman, and acted as the supreme authority of the state. It was quick to assert its religious legitimacy too, although the constitution made very few references to Islam. In a reversal of fortunes, the RCC suppressed the Sanussis and privileged non-Sanussi *'ulama* from the traditional Sunni rites (e.g., Malikites), even placing the Sanussi *zawiyya* under state control.[23] Arabic (not Italian, English, or Berber languages) and the Islamic calendar were required for public usage, alcohol was outlawed, and churches, nightclubs, and cafés (as colonial remnants) were forced to close.[24] By October 1972, more ostensibly Islamic laws were instituted,

88 Libya

including the obligatory payment of *zakat* (alms) and amputation of hands (by surgical removal) for the crime of theft.[25] Yet, despite these superficial odes to Islamic legitimacy, al-Gaddafi was quick to crackdown on any religious activity outside of state control. The Muslim Brotherhood, for example, was condemned by al-Gaddafi as an ally of the colonialists and an opponent of Arab unity.[26] The Muslim Brothers, al-Gaddafi would state, "are actually Muslim traitors because they destroy Islam and they are under the wing of Zionism."[27] In 1974, al-Gaddafi warned Libyan Muslim Brothers to keep their *da'wa* (propagation) efforts outside of the country and several Brotherhood leaders were asked to leave.[28] Many fled to Great Britain and the United States.

Portraying himself as the heir of 'Omar al-Mukhtar, al-Gaddafi had thousands of Italians expelled from Libya, and the American and British military bases (permitted under agreements with King Idris) were closed and abandoned. Even wearing Western-style neckties (as Nasser often did) was condemned and equated with wearing the Christian (Crusader) cross.[29] And as he purged Libya of Italian and other Western elements, al-Gaddafi often quarreled with his fellow RCC members, sometimes to the point of violence. The revolution would increasingly move toward the exclusive, singular and unpredictable vision of al-Gaddafi. The Arab Socialist Union became the sole legal political party in Libya, the same way that Nasser had made the Liberation Rally (later renamed the Arab Socialist Union) the sole legal party in Egypt. And without the king's old Western patrons, al-Gaddafi turned to the Soviet Union for arms and support, as Egypt had done.

Al-Gaddafi's eccentric amalgam of Pan-Arab socialism, Third World anti-imperialism, and Sunni Islam (which he would later reform in heterodox ways), remained an evolving political program subject to the whims of his increasingly detached and volatile personality. Over the 1970s, he started to articulate his views on a number of sociopolitical issues with an almost prophetic posture. Al-Gaddafi's theories were recorded and published in three short volumes from 1975 to 1979, known collectively as *al-Kitab al-Akhdar* or "The Green Book." In these short and confusing writings, which first appeared as extracts in the newspaper *Al-Fajr al-Jadid* (1972),[30] and were subsequently translated into multiple languages for international dissemination, al-Gaddafi attempted to lay out his utopian vision (or guidance) for the world. He rejected all existing notions of legitimacy and loyalty in the Islamic and Arab worlds and asserted that his international revolutionary ideology, called the "Third International Theory," would create a stateless society of the people "based on religion and nationalism—any religion and nationalism."[31] True to his ideology, al-Gaddafi pledged funds and arms in support for a wide and unexpected range of revolutionary groups around the world, including the Irish Republican Army (IRA) and the African National Congress (ANC). Meanwhile, al-Gaddafi crafted new notions of Sunni Islam as well. He claimed that the true Islam of the Prophet had been corrupted by historical errors and accretions. To amend this, the Islamic calendar was changed to start ten years later at the time of the Prophet's death in 632, instead of the traditional date of the *hijra* in 622 observed by all other Muslims.[32] The Hadith, the

Libya 89

second highest textual authority in Sunni Islam, were rejected by al-Gaddafi as corrupt, false, and unnecessary texts.[33] "Religion is the Qur'an and nothing else," al-Gaddafi explained.[34] And the traditional *'ulama*, once supporters of the coup against the Sanussi establishment, were stripped of their privileged posts (and income).[35] *The Green Book*, al-Gaddafi announced, was "the new gospel; the gospel of the masses."[36]

On March 2, 1977, al-Gaddafi transformed Libya into a new political entity based on the teachings of his *Green Book*. Cuba's Fidel Castro even came as a guest of honor for the announcement. The new state was called the *al-Jamahiriyya al-'Arabiyya al-Libiyya al-Sha'biyya al-Ishtirakiyya al-'Uzma* or the "Great Arab Mass of the Socialist Libyan People." The neologism, *al-Jamahiriyya*, which means a state representing the great masses, appeared to derive from a key phrase in a speech by Nasser in 1969, wherein he addressed the nation as "oh ye brethren, oh Libya of the revolution, oh ye rebellious masses!" At the time, Nasser identified al-Gaddafi not as the head of state, but as "Leader of the Revolution" (*al-Qa'id al-Thawra*) or "Brother Leader." In 1977, al-Gaddafi officially adopted the title. In place of the RCC he created a "People's General Conference" (*Mu'tamar al-Sha'b al-'Am*), an annual assembly of people nominated by local committees from across the country.[37] He printed new currency adorned with his likeness and the name of his new state. He also adopted a plain green flag as the symbol of the nation to complement the new constitution based on his book. The *Jamahiriyya*, portrayed by al-Gaddafi as the alternative to the capitalist and communist systems of the Cold War, was envisioned as a model for the entire world. The following summer it faced its first major test.

Since the death of Nasser in 1970, Libya's relationship with Egypt had steadily declined. And like other Arab states, Libya fiercely opposed Sadat's efforts to negotiate a peace with Israel. In fact, Libya encouraged and supported opposition groups in Egypt, urging a revolution of the masses there against Sadat. It is worth noting too that during his last visit to Libya in June 1970, Nasser declared that al-Gaddafi was the heir of Pan-Arabism, and al-Gaddafi believed that Sadat had betrayed the Arabs and submitted to America.[38] On July 12, 1977, al-Gaddafi's spokesperson for the Secretary of Foreign Affairs, 'Ali 'Abdussalam Treki, issued a formal declaration in response to the visit of Egypt's Vice President Hosni Mubarak to Sudan where, according to the Egyptian daily *Al-Ahram*, Mubarak met with government officials in Khartoum opposing "plots fomented by Colonel Gaddafi against Chad." According to the Foreign Affairs Office, the Egyptian delegation traveled to Chad where they met with President Félix Malloum; an act perceived as a coordinated attempt to block Libya's "reconciliation efforts" between the Chadian government and rebel factions. Hence, the Secretariat declared that it was the "right of the Arab Libyan people and the *Jamahiriyya* to pursue its legitimate defense and to go on the attack in the event that it becomes clear the adversarial parties are preparing an assault."[39] On July 22, 1977, citing attacks and kidnappings along the Libyan-Egyptian border where Egyptian forces had amassed for over a year, a spokesperson for the *Jamahiriyya* indicated that Libyan forces had initiated a counter-attack on

90 *Libya*

Egyptian territory near the border.[40] The Egyptian military fought back the inferior Libyan invasion force quickly and occupied parts of eastern Libya. The victory was swift and a larger scale assault against al-Gaddafi may have occurred if not for the intercession of neighboring countries. A ceasefire (established on July 24) was brokered by President Houari Boumediene of Algeria with the support of the PLO and other Arab states. It held and military buildups along the border gradually diminished, but hostilities between al-Gaddafi and Sadat continued. Sadat openly described al-Gaddafi as a madman. And when Sadat was assassinated by Islamist extremists on October 6, 1981, al-Gaddafi applauded the news, stating: "This is the punishment for those who betray the Arab nation."[41]

In May of 1981, a coalition of Libyan opposition groups, including members of the Libyan Muslim Brotherhood, formed *al-Jabha al-Wataniyya li-Inqadh Libya*, or "The National Front for the Salvation of Libya" (NFSL) in Khartoum, Sudan. Backed by Saudi Arabia and the United States (through the CIA), the group trained armed insurgents to fight al-Gaddafi's regime. In 1984, the NFSL carried out an armed coup attempt against al-Gaddafi's fortified Bab al-Azizia compound in Tripoli. NFSL fighters, trained in Sudan, crossed the border into Libya through Tunisia. However, several NFSL operatives were caught while crossing and provided valuable information about the operation under interrogation.[42] The brazen NFSL assault was crushed. Al-Gaddafi ordered a mass crackdown on dissidents in its wake, which was followed by a number of executions. Some 75 allegedly disloyal military officers were executed alone.[43] Publicly, al-Gaddafi also took the opportunity to explicitly blame the attack on the Muslim Brotherhood (rather than the NFSL).[44] After the failed operation, the NFSL redirected their efforts towards more conventional political channels for regime change in Libya. From their centers abroad, the NFSL published journals in Arabic and English, as well as critical pamphlets with titles such as "Gaddafi's Action in Light of the Principles of Islam."[45] In 1987, under the leadership of Rajab Za'atut and Jaballah Matar, a former officer known for his ability to bridge the urban-rural divide in Libya,[46] the NFSL established the Libyan National Army (*al-Jaysh al-Watani al-Libiyya*) in Chad.[47] Among them was the future military core of the National Transition Council (*al-Majlis al-Watani al-Intiqali*), which, based in Benghazi, attempted to facilitate the country's political transition beginning in February 2011. General Khalifa Haftar, the future military leader of the country's elected government (based in Tobruk), was a member of *al-Jaysh al-Watani* in the late 1980s.[48] Jaballah Matar would ultimately be immortalized by his son, Hisham Matar, now one of Libya's most celebrated novelists. In a moving passage from his novel, *In the Country of Men*, Matar writes of his father, who had been disappeared in 1990: "That night I dreamed of Baba floating on the sea. The water was unsettled, moving as it does in the deep, rising and falling in hills."[49]

Throughout the history of the NFSL, violent conflict between Libya and the United States continued. In the early 1980s, the Reagan administration enforced a number of stifling embargos against Libya. Those restrictions, including a ban

Libya 91

on importing Libyan oil, grew more stringent as time passed. Libya's economy struggled and domestic unrest stirred. By 1986, the two countries were unofficially at war. For its part, Libya actively supported terrorist plots against America, including a bombing at a West Berlin disco frequented by American servicemen (two were killed, dozens wounded). On April 15, 1986, the United States retaliated with a series of air-strikes against Tripoli and Benghazi, known as Operation El Dorado Canyon.[50] Meanwhile, Libya was already ensnared in a disastrous conflict in northern Chad, popularly known as the Toyota War. Although Libya was involved in Chad for years, the 1987 campaign reached new heights. Al-Gaddafi's army suffered at least 7500 deaths and lost nearly $1.5 billion in military equipment, including over 800 tanks, to the French-backed Chadian forces, many of whom rode in armed Toyota pickup trucks.[51] Among the Libyan fighters captured by the Chadians was General Haftar. Resentful that al-Gaddafi did nothing to pursue his release, Haftar would ultimately turn to the Americans who secured a life in exile for him in Virginia until his return to Libya in 2012.[52] In addition to its serious economic and military costs, the Chadian adventure prompted a new wave of Islamist opposition groups to try and capitalize on the perceived weaknesses of the regime.

Already in July 1986, a previously unknown group of Islamist militants with ties to Pakistan (and the Afghan *jihad*) attempted to poison several Soviet military advisers in the eastern coastal city of Tobruk.[53] The following February, Libyan state television rebroadcast the execution (by hanging) of six alleged members of the group at a gymnasium in Benghazi.[54] "This is the punishment of ... the allies of Satan and the hirelings of imperialism and Zionism," the broadcast explained to Libyan viewers.[55] And another group, three soldiers in the Libyan army, were arrested for alleged bomb and sabotage plots and subsequently executed by firing squad at their barracks.[56] These events coincided with moves by the regime to crack down on Islamic opposition in Libya. Al-Gaddafi had 48 *madrasas* shut down and increased surveillance of the country's mosques.[57] By the autumn of 1989, al-Gaddafi was warning the nation of the imminent Islamist threat, stating that the Islamists are "more dangerous than cancer and AIDS, even more than war with the Israelis or Americans."[58]

Founded secretly in 1990, the existence of the Libyan Islamic Fighting Group (LIFG) was not discovered by al-Gaddafi's regime until the summer of 1995. Thereafter, the LIFG fought an armed insurgency for years against al-Gaddafi, mostly in northeastern Cyrenaica. What began around Benghazi soon spread to Bayda, Tobruk, and even westward to Tripoli.[59] As a spokesman explained in 1996:

> Qaddhafi, as a ruler who has been forced over the necks of the Muslims in Libya in order to achieve the interests of the enemies of our nation, has fulfilled the role which has been expected from him to the letter; this role required him to break the rules of Islam.[60]

The core members of the LIFG were battle-tested veterans from the famed *jihad* against the Soviet Union in Afghanistan during the 1980s. One of those veterans

92 Libya

was 'Abdelhakim Belhadj, also known by the *nom de guerre* Abu 'Abdullah al-Sadiq, who studied architecture before he took up the banner of *jihad* as a young man. He was only 13 years old when the Soviets first invaded Afghanistan in the winter of 1979. After returning to Libya in 1993, Belhadj was captured (along with his pregnant wife) in Malaysia in 2004 and sent by CIA secret rendition to prison in Libya. Also an Afghan veteran, Belhadj's deputy Salah Fathi bin Suleiman was killed in 1997 by a Libyan air-strike against a LIFG training camp in the eastern mountains.[61] The war against the LIFG served as a pretext for a crackdown against all Islamists in Libya, including al-Gaddafi's longstanding foe the Muslim Brotherhood.[62] These developments coincided with fierce battles against Islamist militants elsewhere in the Maghreb too, most notably in Algeria.

Another armed Islamist opposition movement at the time, less radical than the LIFG, was the Islamic Rally Movement (IRM). The IRM was formed by Libyans abroad in Europe in 1992. Several of its members had ties to the Libyan Muslim Brotherhood. However, they were unhappy with the Brotherhood's unwillingness to pursue armed confrontation with al-Gaddafi's regime. The IRM endorsed armed resistance against the *Jamahiriyya* and attempted to build up a secret fighting force inside the country. However, the movement largely collapsed when several of its imprisoned members died in the infamous Abu Salim Prison massacre of 1996, an event that was a turning point in Libya's modern history.[63]

On the evening of June 28, 1996, inmates at the Abu Salim Prison in Tripoli began a protest against torture and vile living conditions. The protestors captured two guards and sought to use them as collateral for negotiations. In response, Libyan security forces committed an infamous massacre in the prison's courtyard.[64] More than 1200 prisoners were shot and killed, most over the span of a single hour on the morning of June 29. The bodies of the victims were never recovered, despite comprehensive efforts to locate them after al-Gaddafi's death in 2011. One survivor of the massacre, a moderate Islamist prisoner named Mohammed Busidra, would spend 21 years of his life at Abu Salim (without charges) and later helped to draft Libya's new constitution.[65] "I knew my only crime—in the regime's eyes," Busidra told the *Irish Times* in 2012, "was calling people to Islam."[66] A spokesperson for the families of the Abu Salim victims, the human rights activist 'Abdul Hafiz Ghoga later became the Vice Chairman of the National Transitional Council (NTC), the internationally recognized representative of Libya during the revolution. Abu Salim is the place where Libya's Arab Spring revolution was born, long before anyone knew the names of Egypt's Khaled Said or Tunisia's Mohamed Bouazizi.

Imprisoned in Abu Salim many years after the massacre, LIFG leader 'Abdelhakim Belhadj agreed to participate in controversial negotiations with the Libyan regime. Al-Gaddafi's son and presumed heir, Saif al-Islam (imprisoned after the Arab Spring), initiated a "reform and repent" rehabilitation program for imprisoned Islamists that began with members of the Muslim Brotherhood. About 100 Muslim Brothers were freed as a result of the program in March 2006. In 2007, Saif al-Islam started a riskier dialogue with the LIFG and other militant prisoners. After long and tense negotiations, a group of five high-ranking LIFG members, led by Belhadj, issued a set of revisions (*muraja'at*) published in 2009 as *Corrective Studies in Understanding Jihad, Accountability, and the Judgment of the People*.[67] In it, they renounced the armed *jihad* against the Libyan regime as an error. Saif al-Islam reportedly employed a range of coercion and persuasion tactics to achieve the agreement and ideological revisions.[68] On July 3, 2009, a group of current and former LIFG members living in exile issued a statement on the dialogue and revisions. While denouncing the regime in strong terms, the statement also expressed support for negotiations, stating:

> We declare our support for the dialogue underway between the group's leadership and the Libyan regime if it should lead to an end to bloodletting, the release of prisoners, the spreading of security and justice, the reunion of families, and to permitting preaching, educational, and political activities.[69]

The rehabilitation programs were ultimately part of a much larger (and haphazard) project by Saif al-Islam to create an aura of political legitimacy around himself and strengthen his position as his father's political heir as the ruler of Libya.[70] In its wake, a battered Belhadj was finally released from Abu Salim with over 200 other Islamists in March 2010. The final terms for their release were negotiated with assistance from the influential Qatar-based Libyan scholar and *shaykh* 'Ali al-Sallabi.[71] "He not only participated in the negotiations as a trusted figure," Behadj later recalled of al-Sallabi, "but also helped exchange messages between prisoners and officials."[72] Also set free that March was a former LIFG member from the northern port town of Derna in Cyrenaica, Abu Sufian bin Qumu, who later became a leader of *Ansar al-Shari'a* in Libya, which was later implicated in the death of US Ambassador Christopher Stevens in Benghazi on September 11, 2012.

After his release from Abu Salim prison, Belhadj adhered to the LIFG's revisions and transformed the group into the Libyan Islamic Movement for Change (LIMC). The LIMC gave up violence and abandoned armed struggle against the regime. It was now ostensibly a *da'wa* movement akin to the Muslim Brotherhood. Conditions would change when the revolution was underway in 2011 though. Belhadj, an experienced military commander, appeared at the head of a brigade of rebel forces in the western mountains. His brigade laid siege to the fortified Bab al-Azizia compound in Tripoli, where the failed NFSL coup against al-Gaddafi had occurred in 1984. "We kept [our] promise [to renounce violence]," Belhadj later stated. "The revolution started peacefully, but the regime's crackdown forced it to become violent."[73]

When Ben 'Ali fell from power in Tunisia, al-Gaddafi declared that he was "pained" by events there. He lamented that "Tunisia now lives in fear" and urged Tunisians to adopt his Third Universal Theory as the basis for a true "democratic" system of government.[74] But fearful that he would fall too, al-Gaddafi's regime hastily looked to guard itself from an uprising at home. Amidst the crackdown, on the afternoon of February 15, 2011, two leaders from an association of

94 *Libya*

families of the victims of the Abu Salim massacre were arrested. The arrests of these two men sparked local protests in Benghazi that were brutally suppressed by state security forces. This event, in turn, helped to fuel the emergence of Libya's Arab Spring uprising, already riding the remarkable momentum of Tunisia and Egypt. The first of the two men was a young lawyer named Fathi Terbil. He had lost his brother, cousin, and brother-in-law in the Abu Salim massacre, and he was involved in plans for a "Day of Rage" on February 17 to demand political reforms and accountability.[75] The date was chosen because it was the anniversary of the death of 14 Libyans at a similar protest in Benghazi in 2006.[76]

By February 24, the coastal city of Misrata had already fallen to anti-Gaddafi rebels. In March, the rebel NTC in Benghazi had coalesced and declared itself the legitimate representative of the Libyan people. Civil war was underway. From Tripoli, the regime utilized its military superiority to crush the largely inexperienced, undisciplined, and lightly armed rebel forces as it pushed eastward. However, following international outcries, the international community and NATO entered the conflict and carried out airstrikes against pro-Gaddafi forces, eliminating their advantages over the rebels. Tripoli subsequently fell to the rebels on August 23 and al-Gaddafi loyalists, including key members of his family, retreated to al-Gaddafi's hometown of Sirte and the inland desert town of Bani Walid. From an unknown location, al-Gaddafi continued defiantly to urge his followers to keep fighting. Sirte would fall on October 20 and al-Gaddafi himself was caught hiding in a drainage pipe with his bodyguards, appearing disheveled and confused. His captors excitedly recorded the event with their cellphones. The footage shows al-Gaddafi being beaten and then executed with a single gunshot to the head. The NTC subsequently declared Libya officially liberated and announced plans for national elections in eight months.[77] Al-Gaddafi's presumed heir, Saif al-Islam, was caught a month later trying to slip into Niger through the southern desert, dressed as a Bedouin. He was transported to a prison in the western city of Zintan to stand trial for his crimes against the Libyan people.

In 2011, when asked about the Islamist orientation of the rebel militias, Belhadj replied: "I can only say that Libya is an Islamic country and that all our traditions and behavior is built on Islam."[78] He then emphasized that Libyans are moderate Muslims and that extremist elements exist only on the fringes of society and do not represent the Libyan people. Likewise, a prominent member of the LIMC's political committee, Anis al-Sharif, expressed that the Islamists were not fighting under a separate banner, but rather as part of a unified revolution that aimed to create a civil society that respects Libyan identity.[79] Amidst the revolution, the NTC appointed Belhadj as the military commander for Tripoli.[80] Belhadj later resigned in May 2012 to join the Islamist *al-Watan* party, a competitor of the Muslim Brotherhood. However, Belhadj's party would fail to win any elected seats in the new Libyan government.

By March 2012, the Libyan Muslim Brotherhood had established its own political party, *Hizb al- 'Adala wa al-Bina'* (Justice and Construction Party or

JCP), to participate in elections for the national congress. Sulayman 'Abd al-Qadir, longtime leader of the Libyan Muslim Brotherhood, stepped down after Bashir Salim al-Kibti, who hails from Benghazi, was selected to lead the organization in November 2011. The JCP would remain separate from the parent organization though. Mohamed Sowan, a political prisoner from the anti-Gaddafi stronghold of Misrata, was selected to head the political party. Since that time, Kibti would repeatedly state that the JCP is independent of the Muslim Brotherhood and pointed to the fact that diverse members were active in the party.[81] The JCP is a "national political party with an Islamic orientation," he explained.[82] The circumstances in Libya, Kibti further noted, are different than neighboring countries (e.g., Tunisia) because there is no conflict over the authority of Islam. "In Libya," he explained to *Al-Sharq al-Awsat*, "there is unanimity on the authority of the Islamic *shari'a*, the reference of the state is Islam."[83] Even the liberals and Leftists in Libya support Islam, he added. Nevertheless, the expectations for the JCP were high in light of strong Islamist successes in Tunisia and Egypt. It seemed a foregone conclusion. However, the JCP finished second in Libya's first free elections among political parties (some 100 in all) when the results were tallied. It was hardly a defeat for political Islam though.

During his first visit to Tripoli, the non-Islamist chairman of the NTC, Mustafa 'Abdul Jalil, declared that all legislation of the future Libyan state would be grounded in *shari'a*.[84] 'Abdul Jalil had served as the Secretary of the General People's Committee of Justice in al-Gaddafi's *Jamahiriyya* before defecting to the rebels on February 21, 2011. He assumed the chairmanship of the NTC on March 5 and was instrumental in organizing international support for the rebels. Likewise, the National Forces Alliance (NFA), which finished first in the elections for the national congress (defeating the JCP), endorsed a moderate Islamist platform. The leader of the NFA Mahmoud Jibril, a former official under al-Gaddafi known for his liberal economic policies, stated that Libya's future laws should have a reference to *shari'a*.[85] "*Shari'a* law, when it was understood in the proper way," Jibril explained in 2012, "managed to create one of the great civilizations in human history."[86] In his view, there is no question about the applicability and relevance of Islam to society and public life in Libya, the only issue of contention is the interpretation of *shari'a*. "We are Muslims by identity and our identity is Islam," the Muslim Brotherhood's leader Kibti would state in 2012.[87] Indeed, Libya's Arab-Muslim identity (specifically Sunni Muslim) would be affirmed, even without a JCP win at the ballot box.

Stability and security would remain elusive, however. In contrast to the relatively smooth democratic transition in neighboring Tunisia, the months and years after the revolution in Libya remained fraught with violence, lawlessness, and competition between regional authorities. Weapons from al-Gaddafi's depots flooded the countryside and found buyers throughout the region. Benghazi was so plagued by violence and disorder in the summer of 2012 that the international community, including the United Nations and the Red Cross, fled the city entirely.[88] Militias, many of them Islamists, were at the forefront of the disorder, despite the fact that many militias assumed responsibility (with government

96 *Libya*

approval) for policing Libyan cities due to the lack of a well-organized and trained national army. The largest and most powerful of these post-revolution militias was Libya Shield (aka Shield 1). The commander of the militia was a battle-worn veteran and Islamist, somewhere in his late thirties, named Wasim Ben Hamid. On June 8, 2013, a protest against the militia took place in Benghazi and some in the crowd had weapons. When a confrontation with Libya Shield took place, violence erupted and the militia killed 29 civilians (two militiamen died).[89] This came to be known as *al-Sabt al-Aswad* ("Black Saturday").[90] Ben Hamid and Libya Shield subsequently fled Benghazi and claimed that the protestors consisted of al-Gaddafi loyalists and angry tribesman exploiting ethnic tensions. Nevertheless, the weak central government in Tripoli expressed no intentions of disbanding the militia, which was nominally under the auspices of the Ministry of Defense. Rather, the state would have to continue to rely on such groups, Islamist or otherwise, until it had the military forces to replace them.

Notes

1 'Abir Ibrahim Amnina, 2013. "Al-Din wa al-Dawla fi Libya al-Yom," *Al-Jarida.* Accessed April 4, 2017. www.aljaredah.com/paper.php?source=akbar&mlf=interpage&sid=19091.
2 "Wazir al-dakhaliyya al-Tunisi Lotfi bin Jidu fi hiwar li-Al-Khaba." 2014. *Al-Khabar* (Algiers) (November 28). Accessed April 4, 2017. www.elkhabar.com/press/article/75046/#sthash.f3yfI5vu.dpbs.
3 See Martel (1967, 782).
4 See Ziadeh (1958, 44–46).
5 See Martel (1967, 790).
6 See Martel (1990, 149).
7 See Pargeter (2012, 35–36).
8 See Anderson (1986, 67).
9 See Martel (1990, 154).
10 See Anderson (1983, 137).
11 See Otman and Karlberg (2007, 16).
12 See Vandewalle (1998, 47).
13 See Pargeter (2012, 62).
14 Ibid., 64.
15 See Anderson (1983, 139).
16 Ibid.
17 See Pargeter (2012, 38).
18 Ibid., 40–41.
19 Quoted in Pargeter (2012, 68).
20 See Pargeter (2012, 69).
21 See Haykal (1975, 69).
22 Jamal 'Abdel-Nasser. 1969. "Khitab al-ra'is Jamal Abd al-Nasir fi mu'timar al-shabi bi-Tarablus Libiyya." (December 25). Accessed April 4, 2017. http://nasser.bibalex.org/Speeches/browser.aspx?SID=1266.
23 See Anderson (1983, 140).
24 Ibid.
25 Ibid.
26 Ibid., 141.
27 Quoted in Ronen (2002, 2).
28 See Ashour (2012, 1).

29 See Bleuchot (1983, 82).
31 See Anderson (1986, 70).
32 Ibid., 71.
33 See Burgat and Dowell (1993, 155).
34 Quoted in Ronen (2002, 2).
35 See Anderson (1986, 70).
36 Ibid., 71.
37 See Hajjar (1980, 181).
38 See Hagger (2009, 97).
39 See Bleuchot (1983, 240).
40 Ibid., 241.
41 See Stanick (2002, 64).
42 Ibid., 85.
43 Ibid.
44 See Ronen (2002, 1).
45 See Burgat and Dowell (1993, 159).
46 Ibrahim 'Abd al-'Aziz Sohad. "Dhikriyat ma'a Jab Allah Matar," *Libiyya al-mustaqbal.* Accessed April 4, 2017. http://archive.libya-al-mostakbal.org/Minbar-Alkottab/ibrahimSahd/with_jaballah1.htm.
47 Khalid al-Muhir. 2012. "Jabha inqad Libiyya tatahawwal l-il-hizb al-siyasi," *Al-Jazira* (March 16). Accessed April 4, 2017. www.aljazeera.net/news/arabic/2012/3/16/.
48 "Muhtat fi hayat al-rahil 'Abd al-Salam 'Az al-Din al-Madani." 2016. *Al-Wasat* (Cairo) (April 4). Accessed April 4, 2017. www.alwasat.ly/public/ar/news/libya/101557/.
49 See Matar (2006, 83).
50 See Stanick (2002).
51 See Pollack (2002, 397).
52 "Profile: Libya's military strongman Khalifa Haftar." 2016. *BBC* (September 15). Accessed April 4, 2017. www.bbc.com/news/world-africa-27492354.
53 See Burgat and Dowell (1988, 615); Joffe (1988, 615).
54 See Burgat and Dowell (1988, 160).
55 See Ronen (2002, 2).
56 See Joffe (1988, 615).
57 See Burgat and Dowell (1993, 160).
58 Quoted in Ronen (2002, 4).
59 See Ronen (2002, 7).
60 Quoted in Luis Martinez. 2007. *The Libyan Paradox.* New York: Columbia University Press, 62.
61 "Libya's New Generals (II): Conflicting Loyalties." 2011. *Al Akhbar English*, August 30. Accessed April 4, 2017. http://english.al-akhbar.com/node/470.
62 See Ashour (2012, 2).
63 Ibid.
64 See Human Rights Watch. 2006. *Libya: June 1996 Killings at Abu Salim Prison.* Accessed April 4, 2017. www.hrw.org/en/news/2006/06/27/libya-june-1996-killings-abu-salim-prison.
65 Mary Fitzgerald. 2012. "'Unspeakable things happened that no one should ever experience.'" *Irish Times* (March 19). Accessed April 4, 2017. www.irishtimes.com/newspaper/world/2012/0319/1224313527811.html.
66 Ibid.
67 See Pargeter (2012, 203).
68 Ibid., 203–204.
69 Anonymous (LIFG-Britain). 2009. "Statement by Libyan Islamic Fighting Group abroad in support of dialogue with Tripoli: Open letter over ongoing dialogue of fighting group leadership with Libyan regime." *Al-Quds al-Arabi* (July 3). Accessed April 4, 2017. http://search.proquest.com.ezproxy1.lib.asu.edu/docview/458786479.

98 *Libya*

70 See Pargeter (2012, 206–207).
71 "Libya's New Generals (II): Conflicting Loyalties." 2011. *Al Akhbar English* (August 30). Accessed April 4, 2017. http://english.al-akhbar.com/node/470.
72 Umar Khan. 2012. "Exclusive: Interview with Abdul Hakin Belhaj." *Libya Herald* (March 5). Accessed April 4, 2017. www.libyaherald.com/2012/03/05/exclusive-interview-with-abdul-hakim-belhaj/.
73 Quoted in Rod Norland. 2011. "In Libya, Former Enemy is Recast in Role of Ally," *New York Times* (September 1). Accessed April 4, 2017. www.nytimes.com/2011/09/02/world/africa/02islamist.html.
74 Matthew Weaver. 2011. "Gaddafi condemns Tunisia uprising." *Guardian.co.uk* (January 16). Accessed April 4, 2017. www.guardian.co.uk/world/2011/jan/16/muammar-gaddafi-condemns-tunisia-uprising.
75 See Pargeter (2012, 212).
76 Ibid., 214.
77 "Libya Profile." 2012. *BBC Africa* (December 10). Accessed April 4, 2017. www.bbc.co.uk/news/world-africa-13755445.
78 David Poort. 2011. "Q&A: Top NTC commander Abdel Hakim Belhadj." *Al-Jazeera* (September 20). Accessed April 4, 2017. www.aljazeera.com/indepth/features/2011/09/2011920155237218813.html.
79 Murad Batal al-Shishani. 2011. "A Look at Abd al-Hakim Belhadj's Transformation from Jihadi to Libyan Revolutionary." *Militant Leadership Monitor,* 2(9). (September 29). Accessed April 4, 2017. www.jamestown.org/.
80 Hugh Roberts. 2011. "Who said Gaddafi had to go?" *London Review of Books,* 33(22). (November 17). Accessed April 4, 2017. www.lrb.co.uk/v33/n22/hugh-roberts/who-said-gaddafi-had-to-go.
81 Ashraf Abdul Wahab. 2012. "Muslim Brotherhood says it aims to share power," *Libya Herald* (March 15). Accessed April 4, 2017. www.libyaherald.com/2012/03/15/muslim-brotherhood-says-it-aims-to-share-power/.
82 Ibid.
83 Mahmud al-Firjani. 2012. "Libyan Muslim Brotherhood leader interviewed on performance, Islamist rule." *Special Encounter* (TV) on Al-Arabiya Satellite Channel (October 16). Translated and transcribed by BBC Monitoring Middle East, Proquest LLC. http://search.proquest.com/.
84 See Roberts (2011).
85 Jamie Dettmer. 2012. "Libya's Optimistic Leader: Mahmoud Jibril Poised for Historic Election Victory." *The Daily Beast* (July 9). Accessed April 4, 2017. www.thedailybeast.com/articles/2012/07/09/libya-s-optimistic-leader-mahmoud-jibril-poised-for-historic-election-victory.html.
86 Ibid.
87 Firjani, "Libyan Muslim Brotherhood leader interviewed on performance, Islamist rule."
88 Anas El Gomati. 2013. "In Libya, Militias Rule," *Al-Monitor* (June 18). Accessed April 4, 2017. www.al-monitor.com/pulse/originals/2013/06/libya-intelligence-security-benghazi.html.
89 David D. Kirkpatrick. 2013. "Violence Against Libyan Protesters Threatens to Undercut Power of Militias." *New York Times* (June 9). Accessed April 4, 2017. www.nytimes.com/2013/06/10/world/africa/libyan-violence-threatens-to-undercut-power-of-militias.html.
90 Muhammad 'Omar Be'ayu. 2013. "*Milishiyat Libyya: al-Qawa al-Ghashima wa al-Qudra al-Hasha.*" *Al-Hayat* (June 27). Accessed April 4, 2017. http://alhayat.com/Details/527199.

Libya 99

References

Anderson, Lisa. 1983. "Qaddafi's Islam." In *Voices of Resurgent Islam*, edited by John L. Esposito, 134–149. New York: Oxford University Press.

Anderson, Lisa. 1986. "Religion and State in Libya: The Politics of Identity." *Annals of the American Academy of Political and Social Science*, 483 (January): 61–72.

Ashour, Omar. 2012. *Libyan Islamists Unpacked: Rise, Transformation, and Future.* Doha: Brookings Doha Center Publications.

Bleuchot, Hervé. 1983. *Chroniques et documents libyens (1969–1980)*. Paris: Editions du Centre National de la Recherche Scientifique.

Burgat, Francois, and William Dowell. 1993. *The Islamic Movement in North Africa.* Austin: University of Texas Press.

Hagger, Nicholas. 2009. *The Libyan Revolution: Its Origins and Legacy.* Hampshire, UK: John Hunt Publishing.

Hajjar, Sami G. 1980. "The Jamahiriya Experiment in Libya: Qadhafi and Rousseau." *The Journal of Modern African Studies*, 18(2): 181–200.

Haykal, Muḥammad H. 1975. *The Road to Ramadan*. New York: Quadrangle/New York Times Book Co.

Joffe, George. 1988. "Islamic Opposition in Libya." *Third World Quarterly*, 10(2): 615–631.

Martel, André. 1967. "Histoire contemporaine de la Libye: dimensions et recherches." In *Annuaire de l'Afrique du Nord*, 781–792. Paris: Editions du Centre National de la Recherche Scientifique.

Martel, André. 1990. "Le Royaume Sanusi de Libye (1951–1969)." *Cahiers de la Méditerranée*, 41(1): 143–162.

Matar, Hisham. 2006. *In the Country of Men*. New York: Dial Press.

Otman, Waniss A., and Erling Karlberg. 2007. *The Libyan Economy: Economic Diversification and International Repositioning*. New York: Springer.

Pargeter, Alison. 2012. *Libya: The Rise and Fall of Qaddafi*. New Haven, CT: Yale University Press.

Pollack, Kenneth M. 2002. *Arabs at War: Military Effectiveness, 1948–1991*. Lincoln, NE: University of Nebraska Press.

Ronen, Yehudit. 2002. "Qadhafi and Militant Islamism: Unprecedented Conflict." *Middle Eastern Studies*, 38(4): 1–16.

Stanick, Joseph T. 2002. *El Dorado Canyon: Reagan's Undeclared War with Qaddafi.* Annapolis, MD: US Naval Institute Press.

Vandewalle, Dirk. 1998. *Libya since Independence: Oil and State-Building*. Ithaca, NY: Cornell University Press.

Ziadeh, Nicola A. 1958. *Sanusiyah: A Study of a Revivalist Movement in Islam*. Leiden: E. J. Brill.

6 Morocco

The monarchy of the Alaouite Kingdom of Morocco is the last of its kind in the Maghreb. Indeed, it is one of a shrinking number of monarchies around the world that wields any real political power. It is not an absolute monarchy, akin to the gulf kingdoms of Saudi Arabia or Qatar, but a powerful one nonetheless with far-reaching executive powers. The Alaouite royal dynasty traces its roots to the *amir* (originally from the Hijaz) of the Moroccan city-state of Tafilalt in the seventeenth century, and even further through a revered genealogical line stretching back to Hassan ibn 'Ali, the grandson of the Prophet Muhammad. Modern Tafilalt encompasses the remains of what was once the Berber (*Amazigh*) trading city of Sijilmasa, located near the eastern border of the nation-state of Morocco. Seemingly ripe for revolution amidst the democratic uprisings of the Arab Spring, the reigning Moroccan monarch, King Mohammed VI, was proactive in initiating reforms to stem the tide of unrest. He largely succeeded too. However, the Islamists would still make their presence known, even with the country's largest Islamist movement boycotting national elections. The Arab Spring sent a formerly imprisoned Islamist to become Morocco's next prime minister.

When Morocco achieved independence from France and Spain (Ceuta and Melilla aside) in March 1956, the formerly exiled Alaouite sultan, Mohammed V, became king. In his brief reign over the independent Kingdom of Morocco, Mohammed V appointed his eldest son Hassan as crown prince, head of the national armed forces, and finally as his prime minister. King Mohammed V died unexpectedly during minor surgery at the age of 51 in February 1961 and he was succeeded by Hassan. The following year Morocco approved a new constitution, but King Hassan II retained absolute power. Opposition to his rule was not tolerated. Insulting the sacred Alaouite monarchy could bring the most severe penalties. The formidable powers of the monarchy—including its adoption of hereditary succession—caused unrest among devout Muslim leaders from the start. And unlike his father, the French-educated Hassan had a reputation for being a hedonist with an affinity for fast cars and blonde women who adored the spotlight.[1]

As Morocco's new Alaouite king, however, Hassan married two wives (restricted polygamy being legal) and attempted to assume the mantle of the

Amir al-Mu'minin, or Commander of the Faithful. This was a traditionally caliphal title appropriated by many Muslim rulers, including the Moroccan monarch. Hassan was quick to assert state control of Islam, modified as a state cult centered on his personhood, and often donned traditional robes and displayed a look of austerity for his subjects. In October 1968, King Hassan decreed that all Qur'anic schools in Morocco—some 30,000 in all—would be supervised by his government through a cadre of 234 inspectors.[2] Over the course of his reign, he also employed greater Islamic symbolism and language in carefully orchestrated public appearances, marked Islamic holidays—including the sacrifice of a sheep on *Eid al-Adha*—and organized a series of Islamic lectures during Ramadan called the *al-durous al-Hassaniyya* (Hassanian lectures).[3] The king also encouraged an image of himself as a wise and caring father to the people of his kingdom.[4] However, beyond these carefully crafted public facades and the personality cult that he cultivated, Hassan was a brutal authoritarian. Indeed, he populated desert prison camps with anyone he pleased, including political activists of all stripes. And he poured the country's limited wealth into luxurious palaces for his family (including lavish chateaus in France and mansions in the United States), extravagant gifts to those he favored, and custom-designed water-consuming golf courses for his personal amusement. *Sports Illustrated* even published an article with the headline "Where a Golf Nut is King" on September 28, 1970.[5] He was a ruler who was profoundly detached from his uneducated and desperately poor people.

Understandably, the troubled "Years of Lead" or *sanawaat al-rusas* under King Hassan II generated significant political opposition and criticism of the regime. The author of the tell-all *Tazmamart Cellule 10*, Ahmed Marzouki was in the Non-Commissioned Officers training program at the now infamous *Madrasa Ahermoumou al-Askariyya* (The Ahermoumou Military School) when he and 1000 other cadets were armed and transported to the town of Skhirat near the capital of Rabat on July 10, 1971. In Marzouki's words, their orders were to carry out an "obscure mission" that involved encircling two buildings occupied by "subversive elements." They were ordered to fire on anyone who attempted to leave. Other divisions of the Royal Armed Forces were engaged at other locations at the same time.[6] The buildings encircled by the cadets turned out to be a royal palace where a birthday celebration was being held for the king. Marzouki, who led one of the teams (*commando* no. 12), claimed he arrived late and did not storm the grounds and open fire.[7]

In the purge that followed the failed coup at Skhirat, Marzouki was arrested with 57 other officers. He spent two years in prison awaiting trial before he was disappeared to the secret prison at Tazmamart in the Atlas Mountains. After his release in 1991, following mounting pressure on the king from human rights groups and Western governments, Marzouki and two cellmates appeared in Rabat at the Agence France Press bureau. Their subsequent accounts of Tazmamart were the first time the public had heard of the prison, which opened in the 1970s. The coup attempt at Skhirat was just one of several successive attempts by the military to oust King Hassan II. Among those who survived

102 *Morocco*

Skhirat was General Mohamed Oufkir, one of Hassan's most trusted advisors and henchmen.[8] Oufkir led a successful mission to assassinate leftist opposition leader Mehdi Ben Barka in Paris in 1965 and he was inside the palace when the coup struck. In 1972, however, Oufkir was accused of his own coup plot and secretly executed.[9] The monarchy officially claimed his death was a suicide. Yet, as punishment for his alleged betrayal, his entire family was sent to a prison camp where they endured years of torture, isolation, and deprivation—what Oukfir's daughter Malika later described in her memoir as the king's "ancestral tradition."[10] Indeed, *la culture de bagne* ("the culture of incarceration"), as it became known, assumed a life of its own under Hassan.[11] "No one can pretend to have witnessed everything, or to have known everything," Ahmed Marzouki wrote in his memoir, "for the simple reason that each had seen but a portion of events."[12]

The sentiment expressed by Marzouki permeated what became a veritable deluge of testimonials in the wake of Hassan's death, a genre known in its totality as *la littérature carcerál*. Notable examples include 'Abdellatif al-Laabi's *Chroniques de la Citadelle d'Exil: Lettres de prison 1972–1980*, Jaouad Mdidech's *La Chambre Noire*, and Tahar Ben Jelloun's *Cette Aveuglaunt Absence de Lumièr*. In fact, Salah El Ouadie's *Le Marié* was described by Mary Robinson of the United Nations High Commission for Human Rights as an alternative means of "combatting the ignorance and contempt for Human Rights."[13] The Moroccan writers dealing with *la culture de bagne* saw a reflection of the absurd state of social decay that existed under Hassan's authoritarian rule in their experiences. Bensalem Himmich's 2009 novel *Mu'dhabati* ("My Torturess") epitomized this trend. In one of the novel's pivotal scenes the narrator-protagonist, blindfolded and handcuffed, asks his jailor "Where are we?" The jailor points a finger to his head and looks away.[14] As part of his incarceration, the protagonist Hamuda is subjected to a series of bizarre rituals—obscurantist and anonymous judges in the Kafkaesque tradition of Sun Allah Ibrahim's modern classic *al-Lijna* ("The Committee"), and most notably a cabaret-like night club where he and the other prisoners are forced to listen to advertising pitches for Pepsi Cola, a direct reference to the perceived capitalist leanings of Hassan's rule.

This element of critique was long central to the many Islamist campaigns that began to organize against Hassan's perceived pro-Western regime. At the time, the political opposition in Morocco (as elsewhere) was dominated by leftists, especially from the Socialist Union of Popular Forces (French acronym USFP), which split from the pro-monarchy nationalist *Istiqlal* party in 1959. Unlike other postcolonial states in the Maghreb, the Kingdom of Morocco had not imposed a single party system on the state.[15] Rather, multiple parties were permitted to exist, so long as they respected the power and dignity of the Alaouite monarchy. In 1969, a former USFP activist named 'Abdelkarim Mouti formed an Islamist association in Casablanca, consisting mostly of educators and students, called *al-Shabiba Islamiyya al-Maghrebiyya* or the Moroccan Islamic Youth (MIY).[16] Mouti and his group were initially tolerated by the king as a way

Morocco 103

to counter Morocco's leftists, especially Nasserists (as Sadat had done in Egypt), but things changed in 1975.[17] A leading member of the USFP, 'Omar Benjelloun, was assassinated in Casablanca and the monarchy blamed his murder on the MIY.[18] Mouti, who had no connection to the murder, quickly fled Morocco into exile. While living abroad, he was tried for several alleged crimes *in absentia*, including the murder of Benjelloun. He was sentenced to life in prison and later to death by the loyalist Moroccan courts.[19] As an exile in Belgium, Mouti continued to rail against the monarchy in his group's newspaper, *Al-Moujahid*, and a series of Islamist booklets calling for a revolution in Morocco.[20] In 1984, King Hassan's secret services attempted unsuccessfully to kidnap him in Brussels, and still regularly monitored his movements thereafter.[21] Gradually, Mouti faded from the forefront of Morocco's Islamist scene, and he and his family continue to live in exile.

At the same time that the MIY was taking shape, a former school inspector named 'Abdessalam Yassine was parting ways with al-Qadiriyya al-Boutchichiyya *tariqa* (Sufi order) due to its unwillingness to enter Morocco's political arena.[22] Yassine had joined the order in 1965.[23] In 1973, after leaving, Yassine began to write a series of Islamist tracts. In these writings, he proposed Islamic solutions to the problems facing Moroccan society. He called for the creation of a democratic Islamic state—based on *shura* and *shari'a*—to bring justice and prosperity to the marginalized peoples of the country. The Moroccan political scientist Mohamed Tozy has described Yassine as the "the most influential [Islamist] ideologue" in Morocco and "emblematic of Moroccan Islamism."[24] Yassine published ten titles between 1973 and 1996, beginning with the book *al-Islam bayn al-Dawa wa al-Dawla* ("Islam: Between Preaching and the State").[25] But his most controversial work came in 1974 when Yassine dared to address the king directly in a work—written in the style of a letter—entitled "*L'Islam ou le Déluge*." The letter boldly pointed out King Hassan's un-Islamic behavior and rejected his claim to the sacred caliphal title *Amir al-Mu'minin*.[26] Yassine even referenced his own ancestral ties to an earlier (rival) Moroccan ruling dynasty, the Idrisids, and to the Prophet Muhammad, stating: "[I am] a poor Idrisid of Sharifian origins."[27] The message was made public before it was sent to the king, showing that the real intended audience was the Moroccan people.[28] A tremendous uproar ensued.

For challenging the sacred monarchy, Yassine was arrested and imprisoned (without a trial) for more than three years in a mental institution, which likely spared him from the royal executioner.[29] When Yassine was released (under restrictions and surveillance), he did not relent in his controversial views. Rather, he resumed writing tracts against the monarchy. In 1980 Yassine released a new book condemning Western civilization (associated with the king) as decadent, materialistic, and consumed by the acquisition of wealth to the detriment of values, families, and society as a whole.[30] Yassine then organized his growing number of followers. He formed an Islamic association in 1981, which later became *Jama'at al-Adl wa al-Ihsan*, or the Justice and Spirituality Society (JSS).[31]

104 *Morocco*

When Yassine later published a new treatise criticizing the king in 1983, he was arrested and sentenced to two years in prison. After his release in December 1985, the Yassine family was regularly targeted by state security raids and he was sentenced to house arrest in 1989.[32] His Islamist association was officially banned by the king's government and he remained confined to his home for the rest of King Hassan's reign. Shortly after the ban on the JSS, Yassine's son-in-law and five other close followers were arrested and sentenced to two years in prison for membership in an illegal group.[33] When hundreds of JSS members staged a peaceful sit-in to protest the arrests outside of a courthouse in Rabat, riot police rounded them up and savagely beat them with clubs.[34] Yet, the JSS still did not resort to armed confrontation with the regime. Yassine has always firmly rejected violence.

During the 1980s, as 'Abdessalam Yassine languished in prison, a scandal involving the rival MIY ensued. A cache of weapons was found along the Algerian border in the summer of 1985. Twenty-six Islamists, three of them identified as members of Mouti's MIY, were subsequently convicted of a plot to overthrow the monarchy.[35] The next year, a leftist turned Islamist from Rabat named 'Abdelilah Benkirane, who had broken with Mouti and formed his own association (*al-Jama'a al-Islamiyya*) in 1982, publicly declared his intent to pursue political reform through legal democratic channels. Benkirane, as a young man, joined Mouti's MIY group in 1976 when he was a university student in Rabat.[36] He was later arrested in the early 1980s (adding to his credibility) while running a private school, likely due to the provocative writings of Mouti abroad.[37] But some in the Islamist opposition now saw Benkirane as a sell-out, or worse, as a collaborator with the king who was on the royal payroll.[38]

Regarding his 1982 break with Mouti, Benkirane later explained that he and his colleagues came to see provocative attacks against the regime as misguided. In fact, he felt that if the Islamists weakened the regime too much an even more Western and un-Islamic regime could take advantage and fill the power vacuum, contributing to the de-Islamization of Moroccan society. "The elite which had taken power after the [colonial] protectorate was an elite which had essentially been formed in Europe and which saw things in an even more Western manner," he argued.[39] The first priority of the Islamists was therefore to reach the elite and make them "understand that Islam is indispensable."[40] By 1992, Benkirane's evolving Islamist association had become the *Harakat al-Tajdid wal-Islah*, or the Renewal and Reform Movement. In 1996, Benkirane brought together Islamist associations from Fes and Ksar Kabir (both established in 1976) to merge with an Islamist group from Rabat (established in 1986).[41] Those three associations merged and joined Benkirane's group to form the *Harakat al-Tawhid wal-Islah*, or Unity and Reform Movement (French acronym MUR). Thereafter, Benkirane succeeded in bringing another 200 Islamist groups from throughout the country into the new movement.[42] The MUR then became part of the pro-monarchy Popular Democratic and Constitutional Movement (French acronym MPDC). Finally, during the MPDC congress in 1998, the Justice and Development Party (French acronym PJD) emerged as the new political party to contest elections.[43]

Although the spiritual guide (*murshid*) of the JSS could not take an active role in political life due to his house arrest, 'Abdessalam Yassine had a highly educated, charismatic, and trilingual daughter who made up for his absence in public life. Nadia Yassine emerged as the foremost spokesperson and leader of the JSS (although not the Secretary General) and a highly controversial and outspoken figure. Such a figure is not without precedent in Islamist circles (e.g., Egypt's Zaynab al-Ghazali), but Nadia Yassine was still a rather rare character in the story of the Maghreb's Islamists. There is no other woman comparable to Nadia Yassine, insofar as her prominence and leadership in an Islamist movement goes, elsewhere in North Africa. Activist women from the secularist opposition, on the other hand, are relatively abundant. Her mere existence (as well as her *hijab*) seems to agitate her secularist opponents to no end. Meanwhile, hardline Salafis—often tied to groups in Saudi Arabia—fiercely criticize her as well.

After her father's incarceration in 1983, Nadia Yassine laid the groundwork for the Women's Section of the JSS. In time, the Women's Section would emerge as an active organization in virtually every neighborhood of Morocco's major cities and towns, addressing the needs and education of the country's impoverished women, as well as the unique needs of their neglected neighborhoods.[44] She would remain the head of the Women's Section of the JSS until 2012. Her active role in the growth of what became Morocco's largest Islamist organization did not go unnoticed by the *makhzen* (governing elite of the regime), but she had yet to emerge as a public figure at this early stage. It was only after her father's house arrest that she began to publish, permit herself to be photographed (so long as she was wearing her *hijab*), and speak with the media, especially to international journalists. Her husband 'Abdallah Chibani, also a member of JSS, supported her in these efforts. But with the growth of the JSS, King Hassan II sought to divide the Islamist trend in Morocco. He granted the precursor of the PJD increasing room to act legally, accepting Benkirane's recognition of the monarchy, as a means to keep the more formidable (and later banned) JSS of the Yassine family in check.[45] Nevertheless, the JSS thrived, especially on university campuses.

The Sufi orientation of the Justice and Spirituality Society is unique among the Islamist movements of the Maghreb. Although the Muslim Brotherhood also has Sufi roots, the Brotherhood has long since distanced itself from those early years, despite the ongoing use of terms or concepts like *murshid*. The Sufi nature of the JSS, however, is abundantly clear, and its leaders, such as Nadia Yassine, have been outspoken critics of Wahhabism and Salafism, often associated with anti-Sufi sentiments. This has been particularly evident in Yassine's defense of women in the restoration of an Islamic state. Like those in the Wahhabi or Salafi camps, Yassine calls for a radical departure from modern governing structures. However, she locates women at the vanguard of this movement. "It is the Muslim woman," she writes, "that is best prepared to reverse the course of time."[46] The "legitimacy" of women in the Islamic context, she argues, must rely on "theology" and so it is through *ijtihad* and revivalism that women inherently

106 *Morocco*

lead in the movement to "master an ever hostile world."[47] The importance of such revivalism, she contends, became increasingly clear in the Arab-Muslim world after September 11, "*jour zéro*" in international relations.[48] Still, the movement remained "disparate and dispersed," she observes. And "Wahhabism," as a result of its adverse effect on women in governance, remains a "severely inhibiting factor."[49] The most viable Islamist model was that of Rachid al-Ghannouchi in Tunisia, she wrote in 2006, insofar as his was a movement that upheld the "stature of women."[50] But al-Ghannouchi's model was also in jeopardy as it faced systematic oppression by the state.[51] Thus, while the goal of the JSS was the creation of a "true" Islamic state in Morocco that implements *shari'a*, the meaning behind common concepts can differ significantly among different Islamists in the region. "We envision the *shari'a* as a spirit that the heart must discover," Nadia Yassine has explained, clearly hinting at her mystical inclinations.[52]

In her most well-known work, *Toutes Voiles Dehors* ("Full Sails Ahead"), originally published in French in 2003, Nadia Yassine distinguished the identity of the JSS by calling for *ijtihad* that goes beyond the parameters of social reform to reimagine the very foundations of Morocco's existing governing structure. "The more we advance the more we submit ourselves to the political logic of a system that relegates the one to the many and the many to one," she writes. "[It is] a system that empowers those vice-ridden and self-defined demigods who brutalize us in their quest for power."[53] The pyramidal and patriarchal system of *fardiyya*, or the power of the individual (*le pouvoir d'un seul*), extends to the time of the Umayyad dynasty and over the years rendered the *umma* "docile in the face of tyranny."[54] From the death of 'Ali ibn Abu Talib onwards, she writes, the *umma* has passed "from massacre to massacre, from abdication to remission, from torture to treason."[55] Beyond the violence of Western imperialism and the "cancer of the brain" inflicting "modern man,"[56] a condition she attributes to Descartes,[57] Yassine describes the project of *ijtihad* as an intellectual and spiritual diffusion of authority away from the fixed dogma of Western rationalism, individualism, and the capitalist centers of the modern world, towards the more fluid and spiritual field of the *umma*.

Radically anti-Cartesian, the Islam undergirding Yassine's politics is foremost a "belief in the Unseen" (*al-ghayb*). "So even as justice was ousted by our illegitimate rulers," she wrote in 2007, "so too was the belief in the Unseen [ousted] due to our servile imitation of the dominant, materialistic, colonizing West."[58] Her mechanism for recuperating such losses is the restitution of *shura*, a model already well-established by the internal governing structure—"*majlis al-shura*"—of the JSS itself.[59] Indeed, rather than being a fixed system, Yassine contends that the "doors of *ijtihad*" or interpretation are open and that it should be performed by men and women "under the auspices of a real, democratically chosen parliament that springs from the will of the people, unlike the current parliament."[60]

During the 1990s, as Morocco's population grew increasingly young and urbanized, King Hassan II began to lighten his autocratic grip on the kingdom

Morocco 107

and initiate democratic reforms. In 1991, the aforementioned Tazmamart prison was shut down and a number of political prisoners were released, including Ahmed Marzouki. In 1993, two women were elected to parliament for the first time, one from *Istiqlal* and the other from the USFP.[61] And the king appointed 'Abderrahmane Youssoufi, a longstanding leftist opposition leader from the USFP, as prime minister in 1998. His appointment marked the first time that Morocco's government was led by the opposition. But at the start of the decade, the king sparked controversy and unrest by supporting the Western coalition against Iraq during the First Gulf War. In February 1991, between 300,000 and 500,000 people took to the streets of Rabat to express their support for Iraq and opposition to the deployment of some 1700 Moroccan soldiers.[62] Islamists and secular-leftists were united in their opposition. The leftist intellectual Mehdi El-Manjra even characterized the Gulf War as a *guerre civilisationnelle*.[63] As elsewhere, the idea of supporting Western powers against a fellow Arab or Muslim state was unconscionable. The war ended on March 1, 1991, with a decisive rout of Iraq by the Western coalition and this allowed the domestic unrest to dissipate and channel elsewhere.

King Hassan II's final years on the throne were marred by his declining health. As early as the summer of 1995, the king traveled to the United States for treatment of a respiratory infection. He grew increasingly absent from the public eye thereafter. In February 1999, Crown Prince Mohammed was sent in his father's stead to the funeral of another Arab monarch, King Hussein of the Hashemite Kingdom of Jordan.[64] The autocratic Emir of Bahrain, Isa bin Salman al-Khalifa, died the following month. These events marked a great generational shift throughout the broader region. Reports of King Hassan II's decline and speculation about the future of the kingdom grew. On July 23, 1999, the king was rushed to Ibn Sina hospital in Rabat with severe pneumonia and hours later succumbed to a heart attack.[65] After nearly four decades of rule, the tumultuous reign of King Hassan II was over.

On the day of his father's death, King Mohammed VI began his reign. He received his first oath of allegiance (*bay'a*) atop his throne as the *Amir al-Mu'minin*. From the beginning, the young king claimed that he wanted a break from the authoritarian past of his father, and he made many nominal gestures and timid reforms toward that end. His first year in power garnered wild popularity at home and abroad. The spirit of a new era, characterized by reform, modernization, and democratization, did not endure however. King Mohammed VI regressed to behavior associated with his late father. The kingdom remained the land of a privileged few and a secure place for tourist resorts and the Alaouite king's holdings. All the while the king continued to claim, like his father before him, the sacred cloak of Islamic legitimacy and sharifian descent.

Few were fooled or coddled by such political exploitation of Islam though. Rather, it merely provoked the Islamists further. Fear and economic opportunity were the real reason for the deference of the court and the people. Nevertheless, upon assuming power, the new king made many efforts at reconciliation with Morocco's Islamist opposition. 'Abdessalam Yassine was released from his

108 *Morocco*

house arrest in May 2000. It was national (indeed, international) news and the official announcement was made by Morocco's interior minister on state television.[66] This came despite the fact that on January 28, 2000, Yassine demanded in a public letter to the young king, entitled *À Qui de Droit?* ("To Whom it May Concern"), that he use the enormous personal wealth inherited from his father for the benefit of the Moroccan people.[67] The 35 page memorandum furthermore blamed the monarchy for Morocco's social, economic, and political ills.[68] Indeed, the release of Yassine from his house arrest did not mark a warming of relations between the two at all. In December 2000, members of the Yassine family were arrested and given four month suspended sentences for protesting the government's human rights violations.[69] The young king had hoped such gestures would help give him a different image than his late father.

In 2002, King Mohammed VI married at the age of 38. He was reportedly reluctant to do so, as he enjoyed his bachelor lifestyle, but acquiesced to the obligations of his office. Pre-marital sex, of course, is forbidden in Islam. His wife, Salma Bennani, was a 24-year-old computer engineering graduate. As a nod to modernity, the princess consort appeared before the people of Morocco from the start with hair uncovered. It was a startling break from the past where the royal wives (including the king's mother) were completely hidden from view and without official title.[70] The king's wife is known as Princess Lalla Salma. She would later bear him two children, including a male heir named Hassan who will one day inherit the Alaouite throne (assuming it still exists).

At the onset of life as a family man, King Mohammed VI appeared poised to direct his kingdom along a path of relative stability amidst the considerable turbulence of the post 9/11 world. He was among the first in the Muslim world to send his condolences to the United States and pledge support in the campaign to bring the perpetrators of "this cowardly aggression" to justice.[71] While his cooperation was appreciated in the West, some at home objected to the king's efforts. A group of 16 hardline Moroccan *'ulama* issued a *fatwa* (legal opinion) declaring it impermissible for Muslims to join non-Muslims in a coalition against other Muslims, rejecting interfaith worship (e.g., prayers) as a great sin, and condemning the alteration of the Friday prayer liturgies to address the attacks that week.[72] The king's minister of Islamic affairs attempted to persuade the scholars to retract the *fatwa*, but over 200 more scholars, preachers, and Islamic activists soon expressed support for it.[73] Understandably anxious about the pretext that the 9/11 attacks might provide for the regime, Nadia Yassine publicly stated that: "If it is indeed Bin Laden who has done this, then he has done us Islamists a bad turn."[74]

Despite the longstanding existence of Islamists in Morocco, including collaborators with militants operating abroad (e.g., Algeria), the kingdom had yet to face an outbreak of significant violence at home. This dramatically changed on May 16, 2003, with the horrific bombings in Casablanca. Twelve young suicide-bombers (two additional bombers failed), all members of an Islamist militant group called *Salafia Jihadia*, struck multiple sites simultaneously throughout the city. The attacks killed 33 people, most of them Moroccans, and injured many

Morocco 109

dozens more. In its wake, a fierce backlash against Islamists ensued and some called for the dissolution of the PJD, presumably for being complicit in the rise of domestic Islamist militancy. The deputy leader of the leftist USFP went as far as to call for the PJD to apologize to the Moroccan people, citing the Islamist party's longstanding anti-Western sentiments.[75] But assuming a diminished role in public life for a time, the PJD survived the precarious post-Casablanca crisis and went on to contest future elections.[76] Later that summer, after hundreds of arrests, Moroccan courts sentenced four young men, among 87 defendants accused of membership in *Salafia Jihadia*, to death for the crime of premeditated murder.[77] All four men sentenced to death were from the impoverished Casablanca suburb of Sidi Moumen and between 22 and 27 years of age.

In 2004, King Mohammed VI took advantage of the crackdown on the Islamists after Casablanca and sought to reassert the modern nature of his reign (pleasing Western business partners) by reforming the traditional discriminatory Personal Status Code (the *Mudawana*) that treated women as second-class citizens under the control of men. The *Mudawana* was codified after Morocco's independence and consisted of a mixture of classical Malikite formulations of *shari'a* and colonial laws. "We were the first to demand that the old *Mudawana* be abolished," Nadia Yassine explained in July 2006.[78] "The *Mudawana* gave power to men in the name of religion," she argued, "[when] in fact it is not part of religion at all, being only one interpretation introduced by the Umayyads and the Abbasids, who revolted against the true *shari'a*."[79] Nevertheless, Nadia Yassine opposed the king's initial attempts to reform the *Mudawana* in 2000 because secular principles from the West had guided the proposed revisions. In fact, Yassine and members of the JSS, alongside the PJD, marched in a mass protest in Casablanca to demand that reforms to the *Mudawana* follow Qur'anic principles. "We will not import a carbon-copy of Western democracy," she would further explain, pointing to the real heart of the conflict.[80] Meanwhile, the king won great praise from the United States, other Western countries, and international agencies for his efforts to reform the Code.

In the summer of 2005, Nadia Yassine gave an interview with the Moroccan news magazine *Al-Ousbouia al-Jadida* in which she questioned the place of the monarchy in Moroccan society and predicted its imminent downfall.[81] In line with the elders of her party who were openly predicting the arrival of a greater Maghrebian caliphate in 2006,[82] she openly expressed her preference for a republic as system of government in accordance with Islam, rather than an autocratic monarchy.[83] This was not the first time she had made such remarks. For example, at a conference at the University of California at Berkeley, preserved for perpetuity on video online, Nadia Yassine addressed a largely American audience with the assistance of an English translator, stating forcefully the need for real democracy in the Muslim world, the compatibility between democracy and Islam, and the necessity of major economic and educational reforms in Morocco.[84] Such calls for a republic and criticism of the monarchy remained criminal offenses in the Kingdom of Morocco under Mohammed VI. Both Nadia Yassine and the editor of *Al-Ousbouia al-Jadida*, 'Abdelaziz Koukas, were

110   *Morocco*

brought up on charges and sent to trial, facing years in prison for expressing these views.[85] The trial was thereafter repeatedly postponed. "I will never regret what I have said," she would later say. "I am a free woman."[86] Meanwhile, members of the Islamist rival PJD, who accept the legitimacy of the monarchy, dismissed Nadia Yassine as an agitator whose actions and comments are counter-productive to the cause of reform.[87] For her part, Nadia Yassine dismissed the PJD as a party with "very few" supporters beyond the *makhzen*.[88]

The PJD took 47 of 325 seats in the 2007 parliamentary elections, finishing second only to *Istiqlal* with 52 seats. But the PJD had expected to win. It had polled extensively and stressed health, education, and investment throughout the campaign, making few mentions of Islam.[89] After results were tallied, the PJD expressed disappointment in the outcome, and even alleged that the elections were fixed with "dirty money." Lahcen Daoudi, the PJD's deputy leader, told supporters in Rabat that: "It is not only sad for us, it is sad for Moroccan democracy."[90] PJD leader Saad Eddine Othmani similarly added: "We found ourselves in the election campaign facing money instead of political parties."[91] The exact nature of the alleged "dirty money" was never revealed. But within the party, some suggested that the PJD's reluctance to provoke the monarchy and to withdraw from street activism had hurt their base of popular support.[92] The PJD also experienced a break with more ideologically-minded members leading up to the election.[93] Even so, the PJD was already a considerable force in the troubled political landscape of the kingdom. It was positioned well to surge forward amidst the uprisings of the Arab Spring.

In the wake of Mohamed Bouazizi's self-immolation in Tunisia that initiated the Arab Spring, some 20 Moroccan men committed acts of self-immolation with five dying (like Bouazizi) as a result of their horrific injuries.[94] These men, like Tunisia's Bouazizi, were protesting the economic conditions and corruption in their countries. At the time of the Arab Spring, the economy in Morocco was far worse than it was in Tunisia. Meanwhile, King Mohammed VI's personal assets had risen to $2.5 billion, more than Queen Elizabeth II.[95] The gap between the small privileged cabal tied to the king's *makhzen* and the general population was shockingly wide. As protests began to spread nationwide on February 20, the king acted quickly by pushing through a series of constitutional reforms and announcing early parliamentary elections. He agreed to remove constitutional language that conferred a divine right to his rule, but did not relinquish the traditional Islamic title of *Amir al-Mu'minin*.[96] In a major televised speech given on March 9, the king further announced that the selection of the country's prime minister would go to the party that wins parliamentary elections, rather than to his arbitrary royal decree.[97] In addition, the judiciary would become an independent branch and judges would no longer require the approval of the king.[98] Nadia Yassine dismissed the king's overtures as insufficient.

The successes of the Arab Spring uprising in Morocco were less dramatic than elsewhere in North Africa. Sporadic protests and the machinations of the autocratic regime continued. On May 16, a group of protesting public health doctors, calling for better pay and support for their clinics, were severely beaten by state security forces outside of the Ministry of Health.[99] On June 13, a JSS activist named Hind Zerrouq was abducted in Fes by state security agents.[100] She managed to make brief calls to her husband using her cellphone minutes before she disappeared entirely. Her family was subsequently turned away when they demanded information about her whereabouts. Also in June, the regime orchestrated accusations in the media against Nadia Yassine, alleging that she was having an adulterous affair in Greece with another member of the JSS. Yassine adamantly denied the defamatory claims. Indeed, the Qur'an explicitly condemns false accusations of adultery against women to be a grave sin (see, for example, Qur'an 24:4). Meanwhile, on June 17, the king's new reformed constitution was revealed to the public.

When a national referendum on the new constitution was held on July 1, the JSS and several secular and leftist groups, including the revolutionary February 20 youth movement, called for a boycott. The reforms were not produced by a democratically elected commission, but by people nominated by the king, they argued.[101] And, furthermore, the changes did not go far enough. The PJD, *Istiqlal*, and USFP, in contrast, rallied their supporters to support the referendum. In addition, state-employed imams at Morocco's mosques were instructed to preach in favor of the *Amir al-Mu'minin*'s new constitution.[102] The referendum passed overwhelmingly with the government reporting an approval rating of over 98 percent.[103] The results were lauded by Western leaders, including former colonial master France and longtime ally the United States. But those who refused to participate in the referendum were undeterred and continued their protests, sometimes to the dismay of the older working class who simply want to earn a day's wage in peace (especially in the tourism industry).

When national parliamentary elections were held on November 25, 2011, about a month after Tunisia's first free elections, no less than 30 political parties participated. The political spectrum ranged from right-wing Islamists to far-left socialist parties. The PJD, led by Benkirane, finished in first place, winning 107 of 395 seats in parliament. Their tally was nearly double that of the second-place party *Istiqlal*. It was also a significant change from the PJD's disappointing results in 2007. A diverse coalition of eight parties led by the brother-in-law of the late King Hassan II finished in third place. The JSS, meanwhile, boycotted the elections and had no legal status as a political party. In an interview with the French daily *Le Parisien* after the election, Benkirane, clearly seeking to allay fears of his Islamist agenda, stated that "religion should be left to the king" and "we should dedicate our efforts to resolving outstanding problems such as corruption, housing, and education."[104] PJD presented itself as a party with an Islamic reference rather than "Islamist," and Benkirane insisted that religion was the domain of the mosques and the PJD would not interfere in anyone's personal life.[105] Instead, its legislative platform emphasized economic issues, improving education, and fighting corruption. Finally, on November 29, 2011, King Mohammed VI selected the head of the PJD as the winning party, Benkirane, as Morocco's next prime minister. The JSS later posted a statement on its website condemning the PJD's participation in the elections as "political suicide" and for

112 *Morocco*

being a part of the king's attempt to thwart "the people's demands for real change."[106]

A little over a year after Morocco's elections, on December 13, 2012, Shaykh 'Abdessalam Yassine, the founder and revered *murshid* of the JSS, died at his home in Salé at the age of 84. He was buried the next day according to Islamic rite, following Friday prayers at *Masjid as-Sunna* in Rabat. Mohamed Abbadi, a longtime and close confidant of Yassine, was chosen to serve as the organization's new leader in his stead, as Secretary General (not as *murshid*), for a five-year term.[107] Nadia Yassine, passed over for the leadership post, was absent during the official announcement of Abbadi's selection. Meanwhile, unrest in Morocco was growing again, dissatisfied with the pace of change brought by the new PJD government. "If you thought the Benkirane government was going to end corruption in six months," the new Islamist prime minister told *Al-Jazeera*, "there is a problem with expectations there."[108]

Notes

1 See Hughes (2001, 101).
2 See Hefner and Zaman (2007, 143).
3 See Willis (2012, 55).
4 See Hughes (2001, 104).
5 Ibid., 105; Dan Jenkins, 1970. "Where A Golf Nut is King." *Sports Illustrated*, September 28, 1970: 32–39.
6 See Marzouki (n.d., 35–36).
7 See Marzouki's interview with Ahmed Manour: "Shaaheed 'ala 'asr," *Al-Jazeera.* February 24, 2009. www.youtube.com/watch?v=1-MhOJIZeNY.
8 See Marzouki (n.d., 38).
9 See Howe (2005, 5).
10 See Oufkir and Fitoussi (1999). The Oufkirs managed to survive their ordeal. The now-adult children live in France where they have denounced Islam (presumably because of the king's "Islamic" mantle) and converted to Roman Catholicism.
11 Sonia Terrab. 2014. "Maroc le chemin tragique des Oufkir." *Afrique Magazine*, April 14. Accessed April 6, 2017. www.afriquemagazine.com/maroc-le-chemin-tragique-des-oufkir.
12 See Marzouki (n.d., 37).
13 See Salim (2005, 182).
14 See Himmich (2010, 257).
15 See Willis (2012, 163).
16 See Entelis (1997, 53).
17 See Willis (2012, 162).
18 Ibid., 162–163.
19 See Entelis (1997, 53).
20 See Burgat and Dowell (1993, 175).
21 Ibid.
22 See Willis (2012, 163).
23 See Tozy (1999, 189).
24 Ibid., 186.
25 Ibid.
26 Yassine Hicham. 2013. "Imam Yassine's Journey." *Yassine.Net*, May 19. Accessed April 6, 2017. www.yassine.net/en/document/4729.shtml.
27 Quoted in Burgat and Dowell (1993, 166).

Morocco 113

28 See Zeghal (2005, 115).
29 See Willis (2012, 163).
30 See Hughes (2001, 298).
31 See Hicham (2013).
32 Ibid.
33 See Hughes (2001, 295).
34 Ibid.
35 See Entelis (1997, 53).
36 Samir Bennis. 2011. "Abdelilah Benkirane, the mysterious 'Master of the Lamps.'" *Morocco World News/Maghreb Intelligence*, December 16. Accessed April 6, 2017. www.moroccoworldnews.com/2011/12/19356/abdelilah-benkirane-the-mysterious-master-of-the-lamp-party/.
37 Ibid.
38 See Entelis (1997, 53).
39 Quoted in Burgat and Dowell (1993, 177).
40 Ibid.
41 See Zeghal (2005, 214).
42 Ibid.
43 Ibid., 215.
44 See Salime (2011, 19).
45 See Howe 2005, 133).
46 See Yassine (2006, 108).
47 Ibid.
48 Ibid., 105.
49 Ibid., 108.
50 Ibid.
51 Ibid.
52 Kyle McEneaney. 2006. "Interview with Nadia Yassine of the Moroccan Justice and Charity Group." *Sada*, July 18. Accessed April 6, 2017. http://carnegieendowment.org/2008/08/18/interview-with-nadia-yassine-of-moroccan-justice-and-charity-group/6boz.
53 See Yassine (2003, 286).
54 Ibid.
55 Ibid., 287.
56 Ibid., 59.
57 Ibid., 50–64.
58 Quoted in Halverson and Way (2011, 519).
59 See Yassine (2006, 108).
60 Ibid.
61 See Hughes (2001, 305).
62 "War in the Gulf; Huge Morocco March Supports Iraq in War." 1991. *New York Times*, February 4. Accessed April 6, 2017. www.nytimes.com/1991/02/04/world/war-in-the-gulf-huge-morocco-march-supports-iraq-in-war.html.
63 See Bensadoun (2007, 20).
64 Joseph R. Gregory. 1999. "Hassan II of Morocco Dies at 70; A Monarch Oriented to the West." *New York Times*, July 24. Accessed April 6, 2017. www.nytimes.com/learning/general/onthisday/bday/0709.html.
65 See Hughes (2001, 357).
66 Nick Pelham. 2000. "Moroccan Islamist Leader Freed," *BBC News*, May 17. Accessed April 6, 2017. http://news.bbc.co.uk/2/hi/africa/751797.stm.
67 See Vermeren (2002, 107).
68 Associated Press. 2012. "Abdessalam Yassine, 84, Leader of Moroccan Opposition Movement." *New York Times*, December 16: A36.
69 See Howe (2005, 131–132).

114   *Morocco*

70 Anita McNaught. 2002. "The King and the Sheikh's Daughter." *BBC News*, March 28. Accessed April 6, 2017. http://news.bbc.co.uk/2/hi/programmes/correspondent/1899478.stm.
71 See Howe (2005, 16).
72 Ibid.
73 Ibid., 16–17.
74 See Willis (2012, 192).
75 Ibid.
76 Ibid., 192–193.
77 "Death sentences for Morocco bombings." 2003. *BBC News*, August 19. Accessed April 6, 2017. http://news.bbc.co.uk/2/hi/africa/3162285.stm.
78 See McEneaney (2006).
79 Ibid.
80 Ibid.
81 Hassan al-Serat. 2005. "Al-Adil wa al-Ihsaan: tutnaba' bitouli al-khilaafa b-il Maghreb 'aam 2006." *Al-Jazeera*, September 18. Accessed April 6, 2017. www.aljazeera.net/news/reportsandinterviews/2005/9/18.
82 Ibid.
83 "Senior Moroccan Islamist on Trial." 2005. *BBC News*, June 28. Accessed April 6, 2017. http://news.bbc.co.uk/go/pr/fr/-/2/hi/Africa/4630979.stm.
84 See "UC Berkeley: Democracy and Global Islam. Nadia Yassine ¼." *YouTube*, January 2, 2010. www.youtube.com/watch?v=RQ3AGUD__HE.
85 "Senior Moroccan Islamist on Trial." 2005. *BBC News*, June 28. Accessed April 6, 2017. http://news.bbc.co.uk/go/pr/fr/-/2/hi/Africa/4630979.stm.
86 Magdi Abdelhadi. 2005. "Accused Morocco Islamist Speaks Out." *BBC News*, September 30. Accessed April 6, 2017. http://news.bbc.co.uk/go/pr/fr/-/2/hi/Africa/4297386.stm.
87 See interview with PJD representative in the "Maghrib (Morocco): Portrait of Nadia Yassine." *YouTube*, 12 January, 2010. www.youtube.com/watch?v=0v8McoerZAo.
88 See McEneaney (2006).
89 See Wegner (2011, 116).
90 Quoted in "Conservative Party in Morocco Wins." 2007. *Al-Jazeera English*, September 8. Accessed April 6, 2017. www.aljazeera.com/focus/moroccoelections2007/2007/09/200852514653984103.html.
91 Quoted in "Moroccan nationalists in poll win." 2007. *Al-Jazeera English*, September 9. Accessed April 6, 2017. www.aljazeera.com/focus/moroccoelections2007/2007/09/2008525122526993418.html.
92 See Wegner (2011, 118).
93 Ibid.
94 Nicolas Pelham. 2012. "How Morocco Dodged the Arab Spring." *The New York Review of Books*, July 5. Accessed April 6, 2017. www.nybooks.com/blogs/nyrblog/2012/jul/05/how-morocco-dodged-arab-spring/.
95 Ibid.
96 Ibid.
97 See "King Mohammed VI of Morocco Historic Speech/March 9, 2011." www.youtube.com/watch?v=_T-nNedwfoQ.
98 Souad Mekhennet and Maia de la Baume. 2011. "Moderate Islamist Party Winning Morocco Election." *New York Times*, November 26. Accessed April 6, 2017. www.nytimes.com/2011/11/27/world/africa/moderate-islamist-party-winning-morocco-election.html?_r=0.
99 Richard Greeman. 2011. "The Arab Spring in Morocco." *Mamfakinch*, May 27. Accessed April 6, 2017. www.mamfakinch.com/the-arab-spring-in-morocco/.
100 "Maroc: Enlevement de Madame Hind Zerrouq." 2012. *AFD International*, June 13.

Accessed April 6. www.afdinternational.org/index.php/communiques/mena/maroc-enlevement-de-madame-hind-zerrouq.html.
101 Simba Russeau. 2011. "A 'late spring' might reach Morocco." *Al-Jazeera English*, July 1. Accessed April 6, 2017. www.aljazeera.com/indepth/features/2011/07/20117112327327383.html.
102 "A Very Small Step." 2011. *The Economist*, July 7. Accessed April 6, 2017. www.economist.com/node/18929381.
103 "Morocco approves King Mohammed's constitutional reforms." 2011. *BBC News*, July 1. Accessed April 6, 2017. www.bbc.co.uk/news/world-africa-13976480.
104 Quoted in "Profile of Islamist Moroccan Prime Minister Abdelilah Benkirane." 2012. *Open Source Center Report*, February 21. Accessed August 1, 2012. www.opensource.gov.
105 See Dawisha (2013, 210).
106 Quoted in *Open Source Center Report* (2012).
107 Sabah Lebbar. 2012. "Will Mohammed Abbadi Succeed in Preserving the Unity of Al Adl wal Ihssane in this Crossroad?" *North Africa Post*, December 28. Accessed April 6, 2017. www.northafricapost.com/1957-will-mohammed-abbadi-succeed-in-preserving-the-unity-of-al-adl-wal-ihssane-in-this-crossroad.html.
108 Quoted in Suzanne Daley. 2012. "The New Islamists; Moroccans Fear that Flickers of Democracy are Fading." *New York Times*, December 11. Accessed April 6, 2017. www.nytimes.com/2012/12/11/world/africa/moroccans-fear-that-flickers-of-democracy-are-fading.html.

References

Bensadoun, Mickael. 2007. "The (Re)Fashioning of Moroccan National Identity." In *The Maghrib in the New Century: Identity, Religion, and Politics*, edited by Bruce Maddy-Weitzman and Daniel Zisenwine, 13–35. Gainesville, FL: University of Florida.

Burgat, Francois, and William Dowell. 1993. *The Islamic Movement in North Africa*. Austin, TX: University of Texas.

Dawisha, Adeed. 2013. *The Second Arab Awakening: Revolution, Democracy, and the Islamist Challenge from Tunis to Damascus*. New York: W. W. Norton & Co.

Entelis, John P. 1997. "Political Islam in the Maghreb: The Nonviolent Dimension." In *Islam, Democracy, and the State in North Africa*. Bloomington, IN: Indiana University Press.

Halverson, Jeffry R. and Amy K. Way. 2011. "Islamist Feminism: Constructing Gender Identities in Postcolonial Muslim Societies." *Politics and Religion,* 4: 503–525.

Hefner, Robert W., and Muhammad Qasim Zaman, eds. 2007. *Schooling Islam: The Culture and Politics of Modern Muslim Education*. Princeton, NJ: Princeton University Press.

Himmich, Bensalem. 2010. *Mu'dhabati*. Cairo: Dar al-Sharouq.

Howe, Marvine. 2005. *Morocco: The Islamist Awakening and Other Challenges*. New York: Oxford University Press.

Hughes, Stephen. 2001. *Morocco under King Hassan*. Reading, UK: Ithaca Press.

Marzouki, Ahmed. n.d. *Tazmamart cellule 10*. Casablanca: Tarík editions.

Oufkir, Malika, and Michelle Fitoussi. 1999. *Stolen Lives: Twenty Years in a Desert Jail.* New York: Hyperion.

Salim, Jay. 2005. *Dictionnaire des écrivains marocains*. Casablanca: Eddif.

Salime, Zakia. 2011. *Between Feminism and Islam: Human Rights and Sharia Law in Morocco*. Minneapolis, MN: University of Minnesota Press.

116 *Morocco*

Tozy, Mohamed. 1999. *Monarchie et Islam Politique au Maroc*. Paris: Presses de la Fondation Nationale des Sciences Politiques.

Vermeren, Pierre. 2002. *Histoire du Maroc depuis L'indépendence*. Paris: La Découverte.

Wegner, Eva. 2011. *Islamist Opposition in Authoritarian Regimes: The Party of Justice and Development in Morocco*. Syracuse, NY: Syracuse University Press.

Willis, Michael J. 2012. *Politics and Power in the Maghreb*. New York: Columbia University Press.

Yassine, Nadia. 2003. *Toutes Voiles Dehors*. Casablanca: Éditions le Fennec.

Yassine, Nadia. 2006. "Modernité, femme musulmane et politique en Méditerranée." *Quaderns de la Mediterrània,* 7: 105–110.

Zeghal, Malika. 2005. *Les Islamistes Marocains: Le Défi à la Monarchie*. Paris: La Découverte.

7 The Maghreb beyond Islamism

This study has focused on the Islamist political parties that came to power in the Maghreb after the Arab Spring. We have argued that these parties represent an assertion (or reassertion) of Arab-Muslim identities long repressed by colonial occupation, and delayed by secular (i.e., Algeria and Tunisia) or autocratic state-religion (i.e., Libya and Morocco) regimes in anti-pluralist post-colonial state projects. This is not to suggest that conflicting identities do not exist in these states. But given the results of the Arab Spring, we have focused on those who rose to power (to varying degrees), the Islamists.

The Islamist parties of the Maghreb and their leaderships are not monoliths either, but rather come out of a complex array of individual personalities, circumstances, and historical contexts. Morocco's Nadia Yassine is very different from Libya's 'Abdelhakim Belhadj. Likewise, Tunisia's Rachid al-Ghannouchi is quite different from Algeria's 'Ali Belhadj. Indeed, even inside the Islamist cadres of these figures there are significant differences and contending factions. Readers will recall the differences discussed among the various factions of Algeria's Islamic Salvation Front, for instance. Or the break between Ennahdha co-founders Rachid al-Ghannouchi and 'Abdelfattah Mourou in Tunisia. Thus, it is not the contention of this study that the peoples of the Maghreb are some sort of Islamist monolith of one mind. There is always diversity that individuals within societies represent, no matter the geography or religion involved.

At the onset of this book, after exploring the history and establishment of Sunni Islam as the dominant religion of the Maghreb, we discussed the trauma of European colonial occupation in the region. We argued that one cannot truly understand Islamism without acknowledging European colonialism as one of its parents. We reiterate this point because there is a tendency in certain circles, particular in the West, to approach Islamism as a direct product of a text (i.e., the Qur'an). In other words, Islamism is treated as an anachronistic yet allegedly faithful reading of a seventh century sacred text in the modern age (and the two cannot be reconciled). This is a simple, crude and inherently polemical approach to Islamism that we contend is largely devoid of substance. It is furthermore full of contradictions and inconsistencies. The Qur'an is only a very small piece of the puzzle. The more important and substantive answers lie in the people who read that sacred text. Those diverse peoples are the subject of this book. "Who

118　*The Maghreb beyond Islamism*

are these people?" is precisely the question that lies at the heart of *Islamists of the Maghreb.*

An essential part of understanding identity is acknowledging that it is relational. "The Jew is a man," Jean-Paul Sartre famously wrote in his 1946 *Réflexions sur la Question Juive.* "It is the anti-Semite who makes him a Jew."[1] Islamist identities, like any other, emerged from a unique nexus of historical forces. In his seminal *Introduction à la Poétique Arabe*, the acclaimed Syrian-Lebanese poet Adonis wrote:

> consciousness of the other assumes a realization on our part that the opposition between the Arab-Islamic East and the European-American West is not of an intellectual or poetic nature, but is political and ideological, originally a result of Western imperialism.[2]

This notion has been shared widely by scholars of the Arab Middle East. In the *Foundations of Modern Arab Identity*, Stephen Sheehi notes that the dialectical underpinnings of the *nahdha*, a period in which Arab intellectuals who gained access to European education through colonial channels carved out a unique "modern identity" in contraposition to the epistemologies of the West, generated a kind of "intellectual quicksand" whereby subsequent generations,[3] including the postcolonial one we have focused on here, became confined and in a sense obligated to validate the civilizational dialectics of their elders.[4] We see this phenomenon consolidated in the histories we have traced in this book.

The religious gloss associated with the Islamists we have explored should not be unfamiliar to American readers. To understand the blending of religion and ideology that constitutes identity in the American context we need look no further than the Cold War and the polarized opposition to the Soviet Union that emerged in the 1950s and 1960s. So great was the pull of identity politics at this time that the country even altered its pledge of allegiance to include the controversial phrase "under God." This addition to the pledge was a statement that Americans were the champions of religion against the "godless Communists." It may seem ironic that in 2016 America's then President-Elect Donald J. Trump could find common cause with Russia and its president, a former KGB agent. But insofar as identity remains subject to history and the ever-shifting imperatives of "otherness," we can understand this new identity alliance. Under the leadership of Vladimir Putin, Russia too has embraced a religiously-grounded conservatism formed in contraposition to the same "godless Communism" feared by Americans. Previously unimaginable, this alliance would appear to bolster Samuel Huntington's problematic and infamous "Clash of Civilizations" thesis which holds the future of global conflict to be organized less along geopolitical lines (per the Cold War) than cultural and religious ones. Yet, as our study of political Islam has shown, such demarcations can be deceptive and the two have often intermingled.

Islamism did not exist prior to European colonialism. Historically, Islamism emerged in British Egypt and British India, and it developed elsewhere from

The Maghreb beyond Islamism   119

there, including the lands of the Maghreb. Islamism also emerged hand-in-hand with the modern state or nation-state, an imported concept brought to global dominance by the European powers into formerly imperial or tribal lands. It is understandable for contemporary Westerners (or others) to think of it (wrongly) as the natural order of things. This is not so. It is another turbulent child of modernity.

Islamism is a modern political ideology bent on the Islamization of the modern state through the implementation of systems of law and governance attributed to *shari'a* or more broadly in reference to Islam (as opposed to a European or colonial system). The so-called Islamists (proponents of this ideology) are therefore existentially wed to Western colonialism and hegemony. The Islamists exist only via opposition to the trauma of these foreign intrusions into Muslim societies and perceived Western efforts to deracinate traditional life and values. In reaction to such a relational confrontation, identities often become what critical theorist Douglas Kellner has aptly described in the modern context as "a theatrical presentation of the self."[5] Thus, it is insufficient for some among the Islamists to simply profess Islam; rather, they must wear it on their sleeves (metaphorically speaking). The men grow long flowing beards, display large *zabibas* (prayer bruises), wear various head coverings, carry out grand public performances of *salat*, or even don headbands with the *shahada* written across them. There is chanting. There is media. There is performance. People have become more "Islamic" than they ever were before (but it rarely seems to extend into the important realm of ethics). These sorts of performances are most common among the rank and file or the youths (not unlike American gang or sports fan culture with their particular costumes and behaviors), as Islamist ideologues like al-Ghannouchi have no need for it.

The cultural theorist Stuart Hall has noted that: "Identity is a structured representation which only achieves its positive through the narrow eye of the negative."[6] The perception of otherness alone is not enough for the formulation of identity. It is in contradistinction to the menace of a negative force—especially violence—that the collective-self coalesces. In this way Islamism could not have existed in the absence of European colonialism and its derivative postcolonial secular and state-religion projects. "Islam"—meaning its language, symbols, and institutions—was utilized by the post-colonial state regimes of the Maghreb as a means of social control or for an ideological confrontation with the Left in the context of top-down (usually single-party) politics. In contrast, the Arab Spring was a bottom-up social movement. It asserted popular identities rather than the "national identity" dictated by elitist regimes.

By assuming power and some control over the direction of the state, the Islamists of the Maghreb are now being fundamentally altered (since the relationship has changed). They are adapting to new identities as rulers (no longer as the opposition or as pious critics). They must now face the new challenge of governance. They do so at the risk of incompetence, humiliation and failure (as President Morsi in Egypt demonstrated). They can no longer sustain themselves by simply rebuking those in power or offering ambiguous solutions that tap into

120 *The Maghreb beyond Islamism*

ideals of piety and cosmic purpose. The Islamists have to understand economic policy and find people jobs, avoid international isolation, create functioning bureaucracies, crackdown on corruption, eliminate crime, and so on. As Ernest Hemingway wrote in *A Farewell to Arms*: "Put him in power and see how wise he is." This is the next phase, a shift that scholars such as Olivier Roy and Asef Bayat have described as "Post-Islamist."

The Turkish example is a now passé but an oft-repeated model for an Islamist party that transformed into a pragmatic and successful democratic force (crackdowns on the press and perceived Gulenists notwithstanding). When the faltering Ottoman Empire was dismembered by the European powers (especially the British and French) after its defeat in World War I, the military hero that rescued what-is-now Turkey from total colonial control would lead a new republic or state "for the Turks" (to the detriment of other peoples, such as Armenians, Kurds, and Greeks). Mustafa Kemal (Atatürk) created a state where Islam was systematically purged from society, even to the somewhat comical extent that men were encouraged to wear Western-style straw hats and women to wear bonnets (again, theatrical). Like Bourguiba in Tunisia decades later, Atatürk created a fiercely secular state that overtly imitated Western social norms, utilizing the centralized powers of the modern state to enforce them, and cultivated a cult of personality around his own person in Islam's traditional place. But even amidst Atatürk's considerable success, Islam was so deeply intertwined with Turkish history and culture that the cult of Mustafa Kemal Atatürk and his Western secular ways would still spawn an Islamist reaction. And the strength of the Turkish-Muslim identity would be revealed at the ballot box long before the Arab Spring in North Africa.

In 1996, a democratically elected Islamist government came to power in Turkey. However, the new government was overthrown by a military coup in 1997, ostensibly to preserve the secular Kemalist state. The Islamist Welfare Party (*Refah Partisi*) was banned thereafter. This event would trigger the formation of new parties in Turkey, and ultimately the creation of the Justice and Development Party (*AK Partisi* or AKP). The AKP would achieve a great victory in the 2002 elections and remains in power to the present. In contrast to the very different relational contexts of the Maghreb, the AKP's relational context was not one of trauma at the hands of a violent colonial occupying power, but an arch-secular autocratic state regime that failed to acknowledge the cultural identities of the majority of Turks in public life.

Upon achieving power, the AKP did not restore the Ottoman caliphate or impose scarves on the heads of Turkish women. They did not bring the alarmist secular or Western prognostications into fruition. Rather, they set to work attending to the real world tasks of governance. Indeed, the AKP was reelected to power in two subsequent national elections. Under AKP rule, the Turkish economy thrived and became a growing regional power. However, we would be remiss to ignore the deplorable state censorship and heavy-handed responses to political dissent in Turkey, especially in recent years. Erdogan has shown an increasing penchant for heavy-handed autocratic rule. Clearly the AKP is far

The Maghreb beyond Islamism   121

from an ideal governing power (if such a thing exists). Yet, the point is that the Islamist parties will have to govern, and if they do not attend to the dirty complexities of statecraft and meet the needs of their citizens—as the AKP has done—no amount of pious beards and slogans will save them on election day (or sooner).

Let us explore another example from an Arab context. It is an undoubtedly controversial one, but informative nonetheless. Hamas emerged in Gaza in 1987 during the First Intifada (Palestinian uprising) as an Islamist alternative to the leftist PLO confederation. Originating from a branch of the Muslim Brotherhood, Hamas initially seemed to be no threat to the dominance of the PLO. Even Israel allowed the new group to take shape unencumbered (perhaps even more) in hopes that it might weaken its arch-foe Yasser Arafat and the PLO. The PLO was so formidable that it even had ties to non-Arab international Leftist militants (e.g., Japanese Red Army). As Hamas grew, it founded a military wing (the Izz ad-Din al-Qassam Brigades) in 1991, which later infamously employed suicide bombings against Israeli military and civilian targets. This was a tactic it learned from Lebanon's Hezbollah, a Shia organization backed by the Islamic Republic of Iran.

Hamas represented a hardline political opposition force, and it adamantly opposed the 1993 Oslo Peace Accords negotiated by the PLO. Attacks by Hamas' military wing were a major factor (alongside the assassination of Yitzhak Rabin by a Jewish extremist) that significantly disrupted the implementation of the Accords in the 1990s. The ultimate failure of the peace process and the outbreak of the bloody Second Intifada in 2000 in turn helped to win popular support for Hamas as the main rival to the Fatah-dominated PLO confederation. Hamas had refused to participate in Palestinian elections until 2005. But now things changed. In 2006, Hamas won parliamentary elections by taking 74 of 132 seats, defeating the Western-backed Fatah Party. It was no longer an opposition force, but now had to govern. In response to the victory, the United States and Europe, both classifying Hamas as a terrorist organization, stopped all aid to the Palestinians. Meanwhile, tensions between Fatah and Hamas supporters raged. In 2007, gun battles and bombings between the two parties left hundreds of Palestinians dead, and the Gaza Strip (under Hamas) and West Bank (under Fatah) were left divided between the two warring factions.

Hamas, the 2006 electoral victors, had already mastered the "theatrical presentation of the self" with its provocative rallies, parades and masked guerrillas clad in green Islamic banners and explosive vests. It even crafted elaborate songs, media programs (some for children), works of art and graphic design, all extolling "the resistance." The rise of Hamas, coupled with the exodus of Palestinian Christians abroad, the growth of Christian Zionism in America, and threats by extremist Jews and Christians to destroy Islam's *al-Aqsa* compound (to construct a new Jewish temple), have all furthermore helped direct the Palestinian national identity toward an increasingly Arab-Muslim orientation. Yet, since assuming power, Hamas has fought rival Islamists who accuse the ruling party of being too secular and not implementing *shari'a*. As Hamas grappled with the

122 *The Maghreb beyond Islamism*

challenges of governance in the densely populated and impoverished Gaza Strip, it even entered into truces or ceasefires with its sworn-enemy, the "Zionist entity," Israel—something unthinkable to the most hardline Islamists. One of the most hardline groups even denounced Hamas as a "perverted, crooked government" of "abominations."[7]

In 2009, a hardline Islamist group called *Jund Ansar Allah* ("Army of God's Helpers") declared the establishment of an "Islamic emirate" in the Hamas-ruled Gaza Strip. War subsequently broke out between Hamas and *Jund Ansar Allah*. In August, during a prolonged gunfight in the Palestinian border town of Rafah, Hamas security forces killed 15 members of the group and arrested 40 more.[8] Six Hamas members were killed in the conflict. The 2009 gun battle in Rafah was not the first such incident either. In July 2007 Hamas forces stormed the stronghold of another Islamist group called *Jaysh al-Islam* ("the Army of Islam") freeing a kidnapped BBC correspondent.[9] In the wake of the *Jund Ansar Allah* conflict though, Hamas tried to shore up its Islamist credentials. It initiated a morality campaign in Gaza that included checking marriage licenses of couples found out on the street.[10] But it was a short term effort.

Years after the bloody showdown with *Jund Ansar Allah*, Hamas has still not established any sort of "Islamic state." It remains plagued by social and economic crises in Gaza. If the real-world responsibilities of governance have pushed an avowedly militant Islamist group like Hamas, which exists in an active warzone/occupation context, toward pragmatism and away from hardline ideological views, then such responsibilities will undoubtedly have a similar impact on the already far more moderate parties of the Maghreb, such as Ennahdha or the PJD.

Neither the Turkish nor Palestinian contexts are truly mirrors of the circumstances that we have found in the Maghreb states. Far from it, in fact. We have seen in the preceding chapters of this book how the Maghreb states are very different, even from each other. But the broader lessons of the Turkish and Palestinian experiences are still worth noting. The impact of electoral victory through democratic channels and the subsequent accountability of different Islamist parties is significant. And it raises questions about the true nature of Islamist rhetoric, which so often thrives in abstraction when withheld from actual positions of power (and accountability). It would seem that talk of *shari'a* and utopian Islamic ideals is most pronounced when the Islamists exist in the opposition, particularly in the face of perceived threats to Arab-Muslim identities. When that besieged identity is affirmed at the ballot box and an Islamist party assumes control of the state, the business of governance takes hold. These cases are not akin to those such as the Sudanese dictator Ja'afar al-Numayri (originally a socialist). Al-Numayri desperately switched to Islamism and imposed a crude interpretation of *shari'a* on Sudan in 1983 as a last ditch effort to legitimize and secure his un-democratic reign (he fell from power in 1985). Sudan, in fact, was a case of more top-down politics using religion as a means of social control, not unlike Morocco. The Islamist political parties of the Maghreb in the wake of the Arab Spring are a very different matter indeed.

The Maghreb beyond Islamism 123

Let us return to the birthplace of the Arab Spring, where Rachid al-Ghannouchi's Ennahdha party rose to power in 2011. While Egypt struggled after its own elections, facing waves of new protests, clashes, and political infighting, Tunisia (comparatively speaking) seemed to navigate the troubled post-revolutionary waters relatively well. It was still very far from smooth sailing though. The most shocking incident, especially for Western observers, took place at the US Embassy in Tunis on September 14, 2012. It was a Friday and a group of Salafi protesters, gathering after congregational prayers, organized a demonstration outside the US Embassy to denounce a crude American-made anti-Muslim film posted on the Internet called *Innocence of Muslims*. The same film served as a nominal pretext for the horrific assault on the US Consulate in Benghazi, Libya, that resulted in the death of four Americans, including Ambassador Chris Stevens. Ambassador Stevens had been an outspoken champion of the Arab Spring revolutions. The protesters in Tunis, many affiliated with *Ansar al-Shari'a* in Tunisia (AST), stormed the outer walls of the embassy compound, smashed windows, displayed flags associated with al-Qaeda, set fire to cars and trees, and ransacked a neighboring American school. Images of an enormous pillar of thick black smoke billowing from within the compound in Tunis quickly made international news. Tunisian President Moncef Marzouki of the secular-left Congress for the Republic Party (French acronym CPR) dispatched the presidential guard to defend the embassy and subdue the violent protests. During the clashes with security forces, two protestors were killed and 40 were arrested. "Half the arrests were made by our guards, whose job is only to protect the president and his staff," Marzouki's spokesman Adnen Mansar told *TIME Magazine* in the days following the incident.[11] In the aftermath of the attack, which was preceded by other Salafi violence at art galleries and elsewhere in Tunisia, Ennahdha was criticized for being too lax on (or even sympathetic to) the Salafis. In response, a crackdown was launched by the government, sending the leader of *Ansar al-Shari'a* in Tunisia, known as Abu 'Ayyad, into hiding in Libya where he was later killed by an American airstrike in 2015. Sadly, extremist violence would resurface in Tunis less than a year later.

On February 6, 2013, Choukri Belaid, a leader of the leftist Popular Front and a vocal opponent of both Ben 'Ali and Ennahdha, was murdered by an unknown gunman outside his home in Tunis. No one claimed responsibility for the attack. But critics of Ennahdha, including the Belaid family, quickly blamed the ruling Islamists for his death. There was no evidence to suggest this. Nor was it beneficial to Ennahdha for such a crime to take place. To the contrary, few had heard of Choukri Belaid outside of certain circles until his death. As a martyr of the secular Left, however, Choukri Belaid was arguably now more famous and damaging to Ennahdha than he ever was in life. Belaid became the central character in a narrative that portrayed the ruling Islamists as dangerous bloodthirsty zealots engaged in stealth tactics to create an anti-pluralistic autocratic theocracy that was willing to eliminate its critics. The narrative was false, but widely entertained. In fact, Belaid's death resulted in the dissolution of Tunisia's ruling coalition (the Troika) and ultimately the resignation of the Islamist Prime

124   *The Maghreb beyond Islamism*

Minister Hamadi Jebali, after he was unable to forge a new coalition. Prime Minister Jebali was even at odds with his own party, because he had called for an apolitical technocratic cabinet in the wake of the tragedy. This was unacceptable to Ennahdha leaders, who insisted they had a democratic mandate. With Jebali's resignation, Interior Minister 'Ali Laraayedh was selected to replace him. Laraayedh was seen as an Ennahdha hardliner willing to obey the party elders, such as Ghannouchi. His selection proved to be immediately unpopular with many opposition parties, including the small Islamist Popular Petition party, which accused Laraayedh of being responsible for deaths and ill-treatment of protesters in the Siliana region of Tunisia.[12]

On February 26, 2013, the new prime minister-designate announced that four suspects had been arrested for the assassination of Choukri Belaid. A fifth suspect, believed to be the actual triggerman, was on the run, he added. "They belong to a radical religious group," Laraayedh announced, referring to Salafi-Jihadi groups.[13] The news made international headlines. In the wake of the arrests, an official Ennahdha statement, attributed to Rachid al-Ghannouchi, renewed condemnation of the "heinous crime," expressed appreciation for the state security services, and affirmed Ennahdha's right to pursue legal action against "those who accused [Ennahdha's] leaders and incited violence against them."[14] Meanwhile, in the wake of the resignation of Jebali, a new coalition was organized to govern Tunisia. Led by the new Prime Minister Laraayedh, several parties (more than the three of the Troika) joined Ennahdha to form a new government in March 2013 and several coalition partners assumed key ministerial posts, including the minister of the interior, previously held by Ennahdha in the last government. "We see that it is in the interests of the Tunisian government, in the transitional period and for the period to come, to bring together Islamists and secularists, even though we are the majority," al-Ghannouchi told Tunisian radio.[15]

Yet, a far more dramatic gesture from al-Ghannouchi was to come. Amid the tensions and economic uncertainty of 2013, Laraayedh stepped down, and Ennahdha's support at the polls slipped when they won only 28 percent of the vote in the 2014 elections. Again, Ennahdha formed a coalition with secular parties in order to govern the country. Finally, on May 20, 2016, al-Ghannouchi declared that Ennahdha was renouncing Islamism and redefining itself as "Muslim Democrats."[16] Moving forward, religion would be independent from politics and Ennahdha would focus on everyday problems facing Tunisia, such as unemployment. Furthermore, Ennahdha did not wish to exclude portions of the electorate with a distinctly religious platform as it had done in the past. In addition, the rise of the Islamic State in Iraq and Syria (ISIS) movement had irreparably damaged the image of Islamism. Al-Ghannouchi wished to "show the difference between the Muslim democracy we support and the extremist jihadist Islam from which we want to distance ourselves."[17]

In the years to come, we believe that the Islamist parties of the Maghreb will exist in one of two forms. In the first form, the Islamists will decline and exist only as small marginal parties that profess hardline conservative views in the opposition. They will participate in governance through large coalitions with non-Islamist parties that deprive them of ever pushing through their agendas. In the second form, these parties will exist as broad-based, center-right parties with an Islamic reference point, akin to the so-called "Turkish model" or more recently Ennahdha in Tunisia. These examples have invoked comparisons to the Christian Democratic Union of Germany (CDU) by many observers. The CDU emerged amidst the ashes of World War II and the rise of the Cold War when Eastern Europe was dominated by an aggressive Communist bloc that threatened traditional European-Christian identities. By the late 2000s though, with the Cold War long ended, the CDU came to refer only to "values" and tradition in its campaigns rather than any explicit Christian rhetoric. Certainly Islam is a different religious tradition with an arguably richer history of entanglement in politics, so we may never see a CDU-type of transformation, but we must remember that the next generations of the Maghreb, who will have never experienced colonialism or the post-colonial authoritarian states, will have a very different sense of their identities in relation to the world around them.

The theatrics of identity, as a type of performance in the public sphere, will no longer demand such dramatic and impassioned, even aggressive, affirmations. We cannot predict the future or perceive what threats may yet appear on the horizon, but we see no reason to think that the major Islamist trends (as opposed to small extremist fringe groups, which will always exist) will endure in their current (already generally moderate) forms. Indeed, we see increasing moderation and pragmatism taking hold as their participation in national democratic politics continues and new generations of Tunisians, Libyans, Moroccans and Algerians reach maturity. We may still see splinter groups breaking away from the Islamist parties when reforms are perceived to go too far. These splinter groups will criticize their pragmatic governance and reaffirm conservative positions, even questioning the old party's commitment to religion, but they will remain only in the minority.

On this last point, let us clarify what we mean by the term "moderation," because it may mean different things to different audiences. As we use the term, it does not entail a pro-Israel position, despite the fact that Western media outlets and conservative pundits often use the term in this manner. In the West, attitudes toward Israel are often used as an exclusive litmus test for who or what is "moderate" in the Muslim world. These are the same voices who, years ago, regularly called oppressive autocratic regimes, like King Hassan II's Morocco or Mubarak's Egypt, "moderate Arab states" because they maintained a cold peace with Israel. In reality, however, Mubarak's Egypt recognized Israel's existence not as support for Zionism but as part of Sadat's negotiated treaty to have the Sinai returned (lost in the Six-Day War), receive billions in international aid, and alleviate the formidable economic challenges of perpetual hostility with America's most favorite regional ally. The current Egyptian president, 'Abd al-Fattah al-Sissi, appears to share this type of appreciation for the country's peace with Israel and he has even opened the prospect of increased economic and military cooperation between the two countries. But his human rights record remains

126　*The Maghreb beyond Islamism*

troubling and controversial, and the political process in Egypt is hardly inclusive.

"Moderate" or "moderation," we suggest, means a commitment to a pluralistic democratic political process and to the growth of civil society, curbing corruption as much as possible (a challenge even for the United States), and working to uphold a just legal system that allows a large degree of free expression, even if certain legal penalties are implemented to preserve the sanctity of religious texts or persons. When Tunisia debated the contents of its new post-revolution constitution, the Ennahdha-led proposals and drafts that emerged were surprisingly secular in orientation. In fact, the word *shari'a* was completely absent from the text, unlike Egypt where *shari'a* has been privileged in its constitution since long before the Arab Spring. However, the subject of blasphemy (protecting "sacred values") and the limits of free speech or expression remained a point of particular contention in Tunisia. Human rights organizations also questioned the language used in the draft constitution, specifically regarding the subject of women, where "complimentary" (in relation to men) was used instead of equality.[18] The constitution was not rushed through though (as it was after the Arab Spring in Egypt), but continued to be debated before being ratified. It was indeed a slow and carefully negotiated process.

While writing this book, we could not ignore our conflicting feelings about these Islamist parties. We see good governance as democratic and accountable, and based on reason and empirical research, and not ancient revelations from a supreme deity (or any other supernatural entity). That is our bias and personal perspective, coming from our own subjective experience and historical context. We have no say (nor should we) in how citizens of other states in different regions of the world, such as the Maghreb, choose to govern themselves (so long as crimes against humanity do not occur). And we must emphasize the word *choose*. The peoples of the Maghreb have chosen Islamist political parties to govern them. Outsiders must respect that decision, and we hope that this book gives readers a deeper understanding of why the peoples of the Maghreb states may have made those choices at this important historical moment. As we have argued, these developments are not about fanaticism, insidious ideologies, or the content of a venerable old religious text, but rather about identity. Our intentions were never to dismiss other factors at play in these events, such as existing organizational networks that helped support Islamist campaigns or the perception among common people that religious parties are "less corrupt." Rather, human societies are complex and can seldom, if ever, point to single causal explanations for how or why certain events transpired as they did. Identity is most certainly one of those factors and has special significance and importance in this context.

Notes

1　Quoted in Sen (2006, 7).
2　See Adonis (1990, 90).

The Maghreb beyond Islamism 127

3 See Sheehi (2004, 3).
4 The phrase "cultural logic" is common to the Marxist-humanitarian critique of modernity. Quoted here in Kellner (1989, 174).
5 Quoted in Bauman (1996, 19).
6 Quoted in Grossberg (1996, 89).
7 Quoted in Karin Laub. 2010. "Gaza's new crop of zealots turning into a problem for militant Hamas rulers." *Associated Press*, December 2. Accessed April 21, 2017. www.startribune.com/templates/Print_This_Story?sid=111182999.
8 Peter Beaumont. 2009. "Hamas Destroys al-Qaeda Group in Violent Gaza Battle." *Guardian*, August 15. Accessed April 21, 2017. www.guardian.co.uk/world/2009/aug/15/hamas-battle-gaza-islamists-al-qaida.
9 Max Rodenbeck and Nicholas Pelham. 2009. "Which way for Hamas?" *The New York Review of Books*, November 5. Accessed April, 7, 2017. www.nybooks.com/articles/archives/2009/nov/05/which-way-for-hamas/.
10 Ibid.
11 Quoted in Vivienne Walt. 2012. "Tunisia's Political Battles Shade Attacks on U.S. Embassy." *Time*, September 16. Accessed April 7, 2017. http://world.time.com/2012/09/16/political-battles-in-tunisia-shade-attacks-on-u-s-embassy/.
12 Alistair Lyon. 2013. "Tunisia's New Premier Promises Inclusive Government." *Reuters*, February 22. Accessed April 7, 2017. www.reuters.com/article/2013/02/22/us-tunisia-politics-idUSBRE91L0F720130222.
13 Quoted in "Tunisia holds four over Chokri Belaid killing." 2013. *BBC News*, February 26. Accessed April 7, 2017. www.bbc.co.uk/news/world-middle-east-21592419.
14 Rachid al-Ghannouchi. 2013. "Tunisia: Ennahdha Party Statement following announcement of preliminary findings of investigation into assassination of Chokri Belaid." *Ikhwanweb*, February 26. Accessed April, 7, 2017. www.ikhwanweb.com/article.php?id=30692.
15 Quoted in Yasmine Najjar. 2013. "Ennahda to Surrender Sovereign Ministries." *Maghrebia*, March 1. Accessed April 7, 2017. www.magharebia.com/cocoon/awi/xhtml1/en_GB/features/awi/features/2013/03/01/feature-02.
16 Tom Heneghan. 2016. "Key Tunisian Party Renounces Political Islam." *Religion News Service*, May 23. Accessed April 7, 2017. http://religionnews.com/2016/05/23/tunisias-ennahda-movement-renounces-political-islam/.
17 Quoted in Heneghan (2016).
18 See Human Rights Watch. 2012. "Tunisia: Fix Serious Flaws in Draft Constitution." *HRW.Org*, September 13. Accessed April 7, 2017. www.hrw.org/news/2012/09/13/tunisia-fix-serious-flaws-draft-constitution.

References

Adonis. 1990. *An Introduction to Arab Poetics*. London: Saqi Books.
Bauman, Zygmunt. 1996. "From Pilgrim to Tourist – or a Short History of Identity." In *Questions of Cultural Identity*, edited by Stuart Hall and Paul Du Gay, 18–36. London: Sage.
Grossberg, Lawrence. 1996. "Identities and Cultural Studies: Is that all there is?" In *Questions of Cultural Identity*, edited by Stuart Hall and Paul Du Gay, 87–107. London: Sage.
Kellner, Douglas. 1989. *Critical Theory, Marxism, and Modernity*. Baltimore, MD: John Hopkins UP.
Sen, Amartya. 2006. *Identity and Violence*. New York: W.W. Norton.
Sheehi, Stephen. 2004. *Foundations of Modern Arab Identity*. Gainsville, FL.: University of Florida Press.

Index

Abbadi, Mohamed 112
Abbasid caliphate 2, 22, 23, 24, 26, 109
'Abd el-Krim 41
'Abd al-Qadir (Amir) 34, 35
'Abd al-Rahman III 25
'Abd al-Wahhab, Muhammad bin 70; see also Wahhabism
'Abdallah ibn al-Zubayr 13, 14
'Abdel-Nasser, Gamal 33, 42, 47, 48, 51, 65, 66, 75, 86, 87, 88, 89
'Abdel-Wadoud, Abu Musab see Abdelmalek Droukdel
'Abduh, Muhammad 5, 70, 74
'Abdullah ibn Sa'd 12–13, 14
Aboul Fotouh, 'Abdel Moneim 33
Abu 'Ayyad al-Tunisi 79, 123
Abu Bakr 14, 15
Abu Hamid al-Ghazali 9
Abu al-Muhajir 17
Abu Qatada 79
Abu Salim Prison 92, 93–4
Abun-Nasr, Jamal 38
Adonis 118
African National Congress 49, 88
Age of Enlightenment 3, 4
Aisha bint Abu Bakr 14
Ajami, Fouad 54
Akkad, Moustapha 40
Albania 31, 66
alcohol 8, 54, 87
'Ali ibn Abu Talib 3, 9, 14–15, 24, 106
'Ali, Mehmet (Muhammad) 31, 39, 47
America see United States
al-Andalus 20–2, 23, 25, 26
Anderson, Lisa 85
Ansar al-Shari'a 79, 84, 123
al-Aqsa see Jerusalem
Arafat, Yasser 121
Armed Islamic Group 57

'Asharism 69
Association of Muslim 'Ulama 52, 54; see also Ben Badis, 'Abdelhamid
Atatürk see Kemal, Mustafa
Augustine of Hippo 1
al-Azhar 5, 9–10, 17, 31, 51, 67

Ba'athism 46, 66, 67, 87
Bab Souika 76
Baccouche, Hédi 75, 76
al-Banna, Hassan 4, 5, 69, 70, 73, 74, 77
Banu Hilal 26
Bardo Treaty 39
Baring, Evelyn 4–5
Bayat, Asef 5–6, 120
Belaid, Choukri 123, 124
Belhadj, 'Abdelhakim 91–2, 117
Belhadj, 'Ali 54–6, 58, 59, 117
Ben 'Ali, Zine al-Abidine 75–6, 77, 78, 93
Ben Badis, 'Abdelhamid 52
Ben Bella, Ahmed 47, 50–1
Ben Youssef, Salah 65
Benikrane, 'Abdelilah 7, 104, 105, 111–12
Benjedid, Chadli 53, 54, 56
Bennabi, Malik 54, 68, 77
Bennani, Walid 73
Berbers 1, 12, 15, 17, 18, 22, 23, 24, 25, 34, 35, 36, 37, 38–9, 40–1, 47, 50, 56, 57, 100
Bin Laden, Osama 58, 108
Black Saturday 96
Black Thursday 71–2
Bonaparte, Napoleon 30, 31
Bouazizi, Mohamed 78, 92, 110
Boudiaf, Mohammed 56
Boumediene, Houari 50–2, 53, 90
Bourguiba, Habib 48, 64–8, 71–2, 73, 74–5, 79, 120
Bouteflika, 'Abdelaziz 58–9

Index 129

Bouyali, Mustafa 54–5, 57
British colonialism 4–5, 6, 30, 31, 39, 41, 65, 68, 118, 120
Brower, Benjamin C. 33
Buddhism 3
Burgat, François 53
Byzantine Empire 3, 4, 12, 13, 15, 16, 17, 18

Cairo 12, 17, 23–4, 26, 30, 31, 32, 41, 48–9, 51, 52, 66, 85, 87
Catholicism *see* Christians
Chaabani, Mohamed 50–1
Chahine, Youssef 47
Christianity *see* Christians
Christians 1, 2–3, 4, 12, 13, 17, 18, 19, 20–1, 24, 27, 32, 35, 36, 88, 121, 125
Christian Democratic Union 125
Christian Zionism 121
Churchill, Winston 41
Communism *see* Marxism
Connelly, Matthew 49
Constitutional Democratic Rally 64, 75, 76

Damascus 14, 15, 17, 20, 21, 23, 66–7
'Day of the Jackal, The' 49
De Gaulle, Charles 48–9, 50
De Gobineau, Arthur 35
Descartes, René 106
Dib, Mohammed 47
Droukdel, Abdelmalek 58

Egypt 2, 4–5, 6, 12–14, 17, 19, 23, 24, 25, 26, 27, 30–1, 33, 39, 46, 47, 84, 87, 118, 119, 123, 125–6; *see also* Cairo
Ennahdha 2, 6–7, 9, 69, 117, 122, 123–4, 125, 126
Ennaifer, Hmida 66, 67, 69, 71, 72
Entelis, John 57–8
Erdogan, Recep Tayyip 120
Évian Accords 50

al-Fassi, 'Allal 34, 42, 70
Fatah 121; *see also* Palestinian Liberation Organization
Fatima bint Muhammad 3, 24
Fatimid caliphate 2, 3, 24–6
Fes 25, 26, 41, 85, 104, 111
French colonialism 1, 30, 31–5, 36, 37–9, 40, 41, 46, 54, 55, 65, 71, 120

al-Gaddafi, Mu'ammar 7, 84, 86–91, 92, 93, 94, 95, 96
al-Gaddafi, Saif al-Islam 92–3, 94

Germany 41, 65, 91, 125
al-Ghannouchi, Rachid 6–7, 9, 64, 65–70, 71–7, 78, 79, 106, 117
al-Ghazali *see* Abu Hamid al-Ghazali
al-Ghazali, Zaynab 105
'Green Book, The' 88, 89
Guevara, Che 46, 84
Gulf War 51, 107

Hachani, 'Abdelkader 56
al-Halabi, Sulayman 31
Hall, Stuart 119
Hamas 121–2
Harkis 42, 50
Hassan II (King of Morocco) 100–2, 103, 104, 105, 106, 107, 111, 125
Hassan ibn 'Ali 100
Hassan ibn al-Numan 18–19
Hassan, Mona 70
Haykal, Muhammad Husayn 47, 73
Hemingway, Ernest 120
Hezbollah 121
Hinduism 3
Huntington, Samuel 118
Husayn ibn 'Ali 23
Hussein, Saddam 51

Ibadi Islam 15, 22, 23, 25, 26
Ibn Khaldun 26, 73
Ibn Taymiyya, Ahmed 69–70
Idris I (King of Libya) 84–6, 87, 88
Ilyas, Muhammad 68; *see also Tablighi Jamaat*
Imazighen see Berbers
India 4, 6, 30, 41, 68, 70, 118
Islamic Rally Movement 92
Iranian Revolution of 1979 6, 52, 72–3, 75, 78, 121; *see also* Khomeini, Ruhollah
Islamic Salvation Front 53, 54, 55–8, 59, 117
Islamic State of Iraq and Syria ("The Islamic State") 57, 84
Islamic Tendency Movement 6, 69, 73, 74, 75; *see also* Ennahdha
Israel 6–7, 42, 89, 121–2, 125
Italian colonialism 1, 39, 40, 41, 65, 84, 85, 88

al-Jazeera 78, 112
Jebali, Hamadi 7, 74, 75, 79, 124
Jerusalem 15, 26, 121
Jews 1, 2, 4, 7, 18, 19, 21, 22, 24, 26, 38, 77, 118, 121
Jourchi, Slaheddine 6, 72

130 *Index*

Judaism *see* Jews
Jund Ansar Allah 122
Justice and Development Party (Morocco)
2, 7, 104, 105, 109, 110, 111–12; *see also* Benikrane 'Abdelilah
Justice and Development Party (Turkey)
120–1; *see also* Erdogan, Recep Tayyip
Justice and Spirituality Society 103–4,
105, 106, 109, 111, 112; *see also* Yassine, 'Abdessalam

Kairouan 16–18, 19, 22, 23, 24, 25, 26, 68
Kant, Emmanuel 73
Keddie, Nikki 77
Keller, Richard C. 37
Kellner, Douglas 119
Kemal, Mustafa 40, 65, 120
Kepel, Gilles 8
al-Kahina 18–19, 20, 25, 35
Kharijite 15, 22, 23, 24–5, 26; *see also* Ibadi Islam
Khomeini, Ruhollah 72–3, 78; *see also* Iranian Revolution of 1979
Kusayla 17–18

Lalla Fatma N'Soumer 35, 38
Laraayedh, 'Ali 124
Lavigerie, Charles Martial 36
Libyan Islamic Fighting Group 91–2; *see also* 'Abdelhakim Belhadj
Libyan Muslim Brotherhood *see* Muslim Brotherhood

Madani, Abbassi 54, 55–6, 58, 59
Marxism 42, 48, 51, 52, 65, 67, 72, 118, 121
Matar, Hisham 90
Mawdudi, Abul A'la 4, 70, 77
Marzouki, Ahmed 101–2, 107, 123
Marzouki, Moncef 123
Mecca 13, 16, 24, 26, 75, 85
Medina 14, 16, 24, 26
Mitterand, François 53
Mohammed V (King of Morocco) 100
Mohammed VI (King of Morocco) 100,
107, 108, 109, 110, 111
Moore, Clement H. 71
Morsi, Mohamed 2, 33, 119
Mourou, 'Abdelfattah 69, 72, 74–5, 76, 117
Mouti, 'Abdelkarim 102–3, 104
Mu'awiyya 14–15, 17, 22
Mubarak, Hosni 89, 125
Muhammad (prophet) 3, 8, 9, 12, 13, 14,

20, 23, 24, 36, 70, 74, 85, 86, 88, 100, 103
al-Mukhtar, 'Omar 40, 84, 88
Musa ibn Nusayr 19, 20, 21–2
Muslim Brotherhood 2, 5, 9, 33, 59, 67,
69, 71, 72, 73, 79, 90, 92, 93, 94–5, 105, 121
Mzali, Mohammad 74–5

Nakba 6; *see also* Palestine
Nasser, Gamal 'Abdel *see* 'Abdel-Nasser, Gamal
Nasserism 46, 65, 66, 67, 103; *see also* 'Abdel-Nasser, Gamal
National Liberation Front 7, 46–50, 51,
53–4, 55, 56, 57, 58, 59
Naylor, Phillip 30
Neo-Destour Party 65, 68, 71; *see also* Bourguiba, Habib
al-Numayri, Ja'afar 73, 122

Omri, Zeinab 78
Organization of the Secret Army 48, 49
Ottoman Empire *see* Ottoman Turks
Ottoman Turks 1, 17, 26–7, 30, 31, 39, 40,
65, 84, 85, 120
Ouyahia, Ahmed 59

Palestine 6, 7, 22, 49, 66, 67, 121–2
Palestinian Liberation Organization (PLO)
49, 90, 121
Pakistan 2, 68, 70, 91
Paris 20, 31, 37, 48, 49, 65, 68, 69, 78
Personal Status Code (Morocco) 109
Personal Status Code (Tunisia) 66, 75
pied-noirs 46, 48, 49, 50
Protestantism 3, 4

al-Qaeda 22, 58, 79–80, 123
Qutb, Sayyid 42, 54, 67, 68

Rabin, Yitzhak 121
Rida, Rashid 70, 74, 77
Roderick (King) 20–1
Roy, Olivier 7–8, 120

Sadat, Anwar 71, 75, 89, 90, 103, 125
Said, Khaled 92
Salafism 67–8, 69, 79–80, 105, 123, 124;
see also Wahhabism
Salafist Group for Preaching and Combat
58
Salah ad-Din al-Ayyubi 26
Salan, Raoul 48

Index 131

Sanussi *tariqa* 39, 85, 87, 89
Sartre, Jean-Paul 118
Saudi Arabia 68, 78, 90, 100, 105; *see also* Wahhabism
secularism 2, 4, 5, 7, 40, 59, 64, 66–7, 70, 74, 77, 78, 79, 105, 107, 109, 111, 117, 119, 120, 121, 123, 124
Seddik, Youssef 64, 68
Sheehi, Stephen 118
Shia Islam 23, 24, 26–7, 75, 121
al-Sissi, 'Abd al-Fattah 125
Six-Day War 6, 42, 65, 67, 86, 125; *see also* Israel
Smith, J.Z. 4
Soltani, 'Abdellatif 52
Soviet Union 47, 65, 91–2, 118
Spain *see al-Andalus*
Spanish colonialism1, 40, 41
Stevens, Chris 123
Syrian Muslim Brotherhood 67; *see also* Muslim Brotherhood

Tablighi Jamaat 68
takfir 57
Tamimi, Azzam 67
Tariq ibn Ziyad 19, 20–2, 27
Tawhid 8–9, 79
al-Tilmisani, 'Umar 32–3, 67
Toyota War 91
Troika (Tunisia) 79, 123–4
Trump, Donald J. 118
Tunisian General Labor Union (UGTT) 71–2
al-Turabi, Hassan 73

'Ubayd Allah 24–5; *see also* Fatimid caliphate
'Umar ibn 'Abdul-'Aziz 77

'Umar ibn al-Khattab 13, 15
Umayyad caliphate 2, 3–4, 13, 14, 15–16, 17, 18–19, 20, 21, 22–3, 24, 25, 70, 77, 106
United States 2, 7, 10, 48, 51–2, 65, 75, 79, 80, 86, 88, 90–1, 101, 107, 108, 109, 111, 118, 119, 121, 123, 125, 126
'Uqba ibn Nafi 16–18, 23, 25, 80
'Uthman ibn Affan 13, 14, 15

Visigoths 19–20, 21

Wahhabism 68, 105, 106; *see also* Saudi Arabia
al-Walid 21
Warnier law 38
Willis, Michael 59
women, Islamist views on 53, 66, 73, 76–7, 79, 105–6, 109, 120, 126

Yacef, Saadi 47
Yassine, 'Abdessalam 103–4, 105, 107–8, 112
Yassine, Nadia 105–6, 108, 109–10, 111, 112, 117
Yazid bin Mu'awiyya 17
YouTube 78, 79
Yusuf (prophet) 77
Yusuf bin Tashfin 26

al-Zawahiri, Ayman 67
al-Zaytouna 9, 17, 52, 66, 68, 75
Zionism 22, 42, 49, 88, 91, 125; *see also* Christian Zionism; Israel
Zoroastrianism 9, 12
Zouabri, Antar 57, 58
Zuhayr ibn Qays 18

Taylor & Francis eBooks

Helping you to choose the right eBooks for your Library

Add Routledge titles to your library's digital collection today. Taylor and Francis ebooks contains over 50,000 titles in the Humanities, Social Sciences, Behavioural Sciences, Built Environment and Law.

Choose from a range of subject packages or create your own!

Benefits for you
- Free MARC records
- COUNTER-compliant usage statistics
- Flexible purchase and pricing options
- All titles DRM-free.

Benefits for your user
- Off-site, anytime access via Athens or referring URL
- Print or copy pages or chapters
- Full content search
- Bookmark, highlight and annotate text
- Access to thousands of pages of quality research at the click of a button.

REQUEST YOUR FREE INSTITUTIONAL TRIAL TODAY

Free Trials Available
We offer free trials to qualifying academic, corporate and government customers.

eCollections – Choose from over 30 subject eCollections, including:

Archaeology	Language Learning
Architecture	Law
Asian Studies	Literature
Business & Management	Media & Communication
Classical Studies	Middle East Studies
Construction	Music
Creative & Media Arts	Philosophy
Criminology & Criminal Justice	Planning
Economics	Politics
Education	Psychology & Mental Health
Energy	Religion
Engineering	Security
English Language & Linguistics	Social Work
Environment & Sustainability	Sociology
Geography	Sport
Health Studies	Theatre & Performance
History	Tourism, Hospitality & Events

For more information, pricing enquiries or to order a free trial, please contact your local sales team:
www.tandfebooks.com/page/sales

 The home of Routledge books

www.tandfebooks.com